T B Simpson

THE SECOND WORLD WAR

THE
SECOND WORLD WAR

A SHORT HISTORY

by

CYRIL FALLS

METHUEN & CO. LTD., LONDON
36 Essex Street, Strand, W.C.2

First published in 1948

CATALOGUE NO. 5026/U

THIS BOOK IS PRODUCED IN COMPLETE
CONFORMITY WITH THE AUTHORIZED
ECONOMY STANDARDS

PRINTED IN GREAT BRITAIN

                    nor stood at gaze
The adverse legions; nor less hideous joined
The horrid shock. Now storming fury rose,
And clamour such as heard in Heaven till now
Was never; arms on armour clashing brayed
Horrible discord, and the madding wheels
Of brazen chariots raged; dire was the noise
Of conflict; overhead the dismal hiss
Of fiery darts in flaming volleys flew,
And flying vaulted either host with fire.
So under fiery cope together rushed
Both battles main, with ruinous assault
And inextinguishable rage. . . .

                    Deeds of eternal fame
Were done, but infinite; for wide was spread
That war and various; sometimes on firm ground
A standing fight, then soaring on main wing
Tormented all the air; all air seemed then
Conflicting fire. Long time in even scale
The battle hung.
                              Paradise Lost

CONTENTS

MAPS

THIS short history of the Second World War is in the main a
record of events. The war was largely a succession of events,
strange as the notion may appear to certain commentators who
have decided that it was a succession of political and economic
phases or even of frames of mind. War may be, as Clausewitz
holds, an extension of political intercourse, but it differs from
normal political intercourse in that its results are determined by
deeds rather than by words. Words are important, increasingly
so, in war, but not as important as the makers of words suppose.
The results of war are more decisive and less questionable than
political results. Historians may argue endlessly about the results
of political enterprises and issues, or economic developments, or
changes in social habits; but over the results of war there can
commonly be little argument, and none over the results of the
Second World War. The politician may prove to his own satisfaction and that of a varying number of others that he actually
gained the cause which he is generally considered to have lost.
The defeated military commander will find no listeners if he
advances such a plea. The cynic may consider that this is one of
the pleasanter features of war.

Politics and economics admittedly exercised a profound influence upon the war. It is proper that they should be fully discussed, as they will be and indeed to some extent have been. But
I, with little space at my command, have decided to devote the
greater part of it to those events into which politics and economics translated themselves. They themselves are indicated in the
background, but as a rule lightly. Where I have found room for
comment—and there has not been much—I have used it mostly
for military commentary. I have even occasionally tried to pass
beyond the realm of strategy into that of tactics, a bold and indeed
in the circumstances an almost impossible undertaking. It may
not have had great success, but that I have attempted it at all is an
indication of the spirit in which I set about the whole work.

To those who object to my method I can only reply that it
would have been very much easier for me to produce a book in
another form. I have lived so much in the war and become so

familiar with its main phases, characteristics, and innovations, that I should have found little difficulty in producing in the form of an essay a commentary of the same length as this book. I can therefore honestly say that I have put myself to extra pains and trouble in writing a book which is mainly military and at the same time factual.

The pains and trouble have been greater than may appear, and perhaps than the book's merits may seem to warrant. Compression is the most difficult of all tasks in dealing with a contemporary subject when the material is virtually unlimited. I have tried to cover all the ground I could, but there is a great deal which has been of necessity unexplored. To take a single example, the subject of South America is scarcely mentioned in the book. The impact of the war on South America, especially Brazil and Argentina, is of high interest, but there was no room to discuss it within the prescribed limits. I have no doubt that other omissions will be noticed, and, though some may appear strange, I do not think that many of them are unintentional. A far bigger problem, however, has been to find adequate space for the events which are described. The British Home Guard is dealt with in a few sentences. The campaign in Sicily has been allotted what I estimate to be about two pages. Burma, from the British retreat to the Assam border to the recapture of Rangoon, is given one chapter. And one chapter has to cover all the operations in North Africa from the spring of 1941 to the summer of 1942 and events in Iraq, Syria and Persia as well. How then find space for a description of the Battle of Sidi Rezegh, one of the most interesting and intricate ever fought by British arms?

Another characteristic of the book which may require explanation is that it is written mainly from a British standpoint. This does not imply that much more space has been given to British action in the war than to that of the other chief belligerents. It is simply a matter of the point of view. I trust that it has not resulted in an incorrect estimation of the relative importance of events, and there is no good reason why it should.

Nothing official except a considerable number of British despatches and some reports to the Combined Chiefs of Staff had been published when the book went to press. However, a great deal of reasonably well guaranteed information has appeared in other forms or is now obtainable. In this respect I desire to acknowledge with gratitude the aid which has been given to me in clearing up a few doubtful points, but for the most part the sources are those which are open to the general public, supposing the general public to have time or inclination to consult them. For a short and popular history written at this time I consider that these sources are on the whole sufficient. I am acquainted with many formation histories which would have been invaluable in a work of about twice the length of this, in which some detailed description of battles would have been possible, but for my present purposes they afford no help, since they all lead to paths which, as already explained, I have not been able to travel. For the same reason I have devoted scarcely a sentence to the aftermath of the war. To have done so would have necessitated cutting out something else, and I have striven to make every sentence count and in fact make itself indispensable.

C.F.

CHAPTER I

Europe on the Eve of War

THE seeds of all great wars are sown years before the plants break through the soil, and the roots are often long and tangled. In the latter respect, however, the Second World War in its origins will probably appear to posterity as simpler than the First. Before 1914 a number of great States, which seemed on the surface at all events to approach equality in importance—Germany, Russia, Austria-Hungary, France, Great Britain, even Italy—had for some time been involved in intricate political interchanges, combinations, and rivalries. If the political situation were discussed in purely moral terms—an unsuitable medium, it may be admitted—there was room for a good deal of honest doubt about, and even sympathy with, aspects of policy wholly conflicting. There was much to reprobate in some of the manœuvres of Germany, Austria-Hungary, and Russia, while those of the other countries named have not escaped just criticism. Yet though the First World War was mainly due to Germany, and she must be considered the greatest sinner in bringing it about, even Germany cannot be condemned as the unrelieved and wholly responsible villain of the piece. Blunder and destiny, twin sisters who walk about the world with arms entwined and resemble each other so closely that they are often confused, played a great part in precipitating the war of 1914.

The war of 1939, on the other hand, was essentially a war of revenge initiated by Germany. It is not too much to say that German National Socialism, the Nazi creed, stood first and foremost for revenge. The other aims, the "living room" to be obtained by the subjugation of neighbouring states, the absorption of all Teutonic or allegedly Teutonic populations, the colonization of agricultural districts like the Ukraine, the control of all major industries in Europe, were either the means of consolidating the revenge once achieved or the expression of purely predatory instincts such as had always flourished in Prussia and had more recently been diffused by Prussia over all Germany. Adolf Hitler stood first for rearmament and revenge; after that it becomes of minor importance that he stood also for loot and German domination.

He started in a strong position. Not only had he acquired by far the best military force in the world; he had also taken a number of steps towards his goal without having to fight for them. He had remilitarized the Rhineland in breach of the Treaty of Versailles, absorbed Austria, and engulfed Czecho-Slovakia, thus putting himself into a strategic situation which would make the conquest of Poland, when the turn of that country should come, child's play to his overwhelming power. By 1939 he had reached a period favourable from the point of view of armaments.

The mechanization of modern armies has resulted in a state of affairs not previously witnessed in warfare. Outstanding weapons such as the tank and the fighter aircraft pass very slowly through the various stages from experiment to full production, but on the other hand they quickly get out of date. In the Second World War it was not merely the case that there was a rapid development of new weapons, as had occurred in the First; there were also periods in which one country or another would be particularly well situated because its up-to-date and decisive weapons were pouring out of the factories while those of its rivals were in the stage when the machine tools and jigs required to produce them in mass were still being manufactured. It may be nearly a year from the time when the hand-made prototype is approved before a bare factory is tooled up to produce in mass. Germany did not go to war in 1939 simply because she had more weapons than her rivals, but also because at that time she had perfected weapons by experiment—including the experiment of the Spanish Civil War—and was in the midst of a bumper perod of production.

The advantages to the aggressor, always considerable, thus became greater than ever before. Another aspect of this state of affairs is that, while a mass national army can be created in eighteen months or at most two years, the production of modern armaments on a commensurate scale takes from three to four years. If the armies are engaged while short of arms and equipment they are likely to suffer defeat with heavy loss. Germany could thus see ahead of her a substantial period during which she would be all powerful, and with her industry already geared to war might expect to keep ahead even if she had failed to knock out her enemies during that period.

The position of France as she watched the threat of war drawing nearer was pathetic. For some time after 1918 she had assumed in Europe a position of domination which had been made possible, not by her achievements in the First World War, great though they had been, but by the combined efforts of herself and her major allies, Great Britain, the United States, and Russia. The first had gradually retired to her traditional situation of an island power outside the Continent, though intensely interested in its affairs. The second had withdrawn almost entirely from European entanglements and was not even a member of the League of Nations. The third had in the first half of the period between the wars been weakened and distracted by a revolution following upon defeat in war and had not in the second half emerged from the isolation into which she had been originally driven by hostility and in which she had later on deliberately enveloped herself.

France was thus left in a situation which it would have been beyond her power to support even if she had been a united, self-confident, and expanding nation, whereas she was in fact hopelessly divided, timid and uncertain in council, and showing signs of decline in some directions. The system of alliances with the states bordering Germany and Russia with which she had sought to bolster herself up—and, to be just, to maintain European peace —was inadequate for its purpose, and she had lost the keystone of the structure when she and Great Britain failed to support Czecho-Slovakia and allowed it to be overrun by Germany. Now she looked forward to fighting, if battle could not be avoided, with a vague determination to "do her best", which was almost a recognition of the certainty of defeat. The best feature of her armament was her navy, which was strong and up-to-date. Her army had to a certain extent been modernized, but it included very weak elements, and her military doctrine was at once pusillanimous and out-of-date. Her air force was deficient in both quantity and quality. She put any confidence which she possessed in the defences of her frontier facing Germany, the Maginot Line, but this did not cover the Belgian frontier. The Maginot Line was in itself strong, but the "Maginot mentality" of passive defence was disastrous.

Poland, which was to face the first shock, was a country with few major industries, though some attempt had been made to modernize the equipment of her forces. She could hope to survive the onslaught only if great powers, France and Great Britain in the west, Russia in the east, came to her aid. Otherwise her complete and rapid extinction was a military certainty.

Russia stood in the background, a comparatively unknown factor as regards both strength and intentions. It was realized that she had made vast strides in industrial production, notably in agricultural tractors, made by machinery readily convertible to the manufacture of tanks. There was reason to believe that she was already strong in these weapons and even more so in artillery, by which her military authorities set great store. Her vast population would enable her to put into the field any number of men that she could arm, though she had to maintain a powerful army in her easternmost provinces in case of aggression by Japan. She was well provided with raw materials and had within her own territories vast supplies of oil, indispensable for the conduct of modern war. Her chief weakness was the paucity of her communications. Her railways were few and not of the highest efficiency. Only a very few roads were paved or macadamized and all the others were tracks which would not stand heavy traffic, and would dissolve altogether if used in the autumn rain or the spring thaw.

These last constituted serious defects when it was a question of carrying her armies in strength beyond her own frontiers or even fighting an invader within them. But if that invader should effect a deep penetration, as was inevitable if it were Germany, then these very defects might contribute to the handicaps under which the aggressor would have to fight in the heart of the country. Russia's vast spaces were her surest defence, though they would not avail without a spirit of equally boundless self-sacrifice in her armies and her people. Once the enemy became immersed in these spaces, it would be he who would suffer most from lack of communications, particularly since the railways were of a gauge broader than that of the rest of Europe. The outsiders who knew most about the Russian Army, who were probably a few German staff officers—and even they did not know a great deal—were the most disposed to respect her strength, and especially her potential strength.

Italy was a shop with all its goods in the window and nothing on the shelves. The Fascist doctrine and system were on the whole more respectable than the Nazi. They were not without constructive elements and it could not be said of them, as has been said of the latter, that they meant only rearmament and revenge. But the Italian dictator had very different material to work on to the German. Not all the careful historical reconstruction of the Roman empire even down to the symbolism of the lictor's bundle of rods with the axe in its midst, the *fasces* which gave their name to the governing party, had recreated in Italy a martial spirit. The show deceived many observers, but there were large numbers who were not impressed, and even the French General Staff, so fearful of Germany, was contemptuous of Italy. In any case there was some reason to hope that if Germany could be even partially held in check Italy would not join her, though obviously nothing could restrain her if Germany should overwhelm France, in which case she would rush to the aid of the victor.

After Poland and the nations which might be expected to fight if she were attacked, the Low Countries were the most clearly threatened by German aggression. Both Holland and Belgium were firmly wedded to neutrality, and Belgium had deliberately forsworn any responsibilities which devolved upon her after the last war in order to return to the policy of international neutrality in which the kingdom had been born. Of the two she had made by far the more serious preparations to resist invasion, and her forces had been strengthened and modernized within the limits of her resources. In this respect Holland had done little, but she had improved the system of defence by water barriers which might be expected to give an invader serious trouble. Apart from their strategic situation, both countries acquired some importance from their colonial possessions, but Holland much more than Belgium. The Netherlands East Indies provided a vast storehouse of valuable war material.

Little need be said at this stage about the Balkans and other countries of South-eastern Europe, save that old rivalries and memories of strife rendered them tinder to a spark from outside. Turkey, bound by a pact to the western democracies, had no notion in 1939 of the perils which were to come to her door and was then more nervous about the intentions of Russia than of those of Germany. Bulgaria still brooded upon her losses in the

First World War and nursed hostility to Greece and Yugoslavia, who had then acquired territory from her. Hungary felt bitterness against Rumania and Yugoslavia, who had absorbed Transylvania in the former case, Slavonia and Croatia in the latter. Rumania and Yugoslavia, the "haves" of South-eastern Europe, were sitting uneasily on their gains, especially the former. Within Rumania's frontiers were included discontented minorities, and over Bessarabia was written a large note of interrogation as to the probability that Russia would make an attempt to recover the province. Greece was neither extravagantly a "have" nor markedly a "have-not", but she was threatened by Italy, especially since the latter had seized a bridgehead across the Adriatic in Albania.

The United Kingdom was relatively less well prepared for war than in 1914. During the inter-war period when peace at any price and disarmament had been her policy she had pared her fighting services to the bone. Even her navy, relatively the best-off of the three, was dangerously weak for its task of keeping open the trade routes. On the human side it was good, though a batch of exceptionally able officers was nearing the age limit or even past it. Her once great air force had at one moment almost disappeared as an effective fighting instrument, though by the outbreak of war there had been a certain recovery. The personnel was of a very high standard, and where all was so good it is almost invidious to mention in particular the superb quality of the fighter pilots both on the active list and in the reserve. It was, however, to them, and to possession of two good fighter aircraft, the Hurricane, then in fair production, and the Spitfire, not available in any quantity until the following year, that she was to owe her bare salvation after the fall of France. As a result partly of economy and partly of miscalculation, the army was grievously short of tanks. It had no prospect of adequate air co-operation since the R.A.F. was too small and for the time being too much immersed in its own problems to provide this. The training of the small regular army was in general good and there was in it a considerable number of highly capable and enterprising officers who had been anything from lieutenants to lieutenant-colonels in the last war. The training of the second line, the Territorial Army, was inadequate.

Military weakness had handicapped British policy throughout

the years during which Germany was preparing for war. The Government had been compelled to acquiesce in decisions which it disliked, such as the conquest of Abyssinia by the Italians, the invasion of China by the Japanese, and the occupation of Czecho-Slovakia by the Germans. In the last-named case the fear of the bomber, the weapon which now hovered like a malignant bird of prey above all international discussions, was the decisive factor. The country was woefully lacking in anti-aircraft artillery, and in any case there was a well-founded belief that this provided but a very partial defence against air attack. The air menace, far from being under-rated, was if anything exaggerated here as elsewhere, and though it may be said that it was impossible to overstress the potential power of destruction of the bomber, its immediate power, at the start of a war and against unbroken fighter defence, was actually not quite so great as was generally believed.

The nation had for too long refused to look the international situation in the face. For this the Government and all political parties had been largely to blame. Neither Parliament nor press had presented the question to it with the clarity or the persistence necessary to drive home the danger to the mass of the people. The more democratic leaders and organs were particularly culpable because they advocated an adventurous policy in opposing the German and Italian dictatorships while strenuously opposing rearmament. The small Liberal Party was the first to purge itself of this reproach; Labour, far stronger and forming the only potential alternative Government to the Conservatives, remained in error in this respect almost to the last. Its subsequent arguments in favour of this policy—mainly that it did not trust the Conservatives to take a genuinely democratic line in Europe—were respectable, but in the light of the danger, which the Labour Party was as well aware of as any other, they cannot be considered valid. No Government, no party, no organ of public opinion, with the single exception of one statesman who was debarred from office during the critical years, Mr. Winston Churchill, can be absolved.

Nevertheless, none of them can bear the whole responsibility. The nation as a whole must take a heavy share of that. A democracy gets the Government and press which it deserves and which it largely creates. The people at large deliberately thrust its head into the sand, and when it began to look about again was naturally somewhat dazed and bewildered by what it saw. Its outlook upon international affairs was influenced by two conflicting factors, its refusal to affront the possibility of war and its dread of bombing. On the other hand, it accepted without question such safety measures as were taken, especially as the crisis approached. In some respects its reactions to danger were unpredictable and un-accountable. At the time of the Munich incident there was a wild middle-class rush from London. The trains to Ireland in particular were packed, and a considerable proportion of the refugees were, to the scorn of cab-drivers and porters, young men. When war broke out there was no comparable panic.

The liberal humanitarianism which this country professed, and which provided the idealistic element in its political doctrine, had not been entirely unaffected by the materialism of the auto-cracies which had been established in so many other countries, though we had not progressed as far upon the path of materialism as we were to go in the course of the war. Since the last war there had been a general deterioration in standards of international conduct and an increase in national hysteria, cruelty, lack of moderation, and misuse of force, which boded ill for humanity in war. A decline in moral values had contributed to this, but it would be a mistake to suppose that it had been wholly respon-sible. Industrialization and the power to fly had contributed.

Since war had become so dependent upon factories and work-shops and required so large a proportion of the man-power of belligerent states, the means of production—inevitably not ex-cluding the human element, the work-people—became the probable objects of attack. The air arm provided a weapon which could leap all barriers to reach them, but at the same time one which was exceedingly clumsy and as likely to destroy children as machines. The talk about "military objectives", which one belligerent would declare to be exclusively sought by its air force while alleging that its opponent's bombing was unrestrained, was for the most part cant. It was presently abandoned in this country, and before the end of the war it was generally admitted that in bombing Berlin, for example, the policy was simply to shovel out the maximum number of incendiaries and high-explosive bombs roughly over the centre of the city.

The war was to take a surprising form, and no one could have prophesied its remarkable developments. One thing, however, might have been foretold by any competent student of civilization: that it would be a war of singular brutality and absence of scruple, of terrible destruction and widespread suffering.

CHAPTER II

The German Campaign against Poland

THE United Kingdom became involved in war with Germany as the result of the German attack on Poland on September 1st, 1939. The British ultimatum to Germany expired at 11 a.m. (B.S.T.), the French at 5 p.m., on September 3rd.

The British action was taken in fulfilment of a pledge made in the House of Commons by Mr. Neville Chamberlain, the Prime Minister, on March 31st of that year and re-affirmed in the Anglo-Polish agreement of August 25th. This country had committed itself to aid Poland in the event of a clear threat to Polish independence and which the Polish Government was prepared to resist forcibly. France was similarly bound to Poland by treaty.

The immediate issue was the status of the free city of Danzig, of which Hitler had demanded the return to the Reich and the refusal of Poland to hand over to Germany a zone running to East Prussia across the Corridor for a military railway and road—a strategic *Autobahn* of the type the Germans were building in various parts of their own country to threaten their neighbours. Poland might have submitted to the demand if she could have reposed the slightest trust in Germany's word, but it had been proved that this was worthless. Now Hitler and his Foreign Minister, Ribbentrop, gave the Poles a nominal opportunity to negotiate, but in point of fact afforded them no time to do so, and, moreover, gave them only the choice between complete acceptance and complete refusal of the terms on the spot.

Germany was, in fact, determined upon war. She had been strengthening her forces in East Prussia by sea and massing her main armies in Pomerania and Silesia. The latter province outflanked Poland from the south, and this flanking right wing of German power had been prolonged further to the east by possession of Czecho-Slovakia. Militarily Germany had at her disposal a marvellous strategic position which deeply outflanked Poland both to north and south, while any compensating advantage which Poland might have acquired from interior lines was nullified by Germany's overwhelmingly superior strength. The respective merits of interior and exterior lines are often discussed by military theorists, but it has never been denied that exterior lines afford the better chance of crushing a weak opponent thoroughly and rapidly. Germany had to act quickly because she was turning her back on the west, where her most powerful opponents lay. There, however, her frontier defences were strong, while she knew that France and Britain were unready. Provided the Polish campaign went according to plan, she need have no serious anxiety about the west.

What was still more important, she had by a stroke of Machiavellian diplomacy rid herself of all immediate anxieties lest Poland should find a supporter in the east. The United Kingdom and France had realized only too clearly that they could afford no active aid to Poland immediately without the co-operation of Russia. They had therefore approached the U.S.S.R. in the hope, first, that war might be averted by the presence of a supporter behind Poland anxious to keep the peace and, secondly, that if war was inevitable Germany would have to face the active opposition of Russia as well as Poland.

The military talks between their representatives and the Soviet authorities in Moscow broke down. The chief barrier appears to have been Russian insistence upon the necessity of occupying the territories of the independent Baltic States, Estonia, Latvia, and Lithuania, which the United Kingdom and France could not bring themselves to countenance. They were to become less nice and punctilious as the war progressed. A second reason was suggested by the chief Russian representative, Marshal Voroshilov, as reported in the Russian Press. It was that Soviet troops could not intervene in Poland's favour without entering Polish territory and that the Poles would not agree to such a step.

At all events negotiations were rendered nugatory by the conclusion of a pact of non-aggression between Germany and Russia on August 23rd. In this it was stated that "guided by the desire to strengthen the cause of peace between Germany and the Union of Socialist Soviet Republics", the two countries bound themselves to refrain from any act of force or aggressive action against each other. Each power likewise pledged itself that it would "in no manner" support a third power if one or other of the contracting parties were attacked by it. Thus Hitler linked himself to the country which he had most persistently abused and against which his bitterest diatribes had been directed. It may have been suspected, but it was clearly not definitely known to the outside world, including Poland, that there was more behind the treaty than appeared on the surface. It had in fact been agreed between the two parties that at the most convenient moment Russian forces should move in to take possession of the eastern half of the country and that Poland should once again be partitioned.

It has been stated that the Germans had at their disposal greatly superior strength. This, however, was even more in striking power and mobility than in actual numbers. On a full war footing Poland could raise the large force of 30 infantry divisions, 10 reserve divisions, 11 cavalry brigades, and army troops which included 38 companies of tanks and 377 aircraft. The chief weaknesses were in heavy, anti-tank, and anti-aircraft artillery, in the poor quality and small calibre of most of the infantry weapons, in restricted mobility due to lack of motorization, and of course in the deplorable lack of aircraft. In this last respect Germany's superiority in numbers was anything between fivefold and tenfold. It must be added that owing to the sudden and overwhelming German attack, the speed of the penetration, and the disruption of Polish communications, the Polish mobilization was never completed. The forces were disposed in a semi-circle of small armies, known by prominent geographical names of the districts in which they were stationed: Narew Group, Modlin Army, Pomorze Army, Poznan Army, Lodz Army, Cracow Army. In addition there was a small coast detachment to cover the mobilization of the fleet, and a detachment in the Carpathians. The general reserve, situated north-east, west, and south of Warsaw, consisted of 12 infantry divisions and the single motorized brigade which Poland possessed. The Commander-in-Chief was Marshal Smigly-Rydz.

The Polish plan was almost wholly defensive, with a main line of resistance facing northward on the Narew and the Vistula, westward on the Warta, and southward on the slopes of the Carpathians. The armies in the north and west, it is true, took up their positions well in advance of these lines, but their action was to take the form of a manœuvre in retreat in which no ground was to be yielded without pressure, but no decisive action was to be fought in front of the main defences. The basic idea was to hold out in the hope of going over to the offensive later on in

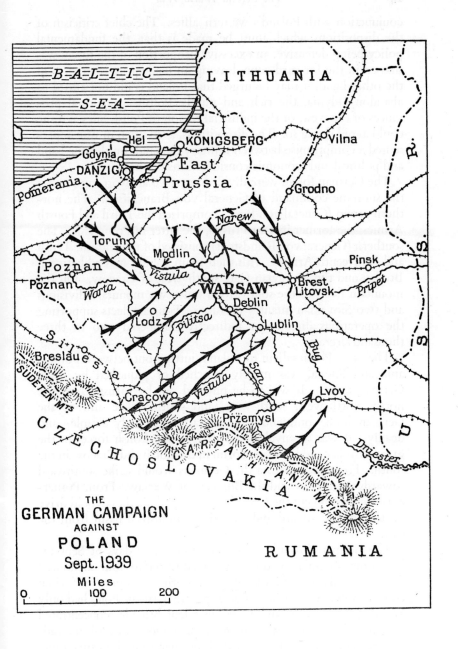

THE
GERMAN CAMPAIGN
AGAINST
POLAND
Sept. 1939

Miles
0   100   200

conjunction with Poland's western allies. The chief criticism of
the dispositions which must be made is that, the fundamental
policy being defensive, an excessive proportion of the forces was
massed in the forward zone, leaving an inadequate reserve. On
the other hand, it may be urged that Poland could not afford to
abandon Gdynia, the rich and purely Polish agricultural provinces of the west, or the industrial region of Polish Silesia, if she
could avoid doing so. The dispositions, as so often in war, represented a compromise between military demands on the one hand
and political and economic considerations on the other.

The German forces were divided into two army groups, under
the supreme command of General von Brauchitsch. The northern group (General von Bock) comprised the Third and Fourth
Armies, the former in East Prussia, the latter in Pomerania. The
southern (General von Rundstedt) consisted of the Eighth, Tenth
and Fourteenth Armies, with their main weight massed between
Breslau and the Moravian Gate south-west of Cracow. On the
mountain front to the south stood only two mountain divisions
and two Slovakian infantry divisions. Four air fleets supporting
the operations directly or indirectly numbered two to three
thousand aircraft.

The great Posen salient of Poland, jutting out between Pomerania and Silesia, was merely watched or piquetted by small
German forces. It was to be pinched out by thrusts from the
north, north-west, south-west, and south. The aim of the
German high command was, in fact, extremely simple—and
deadly. It was to envelop and destroy the Polish forces in the
great Vistula bend between Torun in the north and Cracow in the
south. From East Prussia the Germans would strike southward
towards the Narew and the Bug east of Warsaw. From Pomerania they would cut the Corridor. From Silesia they would drive
north, north-eastward and cut off the industrial basin from the
east.

The Germans brought into action in the first days of September some 38 infantry divisions in addition to four armoured
divisions. By the middle of the month this figure had risen
considerably. As against this on September 1st the Poles had only
16 infantry divisions and 10 independent brigades concentrated
for operations. Owing to the paralysis which overtook the railway system some of the other divisions had to detrain fifty miles

or more from the battle zone and at least one division was never mobilized at all, while mere fractions of another eventually fought at isolated points in the region of Warsaw. It is hard to recall any campaign in which the odds against the weaker belligerent were so heavy. Position, strength, armament, air support, numbers—in all the Poles were hopelessly outmatched.

In the German armies facing Poland were included some of the most competent soldiers in the world, whose names were in many instances to reappear over and over again in the succeeding five and a half years. Brauchitsch, the Commander-in-Chief, was to continue in that post till lack of success in Russia brought about his supersession—by Hitler himself. Halder, his Chief of the Staff, was to be the linchpin of the *Wehrmacht* till much later, though he himself was also to fall from grace. Bock's name was to crop up day after day in Russia. That of Kuechler, now commanding the Third Army, was to be almost as prominent later on: Kluge, commanding the Fourth Army, was to be famous and unfortunate both in Russia and in France. Of Rundstedt it is scarce necessary to speak. His staff officer, Manstein, was to be ranked by many as the ablest of all the German commanders. Reichenau (Tenth Army) was to drop out, but List (Fourteenth Army) was to become more prominent, and Blaskowitz (Eighth Army) was to be one of the last to resist in the *débâcle* of 1945. The commanders of Air Fleets Nos. 1 and 4, supporting respectively the northern and southern groups of armies, were Kesselring and Lohr. It was a good team, but its strength lay in great part in the unknown staff officers who did the planning, the march and concentration tables, the co-ordination between the various arms and the neighbouring formations, the administration, and the intelligence.

Without declaration of war, the German air force began a heavy attack at 4.40 a.m. on September 1st. The first targets were airfields, military bases, and training centres. The second wave of aircraft aimed at the railway junctions and main lines running from east to west and those linking southern Poland to Gdynia. Much damage was inflicted, but it was repaired and the movement of troops continued. At the same time, especially in the section of the Lodz Army, the civil population began to flow eastward into the interior of the country. This movement increased day by day, obstructing communications and creating targets which the enemy was able to attack at his ease with the bomb and the machine gun.

Between 5 and 6 a.m. the German land forces began to make reconnaissances in force, and these were quickly followed by concentrated attacks. Almost immediately the direction and success of the main German thrusts revealed the outline of the plan. From East Prussia the enemy pressed due south in the general direction of Warsaw. From Pomerania he quickly cut the Corridor, so that the German Third and Fourth Armies joined hands, and the Polish force in the area of Gdynia was cut off from the main body, though it successfully resisted attacks. The nose of the Polish Posen salient was entirely disregarded by the Germans, but on its southern flank, led by two armoured divisions, they penetrated deeply between Lodz and Cracow, and by September 2nd had fought their way forward to the Pilitsa, a distance of over fifty miles from the frontier. South of Cracow a lesser but still dangerous thrust took shape.

Generally speaking the Polish forces fell back under pressure on the first two days. Serious losses were suffered in some formations, but no irreparable damage was done. Yet it was already becoming apparent that the prospects were well nigh hopeless. Whenever strong resistance was encountered it was quickly broken by German weight of metal or outflanked by German mobility. Were a German assault held, the command quickly broke it off, reorganized, initiated a fresh artillery preparation, and in nearly every case succeeded at the second attempt. The armoured divisions, closely supported from the air, were extremely effective and made the deepest penetrations, but they were by no means solely responsible for German progress. On September 2nd five had been identified in action by the Poles—one in the Corridor, two on the upper Warta south of Lodz, one west of Cracow, and one south of that city—and it could not be said that the enemy's successes on broad fronts had been entirely due to them.

By the morning of September 7th the whole of the Silesian industrial basin had been over-run by the enemy. His spearheads, thrust up from the south-west, had appeared east of Lodz, 85 miles from the frontier, and the Polish line of resistance in the west was broken. In the north he was at the gates of Torun, and further to the east approaching Warsaw. By the 9th the picture was still blacker. A large Polish force was virtually enveloped in the triangle Thorn-Warsaw-Lodz. In the south hostile forces had reached and even crossed the San, and north of its junction with the Vistula were closing up to the greater river.

On September 10th the Polish Supreme Command issued an order for a retreat to the south-east, in the direction of the Rumanian frontier, leaving behind the isolated garrison of the Warsaw region, covering the retreat by strong rear guards on the Vistula and the San. The manœuvre was successful to a surprising extent because, as was gradually revealed, the German armour and mechanical transport was becoming immobilized for lack of fuel. Certain Polish formations displayed great heroism in this gloomy stage both in defence and in counter-offensive. On the 15th, for example, a Polish force under General Sosnkowski, moving south of Lublin in the direction of Lvov, gained a brilliant local victory, capturing and destroying 20 guns, 80 tanks, and a large quantity of transport.

Were these the death agonies of the Polish Army? They proved to be so, but it was on account of an entirely new factor in the situation. It can never be established with certainty how long the Poles could have maintained resistance or how large a force they could have withdrawn into Rumania but for Russian intervention. Polish writers have naturally striven to put the most favourable interpretation upon the prospects and German the least. At all events the crossing of the eastern frontier by strong Russian forces at dawn on the 17th brought the end. Polish forces, such as the garrison of Lvov, which had been strenuously resisting the Germans, now found themselves enveloped by the forward march of the Russians and had to surrender to one or the other. The Russians had thrown some 30 divisions into the scale. One Polish commander, General Anders, commanding a force of three cavalry brigades, who had greatly distinguished himself in the earlier fighting, was wounded in opposing the Germans in the morning and again in opposing the Russians in the afternoon, before falling into the hands of the latter. His name was to be linked with that of General Sosnkowski as symbols of Polish resistance in later stages of the war.

The defence of Warsaw continued until September 28th. The enemy relied upon continuous air raids and bombardment by heavy artillery. On the 23rd the main water-works were destroyed, and as a consequence the fires started by incendiaries increased. On the 26th the Poles recorded 137 serious fires, and large sections of the capital were burnt out. The population suffered heavy loss. Negotiations for a capitulation were begun on the 28th, and on the 30th the Germans marched into the smoking city. They claimed the capture of 150,000 prisoners. Modlin surrendered on the same day with another 5,000 men. Hel, at the toe of the peninsula north of the Gulf of Danzig, held out until October 2nd. The Polish commander, Vice-Admiral Unrug, had at that time 4,000 sailors and soldiers under his command and almost as many German prisoners in his hands.

The last fight, and a gallant one on the Polish side, was fought by a small force under General Kleeberg. Finding that the Russians had reached Brest-Litovsk in the north and Lvov in the south, he decided to march westward from his frontier position south of the Pripet and join the garrison of Warsaw. Pushing Russian forces out of his path, he crossed the Bug and forced his way a hundred miles to the west until held up by the Germans in strength north-east of Deblin. Despite the enemy's superiority, which was five-fold in artillery, the struggle lasted until October 5th, when Russian armoured divisions closed upon him from the east and the survivors of his detachment were compelled to surrender. In all the Germans captured about half a million prisoners, and the Russians, without any fighting to speak of, a substantial though considerably smaller number. Only remnants, perhaps 50,000 in all, reached the somewhat dubious havens of Rumania and Hungary. The great Polish Army was destroyed.

Poland was once again partitioned, the Germans taking the western and the Russians the eastern half. The Russians could put forward the argument that the territories occupied by them contained a majority of White Russians; the Germans had no such excuse for an act of aggression pure and simple. The war had begun with a terrible martyrdom and with a demonstration of the might of German arms which were to impress the great nations and frighten the small. And yet the full import of the German victory was not driven home because the gallantry and fighting quality of the Polish forces were not fully appreciated.

The outstanding lesson of the campaign was the power of armoured forces backed by air superiority and opposed to a defence inadequately supported by anti-tank and anti-aircraft weapons. In such circumstances, it had been proved, there was no limit to the depth of the penetration which might be effected by the armour apart from the difficulties of fuel supply. Were the tanks supported by dive-bombers, land artillery could be dispensed with in attacking improvised defences, and no others were likely to be encountered after a break-through. In a country of good roads, such as France or Belgium, it would be even easier to maintain the impetus of the armoured divisions than it had been in Poland, especially if supplies of fuel could be captured along the routes. A few voices and a few pens called attention to the deductions to be made from the Polish campaign, but in general they were not understood.

CHAPTER III

The Winter of 1939-1940

ON the outbreak of war the British Government underwent a reconstruction, one of the most important features of which was the appointment of Mr. Winston Churchill to be First Lord of the Admiralty, the post which he had held in 1914. A War Cabinet was formed. Labour, which constituted the chief opposition party, refused to appoint representatives to join the Government, but promised co-operation in the conduct of the war. The Communists provided a display of political acrobatics which did not impress the country favourably. The party began by issuing a manifesto declaring that this was a just war, but almost immediately afterwards announced that it had been mistaken and that the war was in fact "a fight between imperialist powers over profits." The notice of this remarkable change of policy was clearly to please Russia, which was not only bound to Germany by a pact but at the same time critical of British and French opposition to Germany. Thus, when on October 6th Hitler made in a broadcast speech some approaches to the Allies, which they did not for an instant entertain because these involved acquiescence in his conquest of Poland, M. Molotov followed with a statement that Germany was striving for peace, whereas the Allies were opposed to it—a statement literally true but decidedly partial.

The first measure taken by the Government was the issue of a long and comprehensive series of defence regulations designed to establish complete control over every activity which might affect the conduct of the war. They were accepted without hesitation, though their effect was to abrogate liberties painfully won in centuries of struggle. That which was to be chiefly criticized in the course of the war was Regulation 18B, which permitted the confinement without trial of persons considered by the Minister of Home Security and his advisers to be dangerous to the nation at war.

If in many respects this country was ill prepared for the conflict, the provisions for civil defence had on the whole been thoughtfully and energetically worked out. A service of air raid wardens had been in being for some months. The "black out", imposed before the actual outbreak of war, was thorough, probably the best in Europe. The issue of gas-masks was smoothly effected. Public shelters in the cities were utterly inadequate, but the long lull in the early stages of hostilities enabled the accommodation to be considerably increased. Small steel shelters under which two or three people could sleep, named after the Minister of Home Security, Sir John Anderson, were issued gradually. Auxiliary police and fire services were formed. "Light" and "heavy" rescue parties to deal with air raid damage were organized. The public never discovered the dividing line between the two, except that the heavy rescue men were provided with a ladder longer than that of the light, and it is doubtful whether in practice there was much difference between their functions.

Some observers had been so impressed by the power of the air arm against civilian targets that they had taken a pessimistic and even defeatist attitude about the possibilities of civil defence. It was fortunate that the view of the responsible authorities was different. Over and over again in the course of the war the ability of a well-organized civil defence to save life and property even in what were apparently hopeless circumstances was to be proved in many countries. The weakest point in the initial British organization lay in the arrangements for reporting and dealing with incendiary bombs. A large proportion of the damage done by incendiaries in the second winter of the war could have been avoided, and it was not until the great attacks of that period were virtually over that a compulsory "fire-watching" service had been satisfactorily organized.

The evacuation from the cities of children, and in the case of young children of their mothers also, of "expectant mothers", and helpless citizens such as the weak-minded came in for much criticism, though criticism in such cases is easier than performance. A distressing discovery reflecting upon our whole civilization was that some 11 per cent of the children were verminous. There were also numerous instances of conflict between the parents and the families upon whom the children were billeted, and some complaints of the destructive habits of the children themselves. In these personal matters, however, there was exaggeration of the unhappy side because the good side was not "news", and was therefore not so well known. In view of the quantity of grit about, evacuation was fairly smooth in its working. One unsatisfactory feature of it was the tendency of parents to take the children back when the expected air attacks did not occur. This continued during the lulls between attacks, and all through the war there was coming and going of children between the towns and the country. Even without this there would have been difficulties because some of the reception areas, safe in 1939, became unsafe after the fall of France and had to be cleared in their turn, not only of children who had taken refuge there but also of those native to the regions.

The reorganization of the country to meet the needs of total war began immediately, though it could be completed only step by step. Control of labour, transport, foreign investments, were among the most important. Rationing of food began in January, 1940, for butter, sugar and bacon, and was extended to meat in March. Large subsidies were introduced to keep down the price of flour, meat, and milk. Agriculture was put under rigid control, its main feature, viewed with doubt by many sound critics, being a switch-over from stock raising to the plough and a heavy initial killing of stock. War saving was encouraged and made as attractive as possible not merely to finance the war but also to take the rising wages out of the people's pockets and prevent the decreasing supplies of goods from being bought up. Profits were limited by a tax which may have been as good as could be devised, but which worked singularly unfairly as between firm and firm according to their prosperity at a given period before the war.

It was recognized, though perhaps dimly as yet, that propaganda would play in this war a far greater part than in any hitherto waged. Germany already had her machinery, which was an essential part of the National Socialist state, in full working order. In Britain and in France Ministries of Information were set up. How the French would have developed can only be surmised. The British, beyond taking over from London University the finest building in London, made a poor start and produced an astonishing quantity of indifferent matter which went straight into the waste-paper baskets of newspaper offices. It was to improve considerably. The most powerful weapon for the discharge of propagandist ammunition had, however, now become the wireless broadcast, which had outstripped the press in this respect. The B.B.C.'s start was not bad, but it was slow, perhaps necessarily so. Now and throughout the war the Corporation contrived to maintain a very fair standard of dignity with an unusual regard for the truth so far as it could be revealed, and its prestige abroad never ceased to rise.

The self-governing Dominions went straight into the war. The Australian Government indeed considered that no declaration was necessary and that a state of war began automatically on September 3rd. South Africa had adopted a position of neutrality at the time of the Munich meeting, and its government would certainly have done so again, but it was defeated on a resolution. The country then went to war under the leadership of General Smuts. Only the Irish Free State remained neutral, though many volunteers from among its citizens enlisted in the British fighting services. Northern Ireland, which formed part of the United Kingdom, entered the war as a matter of course, but it was not permitted to impose conscription on the ground that, since so many of its citizens favoured the Free State and were hostile to the United Kingdom, such a measure could not have been enforced without turmoil and bloodshed. All the Dominions began to raise expeditionary forces, and the first Canadian troops reached Great Britain in December. In February the advanced guard of the Australians and New Zealanders arrived in Egypt.

One of the most inspired and fruitful decisions of the war resulted in the inception of a vast air training scheme for the Empire in Canada. This proved to be invaluable, perhaps especially in the period when German fighters were constantly over England and British training aircraft ran considerable risks. Work of similar nature but on a smaller scale was carried out in South Africa.

The outbreak of war found Italy in doubtful mood. Some elements even in her government, despite Fascist sympathy for Germany and the "Berlin-Rome Axis" of 1936, were hopeful of keeping her out. For the time being she watched and waited, benefiting by extremely considerate treatment by the Allies; for example, she was permitted to import German coal by sea. Japan was obviously unfriendly to the Allies and still more so to the United States, but she expressed distaste for the German pact with Russia. In the United States the President, a warm supporter of the ideals of the Allies, was checked by Congress in the matter of the neutrality laws when he sought to increase the aid which friends of freedom in Europe might derive from his country. In general the attitude of the United States was sympathetic to Britain and France, but there was also a firm determination not to be drawn into the war if there were any possibility of keeping out of it.

After he had ended Polish resistance it seemed certain that Hitler would at an early date seek a decision against the Allies in the west. Indeed, the chief question was whether he would attack at once or await fine weather in the spring. Preparations for an early attack were made, but the operation was cancelled. Holland and Belgium, of all countries in Europe, had most cause to dread his intentions, since it was certain that he would outflank the Maginot Line by entering their territories. In November their rulers, Queen Wilhelmina of Holland and King Leopold of Belgium, arranged a meeting and issued a solemn appeal for peace. As matters stood it had no chance of success.

It was notable, however, that there were no appeals—until that made by Finland—to the League of Nations, not even by Poland. The League still had some useful work to do, but in its main function as an instrument of peace it was moribund, if not already dead. The splendid experiment had failed.

One side of international affairs, that of the Scandinavian and Baltic countries, had not yet been touched upon. This is so important and considerable a subject that it must be left to another chapter. Indeed, the Russo-Finnish War, though in some respects a side issue, attracted far more interest and attention throughout the world than any event in the "world war" between the cessation of hostilities in Poland and the German attack on Norway. The lull in the west had made the conflict between Germany and the Franco-British alliance extremely dull, and it had been labelled the "phony war" by American journalists. The Finnish war, on the other hand, was to be dramatic in the extreme.

As in 1914, a British Expeditionary Force was moved to the Continent as quickly as possible. The conditions were, however, altogether different. There had been no German offensive in the west; Belgium was uninvaded and a neutral; the French frontier with Germany was strongly defended by the famous Maginot Line. If matters were easier in this respect, the danger of

air attack was greater and made it desirable to use the western
ports of France, instead of as before those of the Channel, both
for the despatch of the force and for its subsequent continental
bases. The troops were landed at Cherbourg, and stores and
vehicles at Nantes, St. Nazaire, and Brest. In order to provide for
expansion, the base and lines of communication services were
built up on a scale greater than the strength of the original force
would have warranted. A third difference was that the British
Expeditionary Force was definitely under French orders. The
British Army was the only one in the world on a completely
mechanical basis as regards transport, and this, though it provided exceptional mobility, created a new problem in transportation. The Commander-in-Chief was General Viscount Gort, V.C.

The I Corps (Lieut.-General Sir John Dill) took up the position
assigned to it by General Gamelin, the French Commander-in-
Chief, on the Belgian frontier east of Lille. It was followed in
October by the II Corps (Lieut.-General A. F. Brooke). By the
spring the British Expeditionary Force consisted of ten divisions,
including one motor division, the 50th, and was disposed on a
front from the Escaut to a point north of the Lys near Bailleul.
Positions of defence were dug. The work was much hampered
by bad weather, and the results did not strike the eye as impressive.
The Secretary of State for War, Mr. Leslie Hore Belisha, after
inspecting it in its early stages, suggested that a series of great contracting firms should be called in to create the nearest possible
thing to an extension of the Maginot Line, which would reach
the sea. He proposed to employ as labour a large proportion of
refugees from Germany. This project went no further. As the
British troops were not in contact with the enemy, brigades were
sent down in turn for experience in the Saar, and in April, 1940,
a whole division, the 51st, took over a sector on this front.

The French Army began by slowly and carefully feeling its
way into the outpost zone or "forefield" of the German Siegfried
Line which covered the frontier. The operation was designed to
put the maximum possible pressure upon the enemy without
launching an attack upon the main defences, for which General
Gamelin did not consider he possessed the means. It may have
caused the Germans some slight qualms, since the Siegfried Line
was lightly held, but it did not embarrass them materially, even
though the French finally occupied over 250 square miles of

hostile territory and claimed to have at least disturbed the working of the Saar coalfield.

In any case the pressure soon ceased. The Germans were quickly in a position to transfer divisions from east to west, and in early October the French discovered that they were mounting an attack to clear their outpost zone. General Gamelin promptly drew back his main body in secrecy to the Maginot Line, and when on October 16th the Germans attacked in force they found only a cavalry screen in front of them. It too was withdrawn, but it appeared that the artillery inflicted considerable loss on the enemy. On the French side the operation had been skilfully conducted, but its effect upon the troops was not good. They were only too ready as it was to consider their part in the war as a defensive based upon the Maginot Line with the minimum of bloodshed. The manner in which their extremely modest offensive had been broken off and its gains abandoned at the first hint of hostile counteraction tended to reinforce this conception. The Germans also embarked upon a propaganda campaign, conducted by various means but notably by loudspeakers in the front line. The main themes were that France, as before, was being sacrificed by Britain and that the Allies possessed no chance of success now that Russia was bound by treaty to Germany. It appears to have exercised a certain effect upon the spirit of the French troops, who were further depressed by exposure and lack of amenities in an exceptionally bad winter.

The war at sea began quietly. The Germans possessed no force comparable to the High Seas Fleet of the last war. Their battleship strength of five, including three "pocket" battleships or battle-cruisers, was in fact similar to that of France, whereas Britain possessed fifteen. Germany was to rely mainly on the submarine for the purpose of closing British trade routes, above all in the Atlantic, thus depriving her foe of, among other needs, the food and oil without which this country could not continue to fight. To begin with, however, a large proportion of the U-boats were training in the Baltic. The enemy, however, gained some striking initial successes, the first being the sinking of the liner *Athenia*, eastbound to Canada, with considerable loss of life. German propaganda revealed the lines on which it was going to work when it alleged that the ship had been sunk on the orders of Mr. Winston Churchill, the new First Lord of the Admiralty, with the object of dragging the United States into the war. Even more significant was the incident in showing that the Germans intended to fight their submarine campaign on the lines which had developed in the later stages of the last war, that is, sinking of liners and cargo vessels without warning or reasonable chance that crews and passengers could be rescued. This disregard of the laws of war was to colour the tactics of the naval forces, both surface and submarine, of all belligerents, and of the air forces.

On September 23rd was fought the immortal but hopeless action of the merchant cruiser *Rawalpindi* against the German battle-cruisers *Scharnhorst* and *Gneisenau*. It was believed at the time that the *Rawalpindi* had been sunk by the "pocket" battle-ship *Deutschland*, and the truth was not discovered until after the termination of hostilities with Germany in 1945. Though British losses from submarine attack were heavy enough during the first few weeks, they afterwards dropped and there was for some time little warning of how serious this form of attack was to prove.

Another dangerous weapon was the magnetic mine, with which British harbours were liberally sown by German aircraft. The feature of this mine was that contact with the ship's bottom was not necessary; it was exploded by the proximity of a metal hull. It was thus at once deadly to shipping and extremely difficult to approach for the purpose of rendering it innocuous. One mine fortunately fell on a sandbank. It was measured by an expert, Lieut.-Commander J. G. Ouvry, and a set of non-magnetic tools was made in order that it might be opened and examined. The next step was the provision of "de-gaussing" girdles to neutralize the magnetic field of an iron or steel vessel. Thus by a combination of fortune, courage, and inventive spirit the first of Hitler's "secret weapons" was defeated. But it had been a terrible threat. The staffs of the naval commands concerned will remember all their lives the sentiment of helplessness in face of a weapon which appeared for a moment destined to starve the country when they woke up to find their harbour approaches bristling with magnetic mines.

The British blockade, with French aid, was from the first largely successful in cutting Germany off from outside sea supplies with the exception of those carried through the Baltic, and this with less friction than had occurred in the last war. As then, the essence of the blockade was the control of contraband carried

in neutral bottoms and the main object of the Allies to make an
end of German trade without unduly prejudicing the neutrals.
Certificates of "origin and interest" were issued to vessels outward bound from Europe where it could be established that
75 per cent of the cargo was of neutral origin. These corres-
ponded to the "Navicerts" issued in respect of consignments from
the United States, Brazil, Argentina and Uruguay to all European
countries except Germany and Russia. A large quantity of contraband was seized, but as in all such cases success could only have
been measured by the quantity of goods which were not shipped
on account of the blockade. This it was impossible to determine,
but it must have been enormous.

There were not wanting critics who urged that Britain was
being too tender to neutral susceptibilities and that the new
Ministry of Economic Warfare was not accorded the prestige or
the power which its importance merited. On the whole, however,
it was realized that a much better start had been made than in
1914. There were some curious arrangements tacitly recognized
by both sides. For instance, Holland divided her surplus agricultural products carefully into two halves, exporting one to Britain
and the other to Germany. The country itself was virtually at
Germany's mercy, but at the same time depended upon Britain
for the power to import from the New World material such as
oil cake without which the livestock could not have been maintained through the winter. Holland thus afforded such satisfaction as she could to her two powerful neighbours and at the
same time preserved her cherished neutrality.

German attacks were not confined to British ships. The enemy
desired to discourage the neutrals from carrying British goods,
and in pursuit of this policy he attacked neutral shipping with
singular brutality, though not yet on a universal scale. It cannot
be denied that he succeeded to a large extent in frightening neutral
states with maritime interests. One proof of this was furnished
by the incident of the *Altmark*. This German auxiliary cruiser,
with 299 prisoners from British ships aboard, was discovered to
be making her way through Norwegian territorial waters and
actually in the inaccessible passage within the islands of the west
coast. To British protests the Norwegians replied that there was
no evidence of prisoners being aboard. On February 19th, 1940,
the destroyer *Cossack* entered Josing Fjord, boarded the *Altmark*,

and rescued the prisoners. The Norwegian Government protested sharply, but the press and public evidently took a more lenient view of the action.

One of the German "pocket" battle ships, the *Admiral Graf von Spee*, slipped out into the Atlantic at an early stage and did a great deal of damage. After sinking a number of ships in African waters she crossed the South Atlantic and appeared on the eastern coast of South America. Here she was engaged off the River Plate by Commander H. H. Harwood with three cruisers, the *Ajax*, *Achilles*, and *Exeter*, on December 13th. She might have been expected to sink them all with her 11-inch guns against the 8-inch of the *Exeter* and the 6-inch of the other two, and she did indeed stop the *Exeter* and put her out of action. She was herself seriously damaged by the fire of the cruisers, which manœuvred with outstanding boldness and skill, but it was a moral rather than a material defeat which finally drove her into the River Plate under a smoke-screen. The British squadron, joined by the cruiser *Cumberland* in replacement of the damaged *Exeter*, waited outside.

The *Admiral Graf von Spee* dropped anchor at Monte Video, where arguments took place about the time which the Uruguayan Government should afford her to repair the damage she had suffered. Eventually she was given up to 8 p.m. on the 13th. Before the time-limit was reached she steamed into the channel leading to Buenos Aires and was there scuttled by order of Hitler. Her captain shortly afterwards shot himself. Her crew were interned by Argentina. The victory was celebrated with rejoicing in the British Empire and undoubtedly damaged the prestige of the German Navy.

So far as the western Allies, the United Kingdom and France. were concerned, the air war began with a feeble and disappointing phase. All too conscious of their own weakness in the air and with an unjustified hope that they would to some extent catch up in production, the French decided upon and won the British over to a policy of confining attack from the air to objectives on the water. The Germans followed suit. The task of the R.A.F. bombers was for the time being largely confined to the dropping of propagandist leaflets over Germany. It is to be doubted whether this policy paid its way, since propaganda was hardly likely to affect a nation such as Germany which had just won an outstanding victory at small cost and with great ease. The flying experience and the information obtained possessed a certain value.

On the western front a good deal of air fighting developed, in which the British Hurricanes, flown by remarkably skilled and daring pilots, defeated superior numbers of Messerschmidts and established a veritable ascendancy. When German reconnaissance aircraft became active on the east coast of England they suffered equally heavy drubbings from the Spitfires. The Royal Air Force also carried out a number of bold raids within the policy laid down, beginning with one at the very start, on September 4th, on the German fleet at the entrance to the Kiel Canal. In general, however, the air war outside Poland took to begin with a form astonishing to those who had expected decisive battles for the mastery of the skies and mass raids on cities in the manner foretold by the Italian writer General Douhet.

CHAPTER IV

The Finnish and Norwegian Campaigns

THE policy of Russia was to create buffers between herself and Germany. Despite the apparent state of friendliness created by the pact, she viewed the Nazi power with extreme suspicion. The pact on her side was, indeed, an instrument to gain time, time to prepare to meet a German assault, time to occupy space beyond her western frontiers which would absorb some of its impetus when it came. She had begun by creating a deep outpost zone in eastern Poland. She was shortly to compel the Baltic republics of Estonia, Latvia and Lithuania to admit her garrisons, a preliminary to their absorption in the U.S.S.R.

In their case resistance was out of the question, but Finland was stronger both in her armed forces and in her natural defences. Yet Finland included territory more vital in Russian eyes than any possessed by the Baltic states: the northern half of the Karelian Isthmus, between Lake Ladoga and the Gulf of Finland, at the southern end of which, only about a score of miles from the frontier, lay the city of Leningrad and near it the island fortress and naval base of Kronstadt. In early October Russia demanded from Finland the cession of a wide zone on the Karelian Isthmus, a lease of the Baltic port of Hangö as a naval base, a number of islands in the Gulf of Finland, and the western part of the Rybachi (Fisherman's) Peninsula in the far north. Some compensation was offered in Russian Karelia to the east.

Finland gave way on certain points but not on all. On November 28th, Russia denounced the pact of non-aggression between the two countries, and two days later she attacked. Helsinki, the capital, and many other towns were bombed from the air. Finland appealed to the League of Nations against the attack of a fellow-member, and on December 14th Russia was formally expelled from it.

The Russian plan was to execute a series of simultaneous attacks, (a) from the south across the Karelian Isthmus, and (b) from the east north of Lake Ladoga, (c) towards the Gulf of Bothnia at Oulu, (d) through Kuolajärvi to cut the "Arctic Road" to Petsamo, and (e) in the far north against Petsamo directly. The isthmus was protected by relatively strong fortifications known as the "Mannerheim Line" from the name of the Finnish Commander-in-Chief, Field-Marshal Mannerheim, an able soldier though over seventy years of age. The Russians had by far their heaviest task in this sector, but it was the only one in which they could concentrate troops and material on a grand scale because the only one reasonably well served by railways. It was perhaps natural that they should have relied upon their flanking attacks, which had no such obstacles to face, to an undue extent, but the result was that they were not only checked sharply in their first attacks on the Mannerheim Line but also suffered defeats when their inadequately supplied columns thrust in from the east.

The half dozen divisions which launched the initial attacks in the Karelian Isthmus (a) made slow progress through the outposts and were repulsed in front of the Mannerheim Line with considerable loss in tanks. North of Lake Ladoga (b), where about four Russian divisions were operating in the first instance, some initial progress was made, but it was soon brought to a halt, and the first of a series of Finnish victories was won at Tolvajärvi. Then a Russian division, checked at Syskyjärvi, in wild country of forest and rock, was surrounded by Finnish ski troops and gradually broken into fragments. In February, 1940, it was completely destroyed. The threat to Oulu (c), through the forests from Suomussalmi was held, and at least two divisions were virtually annihilated. Two Russian divisions, based on the Murmansk railway at Kandalaksha, passed through Kuolajärvi and Salla (d), and at one moment seemed about to reach the "Arctic Road" and cut Finland in two. In the end, however, they suffered the same fate as the others: envelopment, starvation, and almost complete destruction. Only in the far north did the Russians win success. They overran the Petsamo area and held on to it grimly, though surrounded and harassed by Finnish skiers.

The Russian command was not, however, daunted by these reverses. It recognized soon, if it had failed to do so in the first instance, that there was no short cut to victory. The Mannerheim Line must be smashed; good communications were more important than room to manœuvre. Strong reinforcements were assembled. A great concentration of artillery was effected; tanks were brought up in mass; sleighs were provided in which they

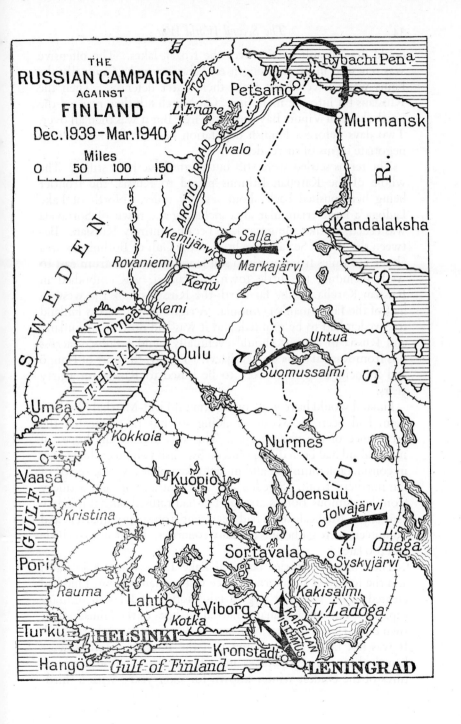

THE
RUSSIAN CAMPAIGN
AGAINST
FINLAND
Dec. 1939 – Mar. 1940

Miles
0   50   100   150

Rybachi Pen.ª
Petsamo
L. Enare
Murmansk
Ivalo
ARCTIC ROAD
Kandalaksha
Kemijärvi
Salla
Rovaniemi
Markajärvi
Kemi
Kemi
Tornea
Oulu
Uhtua
Suomussalmi
Umeå
Kokkola
Nurmes
Vaasa
Kuopio
Kristina
Joensuu
Tolvajärvi
L. Onega
Sortavala
Syskyjärvi
Pori
Rauma
Kakisalmi
L. Ladoga
Lahti
Viborg
Turku
Kotka
HELSINKI
Kronstadt
Hangö
Gulf of Finland
LENINGRAD

SWEDEN
GULF OF BOTHNIA
U. S. S. R.
KARELIAN ISTHMUS

could drag assault parties over the frozen lakes. The offensive was renewed in great strength on February 2nd. Gradually the Finns were driven back from their outer defences. Then the Russians bit into the main line. On March 8th they reached the north shore of Vipuri Bay across the ice. But it was then all over. Two days before a Finnish deputation had left for Moscow to negotiate terms of surrender.

The terms settled were stiff but might have been stiffer. The whole of the Karelian Isthmus passed to Russia, the frontier being here pushed back about seventy miles. North of Lake Ladoga a large triangular area including the town of Sortavala was ceded, so that the great lake became entirely Russian. Between the White Sea and the head of the Gulf of Bothnia an area about 150 miles from north to south and fifty miles from east to west, including the little town Kuolajärvi, was embodied in Russian Karelia. In the far north the Russians took the western half of the Fisherman's Peninsula. A right of way across Finland to Sweden had to be granted, and it was laid down that Finland and Russia in concert should eventually build a railway across this from Kandalaksha to Kemijarvi. Finally, the port of Hangö and its neighbourhood were to be leased to Russia for thirty years.

Finland would have gone on fighting if Field-Marshal Mannerheim had been in favour of doing so, but he advocated the acceptance of the peace terms. This was because the hopes of material aid had been disappointed. Swedish volunteers had come in considerable numbers and in fact taken over a whole sector of the northern front. Sweden had also sent aircraft and artillery from her famous Bofors arsenal, but had refused official military assistance. Medical stores had been sent from many quarters and volunteers were gathering in many countries. But it was too little and too late.

The Finnish victories between Lake Ladoga and Kuolajärvi and the long and stubborn defence of the Mannerheim Line had created in the world at large a false notion of Russian military capacity. The extraordinary martial qualities of the Finns in their own country and in their own winter were insufficiently realized. It was not taken into account that the Russian columns were launched into areas of forest and lake, in the fantastic temperatures of the coldest winter known for sixty years, with a third-rate railway, which at some points was 150 miles from the frontier, behind them. Their leaguers would be surrounded by white-clad Finns on skis. They rarely saw their enemies. Note should rather have been taken of the extreme determination with which they held out in hopeless situations.

And if this state of affairs reflected upon the competence of the command, it should have been noted also that it speedily pulled itself together and set about the reduction of the Mannerheim Line. It applied overwhelming force in a workmanlike way. The infantry maintained the attack with spirit, undeterred by heavy losses. In short, if the Red Army appeared by comparison with the *Wehrmacht* a somewhat clumsy weapon, it was nevertheless an extremely powerful one.

The western allies, Britain especially, had viewed the attack on Finland with disfavour. There was a genuine and widespread sympathy with a little nation subjected to an unprovoked assault. Britain was contemplating the despatch of a small expeditionary force to Finland's aid, and would have sent it through Norway even in face of resistance on the part of that country. Was this purely altruistic sentiment with regard to Finnish liberty? Well, if it sounds cynical, it is yet true to say that no nation committed to a great war permits its attitude to another nation outside the struggle to be governed by altruism alone. If an expeditionary force had been sent to Finland it must have landed in Norway since shipping could not enter the Baltic. Its communications must have been maintained through Norway, and by British forces. And supposing the Russian attack to have been held and peace between Russia and Finland to have been concluded, it was not to be expected that these forces would have hurried home while there remained any danger that the Germans would occupy the Norwegian coast. There was in fact an Anglo-French project for a landing in Norway even after the surrender of Finland.

Germany was aware of this line of reasoning and therefore determined to prevent any allied intervention, though her natural sympathies were with the Finns, and she left the Scandinavian countries in no doubt as to her views on the subject. After the Finnish war was over she decided to forestall the Allies in Norway. She realized that that country would provide good bases for U-boats and in lesser degree surface raiders and aircraft for the attack on British shipping. Even that consideration, however, was subordinate to the transport of Swedish iron ore down the Norwegian coast.

This ore, of the highest quality, was mined near Gellivare in the far north. While the Gulf of Bosnia was open it could be brought down by train to the port of Lulea, but when Lulea was frozen up, as it was all the winter, the only method was to send it by the railway specially built for its export to the Norwegian port of Narvik and ship it there. Unless Germany controlled the Norwegian coast she would be deprived of the Swedish ore for a period of about seven months in the year, to say nothing of the fact that the British might get a proportion of it.

It had been known for some time that Germany was collecting shipping for an expedition in the Baltic, but it was not absolutely certain that Norway was to be the victim. On April 7th air reconnaissance revealed that a considerable fleet was making its way northward from the mouth of the Weser, and the Home Fleet under the command of Admiral Sir Charles Forbes put to sea from Scapa Flow in the Orkneys. The German battleships *Scharnhorst* and *Gneisenau* accompanied the armada up to the neighbourhood of Trondheim and then turned westward, probably with the object of drawing off the Home Fleet. Contact was made, but in thick weather the German ships escaped after a brief engagement. Another British and French naval force had during the night laid a minefield in Norwegian waters near Narvik—a somewhat high-handed proceeding which could be justified only by belief that Norway's neutrality was being abused. This force then drew off westward, losing one destroyer, the *Glowworm*, which, lagging behind to save a man overboard, was caught and sunk after a most gallant fight.

Meanwhile another German fleet of naval vessels and merchant shipping had steamed north through the Kattegat into the great mouth of Oslo Fjord. There was no question of intercepting it by surface vessels, which the British Admiralty was not prepared to risk in Skagerrak for lack of air protection. It was attacked by British submarines and suffered loss, but not of a serious nature. So southern Norway at all events was left to meet the onslaught without outside aid and the Germans had made a good start in their project of subduing the whole country.

Before dealing with the campaign which followed it is con-

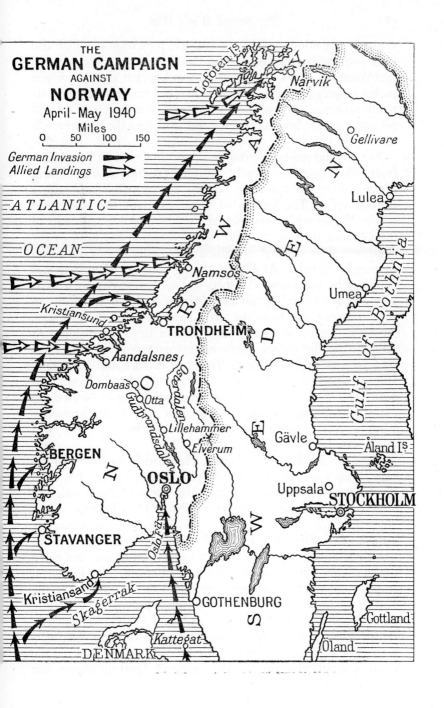

THE
GERMAN CAMPAIGN
AGAINST
NORWAY
April-May 1940
Miles
0   50   100   150

German Invasion ➤
Allied Landings ⇨

ATLANTIC

OCEAN

Lofoten Is

Narvik

Gellivare

Lulea

S
W
E
D
E
N

Namsos

Umea

Kristiansund

TRONDHEIM

Gulf of Bothnia

Aandalsnes

Dombaas

Otta

Osterdalen

Gudbrandsdalen

Lillehammer

Elverum

Gävle

Åland Iˢ

BERGEN

N

OSLO

Uppsala

STOCKHOLM

STAVANGER

Oslo Fd

Kristiansand

Skagerrak

GOTHENBURG

S
W
E
D
E
N

Gottland

Kattegat

Öland

DENMARK

venient to mention the fate of Denmark, possession of which also
came into the German plan. The Danes had long ago concluded
that resistance to a German attack was hopeless and that it was
useless to prepare for it. The country had no defences and virtually no arms. A few shots were fired, but there was no real
resistance to the invasion by sea and land, and the country was
quickly occupied.

Norway did resist, and to some effect. In Oslo Fjord the mine-
layer *Olav Trgdvason* severely damaged the light cruiser *Emden*,
drove a destroyer ashore to become a total wreck, and sank a
minesweeper. The fortress of Oscarborg sank the 10,000 ton
cruiser *Blucher* with torpedoes, and she went down with part of
the German army staff. The capital, Oslo, at the head of the
fjord, was, however, taken without a blow by troops landed on
the nearby airfield. At Bergen the light cruiser *Königsberg* was
damaged by the fire of the forts and sunk next day by a Skua
dive-bomber of the British Fleet Air Arm, flown, not from an
aircraft carrier, but from the airfield at Hatston in the Orkneys.
At Stavanger the destroyer *Aegir* sank a large cargo-ship. At
Kristiansand the cruiser *Karlsruhe* was damaged and afterwards
sunk by a British submarine. The coast defence ship *Norge* sank
another destroyer off Narvik. On the other hand, Trondheim
was taken with little loss to the enemy; the little Norwegian
Navy was destroyed; and the Germans established themselves
ashore at every point at which they attempted landings. They had
all the airfields.

Then the British took a hand. The British destroyers of the
minelaying force which had withdrawn in face of the advance of
the German fleet returned in the early hours of April 10th and
attacked the German destroyer flotilla in Narvik harbour. It
was a fight against odds, five destroyers against eight more heavily
armed. The *Hunter* was sunk and the *Hardy* went aground, but
one German destroyer was sunk, three were set on fire, and half a
dozen supply ships were also sent to the bottom. The last naval
engagement of the campaign was fought on the 13th when the
British destroyers, reinforced and accompanied by the battleship
Warspite, flying the flag of Vice-Admiral W. G. Whitworth,
returned to the scene. The remaining seven German destroyers
were all sunk. Submarines and aircraft continued to strike at the
German supply ships, and in the course of April the enemy lost

100,000 tons of shipping. But in the same space of time the Germans had got 60,000 men into the country.

The King of Norway escaped from Oslo, but subsequently gave an interview to the German Minister at Elverum. The Norwegian Government was prepared to resign in favour of another "which would collaborate with Germany", and the Germans might have obtained an official submission from Norway had they not insisted upon the appointment as Prime Minister of Major Vidkun Quisling, a political adventurer in the confidence of Hitler and his Foreign Minister, Ribbentrop. King Haakon declared that he would abdicate rather than make such an appointment. The Government then decided to fight to a finish, but it was only the King who had come well out of the episode.

On land the Norwegians could effect little because the Germans had rendered impossible the process of mobilization except in the far north. All now depended upon Britain, and the key to the situation was the port of Trondheim, the most northerly which had good communications with the main centres of population to the south. The Allied General Staffs planned a direct attack by naval forces supported by the Fleet Air Arm to silence the batteries and thus permit troops to be landed in the outer part of the fjord. As a preliminary two enveloping forces were to be landed on either side, at the fishing ports of Namsos and Aandalsnes to the north and south-west. The former comprised the 146th Brigade (from the 49th Division) and a demi-brigade of French Chasseurs Alpins, the latter the 148th Brigade (49th Division) followed by the 15th Brigade. The strategy was clever and the prospects at first sight good, since at most 4,000 German troops had landed at Trondheim and Norwegian resistance had prevented reinforcements from reaching them from the south. All things considered, too, the countermove was rapid, the landing at Namsos beginning on April 16th and that at Aandalsnes on the 18th. A third force was landed in the Narvik region, but it was incapable of playing a part in the main struggle and might well have been added to those in central Norway. It consisted of the 24th Guards Brigade with supporting troops and the French 1st Light Division, which included a Polish brigade. The expedition was carried out mainly because it was the original allied project already mentioned.

The main attack was, however, abandoned for lack of air support and fear of naval casualties from bombing. The British were dogged by their inability to obtain an airfield. It was decided, not very hopefully, perhaps, to take Trondheim entirely by envelopment. But the head of the Aandalsnes column under Brigadier Morgan, on reaching Dombaas, was persuaded to move down the long and majestic valley of the Gudbrandsdalen to answer Norwegian appeals for aid. And the head of the Namsos column, moving down to Trondheim Fjord, was held by a force which had come out to meet it, and attacked by two German destroyers in the fjord, which not only shelled it but also landed further troops to take it in the flank. Near Lillehammer in the Gudbrandsdalen Brigadier Morgan's force was driven back, and the Germans pressed north, not only in this valley, but also in the Osterdalen. Some temporary air support was provided by aircraft flown from British carriers and by a squadron of Gladiators which landed on a frozen lake near Dombaas, but the latter were all eventually destroyed after their pilots had performed prodigies of valour. It was lack of an airfield which prevented the landing of supporting arms and supplies, thus paralysing the expeditionary force.

On the 27th it was decided to withdraw from central Norway. This operation was conducted skilfully under the command of Major-General A. Carton de Wiart from Namsos and Major-General B. C. T. Paget from Aandalsnes, though the buildings of these little ports had been laid flat by German bombers and the wooden quays had been destroyed. In the Gudbrandsdalen the Germans were sharply checked in rear-guard actions near Otta and in front of Dombaas by the British regular brigade, the 15th, which had been sent from France. The losses were relatively small and the Germans never claimed more than three hundred prisoners in the whole of this section of the campaign.

The struggle was continued in the north, mainly in the Narvik region, by an allied force consisting of British, French, Polish and Norwegian troops. Here an airfield was secured, and air support made all the difference. After long delay due to bad weather Narvik was recaptured on May 27th. The Germans were driven up the railway towards Sweden and faced with the alternative of surrender or withdrawal to internment over the frontier. They were saved by the bad news from France, which compelled the Allies to take away their troops and above all their shipping. The King and the Government accompanied the force to the United Kingdom. A tragedy accompanied the evacuation, the aircraft carrier *Glorious*, the destroyers *Acasta* and *Ardent*, and the empty liner *Orama*, which had been used as a transport, being sunk.

In view of the state of affairs in France the decision to withdraw was inevitable, though it involved leaving Norwegian comrades in arms to their fate, as had also happened in central Norway. It may be said that on the whole the British, in control of the expedition and supplying most of the forces taking part, had got out of the affair skilfully and cheaply when they realized how badly things were turning out. The employment of raw and ill-equipped troops such as those of the 49th Division looks like frivolous optimism, but there were no others available without drawing further upon the B.E.F. in France, which would have been madness.

Yet the effect was disastrous all over the world. It raised German prestige immensely and correspondingly depressed that of the Allies, especially of Britain. At home, as will appear, it aroused a fierce anger which would not be slaked till it had found victims.

CHAPTER V

Reaction to the Campaign in Norway

THE outcome of the Russian attack on Finland was ill received in the United Kingdom. It was generally considered that Finland's appeals had not been answered as fully as they might have been. Press and Parliament were alike dissatisfied and restless. In a debate in the House of Commons the Prime Minister, Mr. Neville Chamberlain, contended that the Allies had not failed in their obligations, but his speech did not carry conviction. The Labour and Liberal Parties more or less accepted his contention, but damaging attacks were launched by his own supporters, Mr. Richard Law, son of a former Prime Minister, and Mr. Harold Macmillan.

On April 3rd the Cabinet was reorganized, but the shuffle of offices did not increase the prestige of the Ministry. The most important innovation was the abolition of the Ministry for the Co-ordination of Defence, which was replaced by a committee of the service ministers and the Minister of Supply, presided over by Mr. Churchill, First Lord of the Admiralty.

Many commentators had since enlarged upon British good fortune in being prevented from irretrievably offending Russia by the despatch of an expeditionary force to Finland. The region of the might-have-been in history is always somewhat unprofitable to explore, but it may be remarked that this view is too much simplified. It is doubtful whether the arrival of a British force would have embittered the Russians more than they were already by such aid as was actually sent, while Russia would in any case have been glad to accept British aid when attacked by Germany. The worst danger which Britain avoided was the locking up in Finland of reserves which she could not afford.

The half gale which the Government weathered after the Finnish campaign was as nothing to the storm which it had to meet after the withdrawal from central Norway. The press was far more hostile. In a two-day debate which began on May 7th, the Cabinet and the Prime Minister himself were hotly attacked. Once again it was his own supporters, this time Mr. L. S. Amery and Mr. Duff Cooper, who made the most critical and effective speeches, but now Mr. Herbert Morrison joined in the onslaught and announced that the Labour Party would divide the House. The best defence was that of Mr. Churchill, but he was not on strong ground because his office of First Lord involved him particularly in the decision not to attack Trondheim. In the division all the privy councillors present who were not in the Government and many members of the armed forces voted with the opposition. The Government majority sank to 81. On May 10th, despite the fact that the German invasion of Holland and Belgium had been launched that morning, Mr. Chamberlain resigned.

Mr. Winston Churchill was his inevitable successor. He had been long out of office before the war and had persistently striven to awaken the nation to the dangers in which it stood from German aggression. Of hardly another man could it be said that his record was completely clean and satisfactory in those years when the Government had been hiding its head in the sand and the Opposition had been clamouring for strong action and simultaneously voting against every attempt to arm the British forces. At the same time his indomitable spirit, energy, and experience were welcome in this grave hour.

The new Government was a coalition in the fullest sense. The posts of First Lord of the Admiralty (Mr. A. V. Alexander), Minister of Supply (Mr. Herbert Morrison), Minister of Labour (Mr. Ernest Bevin), and Minister of Economic Warfare (Mr. Hugh Dalton) went to the Labour Party, while its leader, Mr. C. R. Attlee, became Lord Privy Seal and deputy-leader of the House. The small Liberal Party was represented by Sir Archibald Sinclair as Secretary of State for Air. A War Cabinet of five was appointed, consisting of the Prime Minister, Mr. Chamberlain (Lord President of the Council), Mr. Attlee, Mr. Arthur Greenwood (Minister without Portfolio), and Lord Halifax (Foreign Secretary), all except the last-named being without departmental duties.

There was some objection in the Labour Party to the retention of Mr. Chamberlain, but none to that of Lord Halifax, though he was regarded by some as an "appeaser". Two outstanding men besides him, Lord Woolton at the Ministry of Food and Sir John Anderson as Home Secretary and Minister of Home Security, retained their former offices and were welcome to all parties. The greatest parliamentarian left out was Mr. Leslie Hore Belisha, who had resigned the office of Secretary of State for War at the beginning of the year. The new Government was in general greeted with enthusiasm and on May 13th it received a vote of confidence which was unanimous but for the opposition of two members of the Independent Labour Party.

Parliament was right in its proceedings if astray in many of its arguments. It was essential that the atmosphere of smug, unreasoned optimism which had enveloped the Government should be dissipated. It was essential that new blood should be brought in. It was essential above all that Labour should participate in the councils of the nation and bear its share of the responsibilities, not because it possessed special ability—for with a few brilliant exceptions its standard was low—but because it had behind it the suffrages of vast numbers of working people who would have to submit to direction and dictation in the interests of total war, and because the burden must be distributed over the greatest possible number of backs. The overthrow of Mr. Chamberlain's Government was a healthy and useful political action.

Yet if the new Government had been in office at the time of the German attack on Norway, or even for three months before, it would have made no difference. If Chatham and Castlereagh and Haldane, Louvois and Carnot and Clémenceau, had returned to assist the Supreme War Council, they could scarcely have changed the fate of the campaign, unless it can be supposed that by some stroke of genius they could have brought about contact between the Home Fleet and the German armada which sailed up the west coast, and could have directed the bulk of the available submarines into the Kattegat to intercept the other fleet which went into the Oslo Fjord. Supposing even that Trondheim had been recaptured, the Germans would still not have been beaten. They already had the measure of the half mobilized, scattered, badly armed, and poorly-trained Norwegians in the south. The capture of an airfield in the Trondheim zone would not in itself have produced air superiority, and if this country had thrown in its reserves of fighter aircraft, small in any case, it would have left itself in a parlous situation. If it had not done so it would have suffered crippling blows to the Navy.

The enemy could reinforce his garrison in southern Norway

without appreciably weakening his strength on the western front and that with relatively well-trained and well-equipped land forces. The United Kingdom and France could not spare troops of equally good quality, and the former's territorial divisions in particular were not at this period a match for German troops or the Austrian mountain troops of which the enemy made large use in Norway. The Allies fought at a heavy disadvantage and did not possess the forces in hand or the war production which would have enabled them to overcome it.

It was clear that one of the main tasks which the new Government would have to undertake with renewed energy was that of putting the nation to work to meet the requirements of total war. Despite the call-up under the National Service Act and over 200,000 voluntary enlistments, the figure for unemployment was still over a million and a quarter by March, 1940. This in itself was proof that the national production was falling grievously short.

Some of the denunciations which fell upon the head of the Government were unjust, since the nation at large and even the majority of its informed public spokesmen did not realize—perhaps happily for themselves and for *morale*—that it takes two years or more to switch a nation such as the United Kingdom over from a peace to a war economy and to gear it to the maximum productivity. It is also the case that in such circumstances it is dangerous to concentrate upon the present and immediate future at the expense of the more distant future—for example, to accelerate production of obsolescent material without modifying plant in order to be able to produce better material. It was none the less manifest that there had been indecision, lack of initiative, and waste over and above what was inevitable and what the country could afford.

In France it was the Finnish campaign which brought down the Government, though as in Britain the former premier obtained a place in the new Cabinet. M. Paul Reynaud represented an improvement upon M. Daladier in ability and courage, but he had less solid party backing. He formed his Ministry on March 21st, bringing in three Socialists. On the 29th M. Reynaud came to London to a meeting of the Supreme War Council. The British and French Governments pledged themselves not to conclude an armistice or peace treaty except by mutual agreement.

German diplomacy was not idle meanwhile. On March 18th

the Axis dictators, Hitler and Mussolini, met in the Brenner and conferred at length. The Führer is believed to have revealed his general intentions to the Duce. But the time for Italy's intervention was not yet come. There was a strong anti-war party in the country which included at that time Count Ciano, Mussolini's son-in-law, and even the Duce himself had probably not decided to go to war as an ally of Germany until he saw the latter certain of victory over the western powers and the way clear for himself to reap territorial advantages in Africa and the department of Alpes-Maritimes in Southern France. Meanwhile he sent reinforcements into Albania, his Balkan bridgehead over the Adriatic.

There was little change in the policy of the United States as the result of the two northern campaigns. Sentiment had been shocked by both of them and realization of the danger that the war might develop into a world war had grown stronger. There could be no doubt, however, that it was both the national policy and the desire of the majority of the people to keep out of the war. That sympathy was overwhelmingly on the side of Germany's opponents and victims was equally manifest. It had already been shown by the acceptance of orders for aircraft on British and French account which by the middle of February, 1940, reached several thousands. American applications for Navicerts had also become numerous, and in general the American attitude to the problem of contraband had been lenient from the allied point of view. President Roosevelt, whose own sentiments were strongly in favour of the Allies and who realized far more clearly than most of the nation the extent of the Nazi menace, not only to free Europe but even to the United States, knew that he could not further force the pace of opinion at present.

CHAPTER VI

The Campaign in the Low Countries and France

ALL through April, 1940, there had been reports of German activity in the west, especially on the Dutch and Belgian frontiers. On May 7th the Dutch received word that a German attack was likely to take place at any moment. All military leave was stopped. The Belgian Government called to the colours some further recruits. There was, however, little the two countries could do. They were already mobilized and had taken such precautions as were in their power. There could be no doubt that it was the German intention to turn the French left as in 1914 by the invasion of neutral territory, but that this time Holland as well as Belgium would be involved.

The Dutch had under arms eight divisions in addition to fortress troops. The armament was deplorably weak and the state of training backward, though it had been somewhat improved during the winter. The defensive system was, as in olden days, based on water. East of the River Ijssel the country was to be held only by an outpost screen. The first strong defensive line lay along the Ijssel and the Maas, the Dutch name for the river known in France and French-speaking Belgium as the Meuse. This could be inundated, though not deeply unless there was ample time. The main line, sometimes known as the "Zuyder Water Line", ran from the southern side of the Zuyder Zee (partly reclaimed in recent years) across the great rivers and then turned west. Further inundations covered "Fortress Holland", which contained Amsterdam, Rotterdam, and the Hague. The defences were well designed. The chief weakness lay in the proposed dispositions. Too large a proportion of the scanty available forces was allotted to the outer defences, so that the reserves within the inner line were dangerously weak for their tasks, whereas there was no real hope of a prolonged defence outside the Zuyder Water Line.

The Belgian Army was a more formidable force, amounting to fifteen divisions. Its armament was superior to that of the Dutch, though lamentably inferior to that of the Germans. The air force possessed about two hundred machines. The military instruction of the officers was also better than that of the Dutch. The main line of defence was the Albert Canal, built for this purpose even more than for that of transport, which ran from Antwerp to near Maastricht on the Meuse. Part of the country north of this obstacle could be flooded, given sufficient time. South of Maastricht the system was based upon the powerful fortress defences of Liége, and south of that upon a series of works running down through the Ardennes and along the frontier of the neutral and defenceless Grand Duchy of Luxembourg. Another line of defence ran from Antwerp to the confluence of the Meuse and Sambre at Namur and thence down the gorge of the river to the French frontier.

There had been no co-ordination in Dutch-Belgian plans and the systems of defence were almost ludicrously incapable of mutual aid. The Albert Canal and the Zuyder Water Line actually faced one another with a gap of some thirty miles between, into which the Germans could penetrate without difficulty to separate the Belgian and Dutch Armies, while the Albert Canal itself could be turned by a passage of the Meuse from Dutch Limburg.

The German attack on Holland and Belgium by air and land began before dawn on May 10th. Following their technique in Norway, the Germans presented memoranda, through their Minister at the Hague and their Ambassador in Brussels, justifying their action and promising to "safeguard" the two countries, after the first acts of aggression had actually taken place. It will be convenient to record first of all the fate of Holland, since the campaign in that country was of a more or less isolated nature.

The Germans quickly reached Maastricht and effected a crossing into Belgium. Further north they lined up on the Ijssel and on May 12th effected a passage at Arnhem, where they secured a bridgehead. They dropped strong bodies of parachutists within the inner fortress. These were overcome in savage and bloody fighting, but they contained a considerable number of Dutch troops urgently wanted elsewhere. The campaign could in any case have had but one ending; that which precipitated its end was the enemy's capture of the great Moerdijk bridges over the Hollandsche Diep, the main estuary of the Maas. The advanced guard which seized it could never be dislodged, and on the 13th an armoured column which had come through North Brabant

THE
GERMAN CAMPAIGN
AGAINST
THE LOW COUNTRIES & FRANCE
May-June 1940

Miles

0   50   100

crossed it and pressed forward towards Rotterdam. That was fatal. Fortress Holland was penetrated. Further north the Ijssel Line was smashed; to the south French troops which were coming up to fill the gap between the Dutch and Belgian defences were pressed back in the direction of Antwerp.

The decisive act was the bombing of Rotterdam on May 14th. The German air arm had been attacking all the time, showering high explosive and incendiary bombs on towns and harbours. Now, when the Dutch air force had been practically destroyed, the Luftwaffe systematically demolished a large section of the city. The Germans threatened Utrecht with a like fate, but that evening the Dutch were ordered to cease fire. The troops in Zeeland were excepted from the capitulation and a number escaped by sea, but about 10,000, hemmed in by bombing and magnetic mines, were afterwards compelled to surrender. Over 80,000 men had been killed or wounded.

The British Navy accomplished some fine work in the course of the brief tragedy and carried out important demolitions, including that of the oil tanks at Amsterdam, before withdrawal. Queen Wilhelmina, her daughter and heir Princess Juliana, and the latter's young children were taken off and carried to the United Kingdom.

The plan of the Franco-British Allies was to swing up into Belgium, hinging on the Meuse at Givet, to the front Givet, Namur, Wavre, Louvain, Antwerp. On the northern flank they would have in front of them the obstacle of the Dyle, on the southern that of the Meuse, but in the centre there was a wide stretch of open country, the "Gembloux Gap". It was a good enough line, but it was certainly not chosen for its military advantages alone. It had also the political advantage of encouraging the Belgians, who might not, it was feared, otherwise have made a prolonged resistance. But for that consideration the Allies would probably have preferred to fight on the Escaut or even on the frontier.

The French strength was now eighty divisions, in addition to the garrison of the Maginot Line. As previously stated, the British possessed ten divisions—including one in the Saar—and the Belgians fifteen. The Germans had at their disposition no more than eighty divisions in first line, including the attack on Holland, but there were thirty to forty more in deep reserve and they were incomparably stronger in striking power. The British did not possess a single armoured division. The French possessed four—and even of these one was improvised in the course of the campaign. The Germans used eight, and six mechanized divisions with light tanks. In the air the German superiority was approximately three-fold. With the aid of wireless the Germans had established a system of co-operation between aircraft and armour such as had not even been attempted by their enemies. The Luftwaffe also included a proportion of dive-bomber squadrons which were intended to act in close support of the land forces. Again, the tactics of the Germans were far more enterprising than those of the French and their staff work was on a higher level.

The Germans had cast aside the linear tactics of the last war because they realized that armour with air support did away with the former disadvantages of the column and permitted it to carry the principle of concentration to its highest point. German tactics in attack were designed to pierce a deep system of defence at several points by armoured columns on a narrow frontage, covered by dive-bombers and supported by motor-borne infantry employed to widen the breaches. Once through the defences one column would converge upon another to envelop a section of the defence, which would then be mopped up by infantry. It was a system which was to meet its match in defence later on and to be modified considerably, but against such a defence as the French could now put up it was well-nigh infallible. The smooth machinery for fuel supply and maintenance, and the mobility and skill of the supporting engineers were other good cards in the German hand. If armoured forces, pushing on fast, became entirely isolated, they would form a leaguer, preferably in a wood, where they were hard to find and, even if found, capable of beating off any attack not strongly supported by artillery.

The allied wheel into Belgium was carried out smoothly and with relatively little interference from the air, no doubt because the enemy did not desire to check it. The leading troops reached their new positions on May 11th. Meanwhile the Belgians had lost important positions on the Meuse and the Albert Canal near Maastricht without having demolished them, and the enemy was crossing. On the 12th an attack of magnificent gallantry was carried out on the Maastricht bridge by five R.A.F. bombers,

3

only one of which returned. The bridge was partially wrecked, but the Albert Canal line was already doomed. This was bad, but by no means disastrous if the Dyle line held. It was now manned by the Belgians in the north from the Scheldt estuary to north of Louvain, by the British thence to Wavre, and by the French First and Ninth Armies from Wavre to the French frontier.

Tuesday, May 14th, was perhaps the blackest day in the war. The Ninth Army, which was covered by the Ardennes, was the weakest and worst equipped of the French forces which had carried out the wheel. Between Sedan and Namur Rundstedt's powerful armoured forces broke through, crossed the Meuse, and made their way into open country, where they met with practically no opposition. While the tanks struck out for the west the breach was widened. The hinge of the wheel into Belgium was smashed.

In the air the situation was equally unfavourable. The little Belgian air force had been almost destroyed. That of the French had been to a large extent driven out of the skies. The R.A.F. squadrons directly under Lord Gort's command fought well and accounted for a considerably larger number of aircraft than they lost themselves, but they were speedily reduced to about fifty machines. Four fresh fighter squadrons were sent out from home, and the British Commander-in-Chief generously allotted three of them to the French front. By the 18th the remainder of the R.A.F. squadrons on the Continent had moved to airfields in central France where they could play only a reduced part in the battle.

In view of the Dutch surrender and the break-through in the Ardennes the French Seventh Army, which had moved up to fill the gap between Belgians and Dutch, was ordered to draw back towards the French frontier in the region of Valenciennes, leaving a corps to hold the Dutch territory south of the Scheldt as long as possible. It had thus to cross the British lines of communication, but this was effected without friction.

The French chain of command was functioning badly, and General Billotte, who was co-ordinating the operations of the allied forces in Belgium, did not receive orders to withdraw soon enough. It was not till after Lord Gort had represented to him the seriousness of the situation that orders were issued, on the

morning of the 16th, to withdraw in three day-stages to the
Escaut. This of course involved the abandonment of Brussels and
Antwerp. The movement began that night.

By the evening of May 17th the breach in the French defences
on the Meuse was sixty miles wide and the enemy's armoured
advanced guard was shearing its way towards St. Quentin. The
roads both in Belgium and France were blocked by throngs of
refugees, who greatly hindered the movements of the troops and
their transport.

The first stage of the British withdrawal was carried out successfully on the night of May 16th and the following day. Three
British divisions, without artillery and with only skeleton signals
and administrative units, which had recently joined the B.E.F.
to work in rearward areas, were now called upon, provided with
field, anti-tank and anti-aircraft weapons from reserve stores, and
disposed in flanking positions, one of them being stationed on the
Canal du Nord between Péronne and Douai. By the morning
of the 18th the British were back on the Dendre. The Belgian
front on their left curved forward in a sharp salient covering
Antwerp. On their right the French line ran south from Ath,
with a similar salient near Maubeuge. But further south the
Germans were unchecked, and their advance guards were at the
gates of St. Quentin and Laon. By the night of the 18th the withdrawal to the Escaut was complete.

On May 18th M. Reynaud assumed the office of Minister of
National Defence, appointed the aged Marshal Pétain Vice-
President of the Council, and brought the determined Jew,
M. Mandel, one of the few really honest, resolute, and able
French politicians, to the Ministry of the Interior. Next day he
appointed General Weygand, who had flown home from Syria,
Chief of the General Staff of National Defence and Commander-
in-Chief in the room of General Gamelin. The moment had
come, however, when the will and power of divisions either to
stand and fight or to counter-attack was more important than
even administration or leadership. And the former seemed to
be deserting the French. In the north too the Belgians were becoming shaky. The British were still steady and well in hand, and
they contrived to take a toll of hostile tanks whenever they were
attacked. It must, however, be admitted, that they had not had
to endure as heavy a pounding as their allies on either flank.

The British Government had decided that the B.E.F. should move out southward to avoid being cut off. Lord Gort felt that it would be impossible to break contact of the Escaut, fight a rear-guard action—because the withdrawal was certain to be followed up—and at the same time cut a way through across the Somme through an area into which large hostile forces had already penetrated. He did make one effort, on May 21st, to clear a way to the south by a counter-attack with elements of two divisions and an armoured brigade. It was partially successful, though the support received from the French was limited, and it inflicted considerable loss on the enemy. But the position reached south of the Scarpe in the region of Arras could not be maintained in view of the threat of envelopment from the west. Lord Gort withdrew the striking force just in time on May 23rd.

By now the Germans were on the coast from the Aa to the Bresle. The British had thrown garrisons into Calais and Boulogne, but the latter was evacuated during the night. From above Amiens, the enemy held an enormous bridgehead over the Somme. The B.E.F., the Belgians, the French First Army, and the French corps which had been left in Dutch territory south of the Scheldt were completely cut off. The British lines of communication were cut, and the force could now be maintained only through the northern ports. The southern flank had, however, been fairly well organized along the canals from the Escaut to La Bassée and thence to St. Omer and the sea along the Aa.

General Weygand's plan was to carry out a large-scale counter-offensive, the B.E.F. and French First Army attacking south-westward across the German wedge while the forces south of the Somme struck northward to meet them. It seemed promising, but it was in fact impracticable. Lord Gort at first allotted to it two divisions but then found he could not simultaneously disengage from increasing pressure, support the Belgians who were now beginning to break up, and thrust southward. The operation was in the end limited to some secondary thrusts, partially successful, by the French against the German bridgehead over the Somme from the south. On this flank there were now the British 1st Armoured Division, which had been landed at Havre, and the 51st Division, which had moved up from the Saar but not soon enough to avoid being cut off from the B.E.F.

The next withdrawal of the B.E.F. and French First Army was to the River Lys. While it was in progress the King of the Belgians, whose army was reaching the limits of endurance, capitulated, the surrender taking effect at midnight on May 27th/28th. This completely exposed the allied left and entailed the risk that German armoured forces, pressing down the coast, would reach the Dunkirk beaches and that all the allied forces in the north would be cut off and compelled to surrender. This danger was parried, but Lord Gort was convinced that there was no alternative now but to form a perimeter round the section of the coast between Nieuport and Dunkirk and embark the maximum number of troops of the B.E.F. In this he had the support of the Government. Lines of communication troops were already being taken off. A considerable German force was contained by the heroic defence of Calais, which held out until May 27th.

On May 28th the front formed a parallelogram nearly thirty-five miles deep but less than twenty miles wide, its southern end on the Lys, its eastern flank on the canals between Comines and the sea at Nieuport, its western flank on the front Dunkirk-Cassel-Hazebrouck. By the 31st it had been drawn in to the small perimeter Nieuport-Furnes-Bergues—west of Dunkirk. The Dunkirk basins had been emptied by bombing and the evacuation had to be carried out from the piers or over the open beaches. The Navy, by a marvellous feat of improvisation, assembled 887 vessels, of which 222 were naval craft, from destroyers downwards, 91 passenger or merchant ships, and the rest small craft of every kind. Yachtsmen and fishermen from all along the coast took part.

Here, however, there arose a controversy which was to poison Franco-British relations and which has even now not been forgotten. The French naval and military commanders had first of all hoped that British and French together would fight it out in the perimeter, though the prospects of holding it permanently were dim. When they found that the British were determined to evacuate they expected that an equal proportion of French and British troops would be taken off. Lord Gort considered that it was his first duty to save his own forces. He did later allot a number of ships to the French and they sent a number of their own, but in the end, while all British troops which had reached the perimeter were taken off, a number of French were left behind.

The Germans bombed the beaches and the shipping lying off them heavily. Now, however, the British fighters could intervene from their home bases. In four days from May 27th, 179 German aircraft were shot down by the R.A.F., with some aid from the Fleet Air Arm, for the loss of 29 British. On the whole the allied naval losses were lighter than could have been expected. Seven British destroyers, a minesweeper, and about twenty smaller craft were sunk, while the French lost about the same number. But a heavy price had to be paid for this concentration of destroyers in the Channel, and the losses from submarines in the Atlantic leapt up.

Fighting fiercely to hold the shrinking perimeter, the British held on to Dunkirk to the end. The last of the rearguard, which had been under the command of Major-General the Hon. H. R. L. G. Alexander since the evening of May 31st, was taken off on the night of June 2nd. In all 335,000 British and Allied troops were saved, a far greater number than the most optimistic had hoped to rescue. They had lost all their equipment and material, and this represented the bulk of what Britain possessed. All the eggs had been in one basket and were now broken. On the other hand, the Allies were very lucky to have saved so many men, and they owed their good fortune not only to the stoutness of their rearguards but also to a lack of forcefulness on the part of the enemy wholly unpredictable in a victorious army and a German army at that.

Meanwhile the French to the south had been given a short respite for reorganization on the Somme (less the German bridgeheads south of it) and the Aisne. General Weygand had created a rudimentary system of defence in depth superior to that of his predecessor. The remains of the French armies, were however, in an indifferent state. It was not merely that they were out-weaponed; in some cases they did not even wait on the ground to which they had been assigned for that to be proved. Officers of the British 52nd Division, which was landed south of the break-through area, took part in the later stage of the fighting, and eventually had to retreat to Cherbourg, noted that whenever their artillery opened fire on the enemy he sheered off and attacked the French on their flank, and that the latter at once gave way.

There was, however, strong resistance in patches at the outset, especially on the Aisne. The first great break-through occurred south of the Somme. The enemy swept through Upper Normandy to Rouen. By June 10th he was over the Seine. And on that day Italy declared war on the Allies. It appeared that the end could not now be far off.

It was apparent that one of the decisive factors in the inability of the French to hold their ground was German superiority in the air. Strong appeals were made—and these came from some British sources as well as French—to the British Government to throw in more of the squadrons, especially those of Spitfires, reserved for the defence of the United Kingdom. The policy had already been bolder than was supposed at the time and perhaps than is generally known now. On May 10th there had been six fighter squadrons in France. During the first week of the campaign the equivalent of another ten squadrons was sent over, and on the 18th, when British fighter strength in France was at its peak, there were therefore sixteen fighter squadrons beyond the Channel. During the first ten days, too, six Hurricane squadrons from Kent regularly flew from Kentish airfields, fuelled on French airfields, operated over the battle area, and returned the same day to their bases. By May 22nd, owing to the withdrawal of the R.A.F. "Fighter Component" with the British Army, only three squadrons remained in France, but when the battle opened on the Somme two more were sent out on June 7th and the five remained until Marshal Pétain had asked for a cessation of hostilities. The effort over Dunkirk had been tremendous, and by the end of the evacuation only three of the day-fighter squadrons of Fighter Command had not been involved in Continental fighting.

The British Government, however, acting on the advice of the heads of the services, regretfully but firmly refused to part with its last reserve. It knew that the squadrons could get out to France but that not a fraction of their ground staffs or material would reach them. They would thus be deprived of half their value. They would likewise be hunted from airfield to airfield as the French gave way, perhaps finally to be bombed on the ground when out of fuel. The British Government did not believe that this sacrifice would save France, but they did believe that it would deprive Britain of her most precious weapon against invasion. It may not appear a magnanimous decision, but any other would have been suicidal. The world must be grateful that it was taken. Otherwise Britain might now be a German colony, in which case France herself would not have been liberated.

The French Government on June 12th declared Paris an open town and retired to Tours. On the 15th it moved to Bordeaux. Fervent appeals were made to Britain and the United States for aid. The British Government, realizing that France might at any moment throw up the sponge, made a remarkable offer to the French, an offer of a complete union between the two nations. But M. Reynaud resigned. Marshal Pétain formed a new Government which was determined to surrender and had been purged of those elements in the former Cabinet who had advocated withdrawal to North Africa with the fleet, France's last powerful weapon. Late in the night of June 16th he got in touch with the Germans and asked for a cessation of hostilities.

The Germans did not reply for three days, during which they continued to pour southwards towards Lyons and Bordeaux and westward into Brittany to Brest. Ships carried off the remainder of the British forces and numbers of refugees of many nationalities from the western ports. On June 22nd the Italians attacked in the south. Though the odds in their favour were about six to one, they scarcely dented the French position. But in the evening of the 24th the French Government signed an armistice convention with Italy. The Germans had had their armistice terms accepted on the 22nd, but they did not order the cease fire till six hours after learning of the Italian armistice, professedly to safeguard their ally but perhaps also to ensure that Mussolini should not be able to boast that, even for a moment, he had fought France single-handed.

The German terms, dictated in a theatrical setting chosen by the Führer, at Rethondes in the Forest of Compiègne and in the very railway salon carriage in which Foch had handed those of the allies to the Germans in 1918, were severe. They compelled the French to put their territory and their people at the disposal of Germany for the purpose of attacking their ally and actually forced them to hand over the refugees who had found asylum in France to the Gestapo. The most important clauses were as follows:—

French territory to be occupied north and west of a line from the Swiss frontier at Geneva through the centre of France at

Bourges to a point twelve miles east of Tours and thence south to the Spanish frontier at St. Jean Pied de Port. That is to say, the Germans were to take over the northern half of the country and a coast strip averaging about seventy miles of the southern half, so that they possessed all the ports. In the occupied area the Germans were to have all the rights of an occupying power except that of local administration.

French forces were to be demobilized and disarmed.

The Germans were empowered to demand the surrender in good condition of all such weapons and equipment as they required, and all defences were to be handed over in good condition.

The French fleet was to be disarmed, but Germany declared that she had no intention of using it or claiming it at the conclusion of peace.

No French shipping was to leave harbour and merchant shipping at sea was to be recalled or to make for neutral harbours.

All wireless transmitting stations in French territory were to stop.

The cost of maintenance of the occupation was to be paid by France.

All German prisoners of war (and this included a number of airmen shot down by the British) were to be released. All German subjects indicated by the German Government were to be handed over. French prisoners of war were to remain in German hands until the conclusion of peace.

The Italian terms were of less importance, Italy being the lackey of Germany, and Hitler being determined not to satisfy her demands on France until he had discovered how much collaboration he could get from the latter. The chief points involved the demilitarization of zones in southern France, Tunisia, Algeria and French Somaliland, together with the naval bases of Toulon, Bizerta, Ajaccio and Oran; the surrender of all material of the French forces which had been facing Italian forces.

The French Government moved to Vichy, henceforth to serve as the capital of the unoccupied zone. General de Gaulle, who had been head of the Military Cabinet of M. Reynaud for a few days after serving with great distinction in command of an armoured division which carried out successful counter-attacks near Laon and Abbeville, reached London. On June 18th he broadcast a message protesting against surrender and on the 23rd announced that, by agreement with the British Government, he was setting up a Provisional National Committee to work for the recovery of national independence and to honour French alliances.

CHAPTER VII

The Battle of Britain

NOW, in all Europe, the United Kingdom stood alone. Hitler had spoken, in laying down the terms of the French armistice, of reducing to a minimum the occupation of the west coast of France "after the cessation of hostilities with Great Britain". It was an indication of his intention to make use of that coast for the subjugation of the country and the nation. Mussolini, in a speech on the declaration of war, had announced that his object was "to break the territorial and military chains that are strangling us in our sea", another way of saying that he intended to establish an Italian hegemony of the Mediterranean. And in the Mediterranean he had at his disposal a powerful fleet, including ten battleships old or new. This constituted a deadly threat to British communications.

It seemed possible that the threat might be increased by a German occupation of Gibraltar, especially in view of the friendliness expressed to the Nazi and Fascist states by the government of General Franco. Whatever the sympathies of the Spanish rulers, however—and they were certainly more anti-democratic than pro-German—Spain was worn out by her civil war and wanted to remain at peace. There was no invitation to German arms to enter the country and Hitler did not choose to do so by force.

In addition to the new factor of the Italian fleet there was that of the French to be considered. It was lost to our cause, it seemed, but there was the worse probability that, by a denunciation of the armistice terms, it might at any moment pass to the side of the enemy. Britain had offered to release France from her alliance and pledge not to conclude a separate peace on condition that the fleet should be sent to British ports before the negotiations with the enemy were completed. Now a great proportion of the fleet was effectively in the enemy's hands. The British Government decided that in such circumstances its action could be confined by no pedantic scruples.

On July 3rd that proportion of the fleet under British control was taken over at Portsmouth and Plymouth, while at Alexandria the French squadron was immobilized under threat of sinking. Some hundreds of the crews in the British ports volunteered to serve under General de Gaulle or applied for British nationality. It was arranged that the rest should be repatriated as soon as possible, together with the bulk of the troops taken off from Dunkirk, only a small proportion of whom retained sufficient spirit to desire to continue the struggle. These measures could not be criticized, but the action taken against that part of the fleet at Mers-el-Kebir, the naval port of Oran in French North Morocco, was graver and more painful.

Here the grim task was allotted to Vice-Admiral Sir James Somerville, who had played a distinguished part in organizing the evacuation from Dunkirk. The French admiral was offered three alternatives: to sail with the British fleet and continue to fight, to sail with reduced crews under British control to a British port, to sail with reduced crews to a French port in the West Indies. It was hoped that one would be accepted, but the armistice commission which was then in session at Wiesbaden ordered the admiral to refuse them all. Admiral Somerville then opened fire. The French ships, almost helpless because at anchor, defended themselves with courage, but suffered crippling losses. Four days later the battleship *Richelieu*, lying at Dakar, was damaged by depth charges. These attacks aroused bitter feeling in France, and, what was worse, in the French colonies, where they undoubtedly damaged such prospects as existed of declarations in favour of General de Gaulle and his organization, Free France.

In the United Kingdom strenuous preparations were made to face the invasion which was to be expected. The most capable officers available were placed in the key posts. General Sir John Dill became Chief of the Imperial General Staff and General Sir Alan Brooke—the ablest soldier the country possessed—Commander-in-Chief Home Forces. Lord Gort was somewhat ungratefully relegated to the post of Inspector-General. Immense works of fortification were carried out on the south and east coasts of England and to a lesser degree inland. The troops taken off from Dunkirk were reorganized as quickly as possible, but there was a deplorable shortage of material of all kinds, and the standard of armament remained low for a long time to come.

Northern Ireland was constantly in the minds of those responsible for the defence of the United Kingdom. On the one hand it provided an indispensable outpost to the sea approaches to the Clyde and Mersey now that the British could not, in view of the neutrality of the Irish Free State, use Queenstown or Lough Swilly. On the other hand, it was the only Irish soil on which a fully armed garrison could be assembled to meet invasion. The Free State was practically unarmed and seemed to invite invasion. Forces of all three services were established in Northern Ireland—those of the land only two divisions and one brigade—and a scheme for entering the Free State if invaded was worked out. Another outpost, the Channel Islands, had to be abandoned and was occupied by the enemy.

As a second line of defence there had been formed while operations on the continent were still going on a corps called the Local Defence Volunteers. In origin it was mainly intended to deal with parachutists and to protect points such as power stations until regular troops could reach the scene. These part-time volunteers, however, who were not called upon to abandon their ordinary occupations, gradually developed into a true second line, which took over all local defence except that of the coasts from the regulars and allowed the latter to concentrate to an extent much greater than would otherwise have been the case. Early in its career the force was renamed—to great advantage—the Home Guard. Its armament was primitive, including shot guns and pikes, and even when old rifles were procured from the United States there was an extreme shortage of ammunition. In the end it was to become, so far as light weapons were concerned, a relatively well-armed force, but not until the pressing danger of invasion had already been removed.

The new Government provided itself with new powers of a type hitherto unknown. The Emergency Powers Act gave it control of all persons and property in the country. The man in the street, perhaps fortunately for himself, had a comfortable feeling that the nation had now gone over to full war production, but in fact it was still groping, often ineffectively and with many blunders, to that situation. Registration for military service was hastened. Men aged from 25 to 29 registered between April 6th and June 22nd, producing a million and a quarter potential recruits for the three services. A new proclamation under the

National Service Act rendered liable for service all British subjects between the ages of 19 and 36.

The nation, which all the world believed to be doomed, met the menace with unshaken spirit. As was so often to be the case, its attitude was embodied, though at the same time exalted, by the final words of Mr. Churchill's speech in the House of Commons on June 18th:

"Hitler knows that he will have to break us or lose the war. If we stand up to him all Europe may be free, and the life of the world may move forward into broad sunlit uplands; but if we fail, then the whole world, including the United States, and all that we have known and cared for will sink into the abyss of a new dark age, made more sinister and perhaps more prolonged by the lights of a perverted science. Let us therefore address ourselves to our duty and so bear ourselves that if the British Commonwealth of Nations and Empire last for a thousand years men will still say: 'This was their finest hour.'"

Doubtless military ignorance and failure to realize the full extent of the danger formed an element in the country's fortitude, but it is none the less true that the people went about their tasks with a cool and steady courage which was worthy of their highest and fondest traditions. They could not divine what form the test was to take, but they were in no doubt that a most searching and cruel test was coming.

The Germans began to launch air raids on a limited scale before the armistice with France had been concluded. On July 20th over a hundred bombers crossed the coast. On August 8th the real "Battle of Britain" began with heavy attacks on two convoys off the Isle of Wight and Bournemouth. On the 11th 200 bombers attacked Portland, Weymouth and their shipping. On the 12th Dover was the main target. Then the enemy switched mainly to fighter airfields in the south and south-east. On the 15th he suffered heavy defeat after fierce fighting, losing 76 aircraft. In the first ten days his losses numbered several times the R.A.F. loss of 153, with 60 pilots saved, without taking into account the fact that all our losses were in single-seater fighters and a large proportion of his in bombers carrying crews of about five or in two-seater fighters.

The problem before Goering and his advisers in the *Luftwaffe* was simple. The main British naval forces in home waters were based on Scapa Flow, except for the units employed on convoy work, and in the present state of air power, with the balance heavily on the German side, ran great risks if they operated anywhere except in the open North Sea or the Atlantic. Smaller and faster craft presented a formidable obstacle to invasion, but this would be greatly decreased if they and their bases were altogether deprived of air cover. The second defensive role of the Royal Air Force in the event of invasion would be to attack the barges and other vessels in which the enemy sought to cross. Here it was the bomber that was feared rather than the fighter, but the bomber without fighter cover, and especially the slow and clumsy British bomber of that day, was not to be feared. Two other tasks which lay before the Royal Air Force were the interruption of supplies after an invading force had landed and the support of the Army opposing this force.

The German aim was therefore to inflict defeat upon the R.A..F, to break its back. How was this to be done? In the first place by driving it away from all its advanced airfields. In the second by attacking targets which it would be forced to defend and bringing on engagements with the British fighters in the greatest possible numbers. The battle to begin with would be against Fighter Command—a certain amount of bombing of airfields used by bombers being purely incidental—but victory over Fighter Command meant victory over the R.A.F. and then the opening of the way to invasion.

But this excellent plan depended for success upon beating the British fighters in the battles which were to be brought on by the *Luftwaffe*. Here, to the surprise of the Germans, difficulty arose. They found they were not winning. In fact, for the first time that this had happened to any German forces since the beginning, they were getting one drubbing after another.

Among the factors contributing to this result there was first the slight but consistent superiority of the Spitfire over the enemy's single-seater fighter, the Messerschmidt 109, and his even faster but less manœuvrable two-seater, the Messerschmidt 110. The British Hurricane, slower than any of these three, was also extraordinarily effective, especially against the enemy's bombers. Secondly, there was again a slight but consistent superiority in dash and enterprise on the part of the British fighter pilots. Thirdly, there was the excellent organization in groups and sectors and the able control of Fighter Command (Air Vice-Marshal Sir Hugh Dowding). Fourthly, there was the advantage of fighting "on the home pitch", which saved large numbers of British pilots. There were many instances of British pilots reaching the ground by parachute and going into action again almost at once, whereas every German pilot who did so was lost, though a number who fell into the sea were rescued by means of boats, floats, and seaplanes. Finally, there was a certain advantage on the side of fighter squadrons, the sole task of which was to attack the enemy as against those tied to formations of bombers which they had to defend.

British strength on August 8th was 55 operation squadrons in Fighter Command, including six night-fighter squadrons flying Blenheims which took little or no part in the battles in daylight. In a considerable proportion there had not been time for full recovery from the effects of the fighting on the Continent. The day-fighter squadrons were equipped with Hurricanes and Spitfires (the former outnumbering the latter by about four to one) and in a couple of cases with Defiants. By September 30th, when the enemy was nearly beaten, British strength had grown to 59 squadrons, eight of these being assigned to night fighting. All the hottest fighting was in the south-east, though attacks ranged up to the Tyne, but as fighter groups and squadrons became exhausted they were exchanged with others from quieter areas. By the end every day-fighter squadron but one in Fighter Command had been engaged, and squadrons outside the danger area had been stripped of three-fourths of their operational pilots and turned over to training, though still capable of defending their sectors against unescorted bombers. Owing to the losses in pilots —more difficult to replace than the aircraft, which were now coming out at a good rate—many were brought in from other commands and a large number of naval pilots also volunteered for the great task.

The enemy's reaction to the painful lessons he had learnt was to increase the proportion of fighters to bombers. After resting his aircrews for a few days, he began a fresh series of attacks, directed mainly against inland fighter airfields and aircraft factories. British tactics were altered so as to encounter the enemy in greater strength and farther from his objectives. Between September 1st and 5th there were eleven major attacks, and by the latter date the R.A.F. claimed in this second phase 562 aircraft against a British loss of 219, with 132 pilots saved. It is now known that our estimates of German losses were altogether excessive, but the actual losses, since established by captured documents, were far beyond the enemy's expectation or what he could long continue to bear. Yet he still saw hope of victory.

September 7th marked a new phase. The enemy on that day made a tremendous effort to reach London, throwing in 350 bombers and fighters which flew in two waves east of Croydon. How are the results of that day to be summed up? First, the Germans suffered losses which must have brought nearer the end of the mass daylight attacks. But, on the other hand, they broke through on a very big scale. They reached Dockland, where they started huge fires; they inflicted damage on railway sidings and buildings, gas and electricity stations. Guided by the flames, the night bombers for the first time attacked London in force and continued to do so until just before dawn on the 8th. Three hundred and six people were killed that night and 1,337 seriously injured. The attack was renewed on the following night and again on that of the 8th. It was to be kept up steadily for some time to come.

The daylight attacks were, however, not over yet. September 15th was, in fact, the day of the greatest onslaught of the whole conflict. Two hundred and fifty aircraft in the morning and about the same number in the afternoon fought a series of great engagements with the R.A.F. over an area covering the Straits of Dover, Kent and part of Sussex, and west to the outskirts of London. It cost the enemy 56 aircraft. The claims at the time were over three times as great, but the losses were now too heavy to be endured, even by pilots of the utmost determination, as those of the *Luftwaffe* certainly were. The assaults began to tail off. By about October 5th the bombers had ceased to come at all by day. The enemy now relied on fighter bombers, mostly Me. 109s carrying a pair of bombs, heavily escorted and generally flying at extreme height. They met the same fate, and the Battle of Britain may be said to have ended with the end of October. In this last stage the disparity between R.A.F. claims and the losses of the enemy became much heavier than before because, with fighting at heights of 30,000 feet or so, it was so often impossible to observe the fate of hostile aircraft which dived out of sight, and no point is to be gained by quoting the sensational figures which then so much impressed the country.

It has, however, been definitely established that the enemy lost 1,733 aircraft in the struggle. It was a battle of a type new to history. The work done by anti-aircraft artillery, balloon barrages, searchlight sections, and even on occasion machine guns on the ground made a contribution without which the defence could not have been maintained, but the part played by British land forces was secondary. That played by naval forces on both sides was small, while the German land forces could not intervene at all. It was in the main air force against air force, and the prize of battle was the fate of Britain. The enemy had fleets of barges ready for the invasion. It is now established that he intended to launch them in early October, by which time he was confident of attaining his object and breaking the back of the R.A.F. About twenty divisions were to have been devoted to the task, and in view of the disparity between their training and armament and those of the defence there is little doubt that the invasion would have been successful if the air war had been won first. Some even believe that it might have succeeded, though at fearful cost, if launched while the battle was still in progress. As it was, the project was now abandoned at the instance of the beaten *Luftwaffe*. There is some evidence that it had been abandoned earlier, and that the enemy counted upon the *Luftwaffe* to win by itself, through completely paralysing and starving out the country, but this is not certain.

It was a great British victory, one of the two or three most decisive of the war, though in using that adjective one must not forget the foreigners who fought in the R.A.F., least of all the Poles, who included some of the finest fighter pilots in the world. It did not break the *Luftwaffe*, as future events were to prove, but it took the bloom off it. On the other hand, it exhausted Fighter Command to an extent which neither the Germans nor this country fully realized.

The new phase, that of night bombing, was a different matter. Neither night-fighters nor the anti-aircraft barrage could account for more than a fraction of the attackers. The enemy flew above the range of illumination by searchlights. The first radio-location apparatus had already been fitted in night-fighters, but to begin with the results were disappointing. Night after night the bombers came over London, concentrating particularly on the working-class and business areas, though there was none that they left untouched. Very heavy damage was done and the business life of the capital was seriously interrupted. The people generally stood up well to the test, though more and more who could do so took to sleeping outside, in many cases travelling long distances to work each day.

Among the provincial objectives the ports were the chief sufferers. Southampton, Plymouth, Bristol and Liverpool had to endure particularly heavy attacks during the remainder of the year. On the night of November 14th all central Coventry was virtually destroyed. Next night the Germans came back to London in strength, and then followed three heavy attacks on Birmingham. There were terrific attacks on Southampton on the nights of November 30th and December 1st. The civilian casualties in the country amounted to 1,075 killed in August, 6,954 in September, 6,334 in October, and 4,558 in November.

Needless to say, the Germans held a great advantage in the duel of night-bombing, since their airfields were so much closer to their targets than those of the British. A series of attacks were, however, launched by the R.A.F. In August and September these were largely directed against synthetic oil plants in Western Germany. The Ruhr was another objective, and there were assaults on ports and dockyards. In the autumn, raids on Berlin increased and huge flights across the Alps carried the British bombers to Turin and Milan to attack motor and electrical works. It was estimated in the winter that the industrial capacity of Germany had been reduced by 20 per cent. In the light of later information this has been shown to be a fantastic exaggeration, but the attacks were already perturbing the Germans somewhat, because it was clear that, if the invasion of Britain did not take place, they would increase in weight. It was the clumsiest, most brutal, and most wasteful of all forms of warfare, this bombing and counter-bombing, but it had its effect, though the industrial effort required to make it was so great that the advantages created by the destruction were not nearly as important as was commonly supposed.

By comparison with the Battle of Britain, applying that term to the German effort to knock out the R.A.F. in daylight fighting, this night bombing campaign was a secondary affair. And, whereas its effects were difficult to estimate—as they are even now—there could be no doubt about those of the Battle of Britain. It was realized in this country, to a somewhat lesser extent in the world at large, and presently more dimly in Germany, that Britain had won her first great victory and Germany had suffered her first major defeat.

CHAPTER VIII

The Mediterranean and Africa

THE prospects of keeping open the Mediterranean looked black after the fall of France. The Italian peninsula jutted out deeply into the heart of this land-locked sea. The gap between the southernmost point of Italy and the African coast was to a large extent blocked by the big Italian island of Sicily, south of which lay the now isolated British fortress and base of Malta. From the Egyptian frontier to the frontier of Tunisia was hostile Italian territory. From thence to the frontier of Spanish Morocco was the territory of a defeated and now somewhat unfriendly former ally, to a certain extent in the hands of the armistice commissions of the conquerors. And from thence to the Straits of Gibraltar was territory potentially hostile. Malta, as has been said, was isolated. Gibraltar was not, since it could be reached by sea and air without difficulty, but it appeared to be threatened by a German invasion of Spain or even by Spanish aggression, and it was very open to sabotage. In addition every move of the fleet stationed there could be immediately reported to the Germans.

There was no possibility of affording air protection to shipping in Mediterranean waters except by means of aircraft carriers. There was a powerful and in most respects modern Italian fleet provided with good bases. There was a numerically strong Italian force. There were at least 200,000 European troops, irrespective of natives, in Libya. At the same time British forces in the Middle East were threatened by another considerable Italian force in East Africa, which had actually been reinforced through the Suez Canal while the war was in progress, but before Italy had begun to take part in it. Against all this strength and these strategic advantages the British could muster, besides the garrisons of Malta and Gibraltar, only a few divisions in the Middle East Command, a handful of fighter squadrons flying the obsolete Gladiator biplane, and two small fleets, one based on Alexandria, under the command of Vice-Admiral Sir Andrew Cunningham, the other based on Gibraltar under the command of Vice-Admiral Sir James Somerville.

The eastern fleet was relatively constant in strength, containing at least three battleships and a modern aircraft carrier, but the western, which could be readily reinforced or drawn upon, varied in accordance with convoy requirements in the Mediterranean on the one hand and the demands of Atlantic warfare on the other. It was generally based upon the *Renown* and the famous old carrier *Ark Royal*. It was, somewhat surprisingly, found possible to pass convoys to and fro, despite the strength of the enemy's resources and strategic position, and it was not until the German *Luftwaffe* came into the Mediterranean in strength that affairs became really hazardous in this respect.

The first Italian air attack on Malta was carried out on June 11th, the day after Italy's declaration of war. Thereafter there was constant raiding, causing considerable damage. The Italians also attacked from the air Mersa Matruh, a British outpost in the Western Desert of Egypt. Bombs were later dropped on Alexandria and Cairo, causing a certain perturbation in the country. The British for their part attacked Italian airfields and landing grounds in Cyrenaica. From Aden the R.A.F. and from Kenya South African aircraft did what was possible to worry the Italians in East Africa.

On the Libyan frontier the British engaged in bold harassing tactics and gained a number of small successes despite the vast Italian superiority. On the frontiers of the Sudan and Kenya there were local combats, in which the enemy gained relatively little advantage with even greater odds in his favour. In August, however, he won a success of some importance. He invaded British Somaliland with the greater part of two divisions and rapidly overran the country, which was defended by little more than a single brigade. The garrison was withdrawn by sea from Berbera with small losses. The strategic gain was small, since in Eritrea the Italians were already in a position to attack Aden or close the Red Sea if they were capable of doing either, but the loss of prestige to the British in the Middle East was not to be under-rated.

The first action against the Italian naval forces took place on July 9th, 1940. An Italian fleet was returning from escorting a convoy to a Libyan port when it was attacked by Admiral Cunningham. The enemy escaped under a smoke-screen after suffering some damage. On the 19th came a real success. The Australian cruiser *Sydney*, with four destroyers, met two Italian light cruisers off Crete. The *Bartolomeo Colleoni* was sunk, but the *Giovanni delle Bande Nere* got away, though repeatedly hit. It had already become evident that the Italian Navy was in somewhat coy mood.

Meanwhile the Italians in Cyrenaica under Marshal Graziani had been preparing for an attack on Egypt. The advance along the coast began on September 13th. It was harassed by British land and air forces, but the advanced guard covered some seventy miles to reach Sidi Barrani on the 16th and then, pushing on a few miles further, halted to sink wells, bring up material, and construct a series of entrenched camps. It was generally expected that Graziani would soon come on again, but throughout October and November he stayed where he was, building up his strength.

The British might have struck back at him earlier than they did but for the necessity of sending air support to the Greeks, who had been attacked by the Italians from Albania. The British Government had taken a bold decision. Despite the peril at home, it had despatched to the Mediterranean some of its most precious material and reinforcements, including the heavy tanks known as "Matildas", which were then among the most formidable in the world. A great sweep by Admiral Cunningham had kept the main Italian fleet in its harbours. Now there was at the disposal of the Commander-in-Chief Middle East, General Sir Archibald Wavell, and his subordinate Lieut.-General H. M. Wilson commanding the British forces in Egypt, a striking force which appeared to be adequate to deal the enemy a blow. General Wavell kept an open mind as to future plans, which depended on the strength of the resistance and the fighting qualities of the enemy, an unknown factor. If the Italians proved sturdy he would have to pull out after inflicting what damage he could; otherwise he would exploit his victory to the limit of his resources.

The British force in Egypt, as well as Britain's Greek allies, received strong support from Admiral Cunningham at sea. The culmination of some brilliant operations was an attack on the night of November 11th on the Italian battle squadron at Taranto by aircraft of the Fleet Air Arm. The modern Italian battleship *Littorio* was left down by the bows with her forecastle under water. One of the older *Cavour* class battleships had to be beached;

a second was aground; and in the inner harbour two cruisers were left with heavy lists and surrounded by oil fuel. The effect on the Mediterranean war was important, since such ships as could be moved from Taranto retreated to the western ports of Italy or up the Adriatic and the powerful *Littorio* was put out of commission for some months. In a running fight on November 27th Admiral Sir James Somerville's squadron inflicted further damage on the enemy off Sardinia before the Italian ships encountered escaped under a smoke screen.

It was estimated that there were 15 Italian divisions in Libya in December, three of these being stationed in Tripolitania to maintain order and keep an eye on the French in Tunisia in case they should declare for the Free French régime of General de Gaulle, as the French Congo, the Cameroons, and the Chad Territory had done in August. On Egyptian soil about Maktila and Sidi Barrani stood five divisions, one armed with light tanks, one regular, one "Blackshirt" or militia, and two of native troops. Back on the frontier there were four divisions, and at Tobruk two more. The advanced force held a series of entrenched camps stretching from the coast to a low escarpment 25 miles south of Sidi Barrani. The Italian air force in Libya, with some 500 aircraft, outnumbered the British directly opposed to it by upwards of two to one.

Based on Mersa Matruh, General Wavell had at his disposal the 7th Armoured, 4th Indian, and 6th Australian Divisions. The R.A.F. Middle East Command under Air Marshal Sir A. M. Longmore had at its disposal $10\frac{1}{2}$ fighter, $18\frac{1}{2}$ bomber, one bomber-transport, and a few army co-operation and reconnaissance squadrons. These, however, included the force sent to the aid of the Greeks and were spread over Egypt, the Sudan, East Africa, Palestine, Irak, and Malta. Among them were one Australian, one Rhodesian, and seven South African squadrons. General Wavell's intention was to break through north of the southernmost camp, widely separated from the rest of the series, penetrate to the rear of these, and cut them off from Sollum and their forward base at Buqbuq, half way between Sollum and the front.

During the night of December 7th the 7th Armoured Division moved towards the gap in the line of forts. The 4th Indian Division, after feinting directly towards the southernmost at Bir

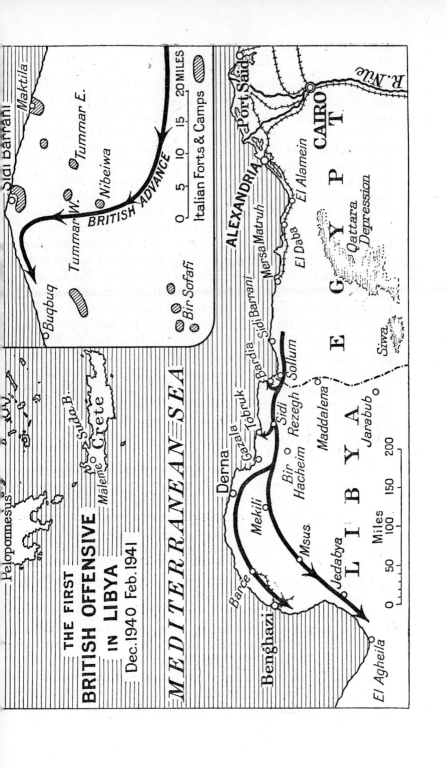

THE FIRST
BRITISH OFFENSIVE
IN LIBYA
Dec.1940 Feb.1941

MEDITERRANEAN SEA

Pelopponnesus

Crete
Suda B.
Maleme

Benghazi
El Agheila
Jedabya
L I B Y A
Barce
Mekili
Msus.
Derna
Gazala
Tobruk
Bir
Hacheim
Sidi
Rezegh
Bardia
Sollum
Maddalena
Jarabub

Miles
0 50 100 150 200

EGYPT

ALEXANDRIA
Mersa Matruh
El Daba
El Alamein
Sidi Barrani
Siwa
Qattara
Depression
Port Said
CAIRO
R. Nile

Sidi Barrani
Maktila
Tummar E.
Tummar W.
Nibeiwa
Buqbuq
BRITISH ADVANCE
Bir Sofafi

0 5 10 15 20 MILES
Italian Forts & Camps

Sofafi, passed through on the 8th and early on the morning of the 9th assaulted the central forts at Nibeiwa, while part of the armoured forces masked the Italian infantry division and the section of the armoured division which constituted the garrison of Bir Sofafi. Had this force shown enterprise and moved out at once to support the front further north, the fortunes of the day might have been rather different, but it hesitated too long. The Nibeiwa forts were overwhelmed and the bulk of their garrison killed or captured. Without delay the British armour—a single regiment with heavy tanks—reformed and, with a second Indian brigade, went on to attack the next group. These too fell after sharp fighting, and by the night of December 9th a detachment of the armoured division reached the sea at Buqbuq. The force at Maktila, a division in strength, evacuated its camp and fell back towards Sidi Barrani, only to be caught and compelled to surrender. That at Bir Sofafi fled westwards, but was pursued by British and Australian aircraft and then broken up by the British light tanks. Finally a division which had advanced from the region of Sollum to support the front was surprised on the march by the British armoured brigade which had reached Buqbuq and captured practically *en bloc*. Upwards of 40,000 prisoners and 400 guns had been taken. The pursuit was continued by the air forces, which not only took toll of the land forces but almost shot the Italian aircraft out of the skies.

Such was the battle of Sidi Barrani, which was extremely heartening at a moment when there had been no previous good news from the land war. General Wavell, well seconded by the Navy, pressed his advantage. On December 16th, after reoccupying Sollum, his advanced guard crossed the Cyrenaican frontier. The enemy fell back on Bardia, and a large force was hemmed in there by the cutting of the road to Tobruk. By the 23rd the British artillery, hauled with great effort up the Halfaya Pass beyond Sollum, was shelling the place.

On January 1st, 1941, the R.A.F. attacked in force, bombarding Bardia and at the same time dealing so effectively with the Italian airfields far to the west that few aircraft were able to intervene. At 5.30 a.m. on January 3rd the armoured forces and the 6th Australian Division launched their assault, and presently naval guns began to pound the rear of the Italian entrenched camp. The Australians swarmed over the anti-tank ditch, and at certain points it was quickly filled in sufficiently for tanks to cross it. By nightfall the advance had penetrated to a depth of two miles. It was renewed next morning, and presently the defence collapsed. The haul of prisoners, guns, and tanks, was even greater than at Sidi Barrani, the former numbering close on 45,000. The British, who had suffered about 800 casualties at Sidi Barrani, lost about another 600 here.

Naturally, British reports made the most of any stout qualities displayed by sections of the defence, and some there were. It was, however, clear to every experienced eye that the Italians were not a first-class foe. They fell below this standard in resolution, somewhat surprisingly also—since they had been considered quick-thinking soldiers—in initiative and manœuvre, and even in armament, though this to a lesser extent.

The British wasted no time. They pushed on quickly to Tobruk, the chief Italian naval base. The Italians showed themselves sluggish. They allowed the neighbouring airfields to be occupied and Tobruk to be invested without resistance in the open. Sandstorms caused a delay, but on January 21st an assault was launched, again by the 7th Armoured and 6th Australian Divisions. The relatively strong defences were speedily breached and the place was captured next with 25,000 prisoners, again for but a slight British loss. The British pressed on and took Derna in the same way, resistance collapsing as the Australians got to close quarters. There was no stand at Benghazi.

Then came an operation as brilliant as any in the war. As the remnant of the Italian army fell back along the coast a brigade of the 7th Armoured Division followed the chord of the arc, over rocky and almost waterless country and reached the main highway on the coast about sixty miles south of Benghazi just as the head of the Italian column came in sight. It was surprised and destroyed undeployed. But on the following morning, that of February 6th, a ferocious struggle began with the main body, which included over seventy tanks. At times it seemed certain that the enemy would break through and even that the frail British advanced guard would be destroyed, but a brigade equipped with cruiser tanks reached the scene just in time. The last desperate assault of the Italians failed, though not by much. Then white flags began to appear in the dunes. The Italian force, still 15,000 strong, surrendered.

The inland oasis of Jarabub held out till March 21st, when it was taken by troops of the newly-arrived 9th Australian Division, but meanwhile the British had pushed on their advanced guard to the region of El Agheila on the Gulf of Sirte. Meanwhile also the Germans had come to the aid of their shaky ally. They had established a strong air force in Sicily and with remarkable promptitude had landed a well-equipped armoured corps in Tripoli under an able commander, Erwin Rommel. General Wavell had been compelled to despatch a considerable force to Greece and had transferred the 4th Indian Division to the Sudan. It will always be a matter of controversy whether from the strategic point of view a serious error had not been made in sending the expeditionary force to Greece and thus gravely weakening the army in the Western Desert. It was a political decision, but not necessarily wrong for that reason. If Britain had left Greece unsupported in her extremity she would have been shamed before the world. Militarily, however, the decision was calamitous as regards the situation in North Africa.

On the Tripolitanian frontier there was now only a single British armoured brigade, in part equipped with captured Italian tanks and a brigade of the 9th Australian Division. At the end of March the Germans and Italians launched a counter offensive and over-ran the armoured brigade. The Australians, fighting rear-guard actions along the coast route, fell back. General Wavell had taken a very daring decision, to drop a force, mainly consisting of the Australian division, in Tobruk and keep it supplied by sea. He intended that it should provide him with a firm footing behind the enemy's front against the time when he should find himself in a situation to renew the offensive.

Meanwhile the dangers of the eastern Mediterranean had been lessened by a remarkable victory gained by Admiral Cunningham, to which the name of Cape Matapan, the southernmost point in Greece, has been given. The intention of the Italians was to attack convoys bound for Greece. Their fleet, consisting of a battleship, six cruisers, and seven destroyers, was sighted south of Crete. The British light forces under Vice-Admiral H. D. Pridham-Wippell, with the cruisers *Orion*, *Ajax*, *Gloucester* and *Perth* (of the Royal Australian Navy), and destroyers, encountered the enemy and endeavoured to draw him towards the main fleet, the flagship *Warspite* with the battleships *Valiant* and *Barham* and the

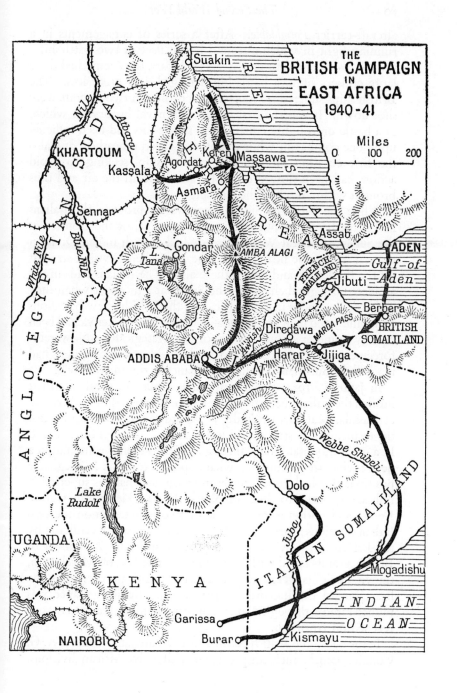

THE
BRITISH CAMPAIGN
IN
EAST AFRICA
1940-41

Miles
0   100   200

Suakin
KHARTOUM
Kassala
Agordat
Keren
Massawa
Asmara
Sennar
Assab
ADEN
Gulf of Aden
Jibuti
Berbera
BRITISH SOMALILAND
Gondar
L. Tana
AMBA ALAGI
FRENCH SOMALILAND
Diredawa
MARDA PASS
Harar
Jijiga
ADDIS ABABA
Awash
Webbe Shibeli
Dolo
Lake Rudolf
Juba
ITALIAN SOMALILAND
Mogadishu
INDIAN OCEAN
UGANDA
KENYA
Garissa
Burar
Kismayu
NAIROBI

Nile
Atbara
SUDAN
White Nile
Blue Nile
ANGLO-EGYPTIAN
ABYSSINIA
ERITREA
RED SEA

aircraft-carrier *Formidable*. After a series of engagements in a running fight in which a second Italian fleet of two battleships, three cruisers, and four destroyers took part, the enemy had three large cruisers sunk, a battleship damaged, and other loss. The British ships suffered no loss whatever, though two aircraft were shot down. It was the first occasion in naval history on which, in a battle on roughly equal terms, severe loss had been inflicted upon one combatant while the other escaped unscathed, and also the first occasion on which ship after ship, seeking to avoid action, had been slowed down by attacks from the air and thus brought within reach of the pursuer.

While the battle of Sidi Barrani was in progress the Italians in Eritrea began to put heavier pressure against the frontier of the Sudan. General Wavell already had the 5th Indian Division on that front. He now plucked the 4th Indian Division straight off the battlefield and sent it there also. The Italians had missed an incredibly good chance in the Sudan at a moment when they had 300,000 troops in East Africa and the British a few battalions and some 5,000 men of the Sudan Defence Force. Kenya had been equally vulnerable, but less important strategically. Now reinforcements were hastening to it also. Hurricane fighters had reached the Sudan, and Italian ascendancy in the air was gone.

In January, 1941, the Indian troops under General W. Platt hustled the Italians back from the frontier, which they had crossed at Kassala, beat them soundly at Agordat, but came up against the tremendously strong position of Keren, 40 miles further east. In a great mountain mass, through which the only route ran in a deep ravine, the enemy had what appeared to be an impregnable position. He had good European troops and natives superior in military qualities to those of North Africa. He fought well at Keren, and within a square mile or two inflicted upon the two Indian divisions a large proportion of all the casualties suffered by the British in the whole course of the campaign. A number of British assaults failed with heavy losses, but at last, on March 25th, the vital heights were cleared. The loss of this position took the heart out of the Italians in Eritrea. The British advance was pushed rapidly through Asmara, the capital, to the sea at Massawa, reached on April 8th.

In the south the British commander, Lieutenant.-General A. G. Cunningham, had at his disposal two small native African divisions, the 11th and 12th, containing troops from both West and East Africa, and the 1st South African Division from the Union, which arrived in stages. He began his advance at approximately the same time as Platt. Its main line followed the coast to Kismayu, the capture of which gave it a new base and allowed it to cut loose from its difficult road lines of communication from the far-off railhead in Kenya. It then pushed on to Mogadishu, where another new base was established and vast quantities of fuel were captured. From here it travelled by the fine road to the north to Jigjiga and Harar recently made by the Italians.

In actual fighting quality Cunningham's force proved itself the superior of the Italians on every occasion, but the main cause of its wonderful success was that it was mobile and dashing while they were sluggish and unenterprising. Brilliant use was made of its lavish transport—the third-line alone consisted of forty reserve companies, each of 75 two-ton or three-ton lorries—to make rings round the Italians, to anticipate all their moves, and to beat them piecemeal. Cunningham fought a successful action on the Juba on February 16th, but thenceforward was not seriously opposed till he had raced up the great road to Jigjiga and had to force his way through the Marda Pass a month later. After that Harar fell like ripe fruit into his hands and he dashed westward, 300 miles to the capital of Abyssinia, Addis Ababa, which surrendered on April 6th. He had covered roughly 1,700 miles in 57 days, a pace seldom if ever surpassed in war. On May 5th the Emperor Haile Selassie, who had struck in with a column from Sennar on the Blue Nile, reached his capital and regained his throne.

There was a great deal more fighting and marching in Italian East Africa after the northern and southern claws of the British pincers had met at Amba Alagi, where the Italian Commander-in-Chief, the Duke of Aosta, surrendered on May 18th. The rainy season between mid-June and mid-September gave the Italians some respite, There was, however, little but mopping-up to be done, though this was a trying task in broken and almost road-less country. The end came in the mountains at Gondar, north of Lake Tana, on November 27th.

The campaign provides a rare example of successful operations on exterior lines against an enemy of considerably greater numerical strength and possessing superior armament. Like nearly all the victorious campaigns of the war it owed its success in large degree to ascendancy in the air, which made the Red Sea safe for British shipping. The handling of the reserves was notable. The use of the 4th Indian Division has been mentioned, and it may be added that the South Africans also began moving from Southern Abyssinia to Egypt in early March. But the two vital factors were, first, the dash and drive displayed against a slow-footed enemy, and, secondly the skilful management of the supply routes and the feeding of the campaign from Nairobi and Mombasa in the south, Cairo and Port Sudan in the north, and even across Central Africa through Nigeria and the French equatorial station of Fort Lamy to Khartoum in the north-west.

CHAPTER IX

The Baltic to the Balkans

THE U.S.S.R. continued to erect buffers against the possibility of German aggression. It had already set up new Governments in Estonia, Latvia, and Lithuania. In the summer of 1940 elections were held in which only those in favour of amalgamation with Russia were permitted to vote. After the elections the three states applied for admission to the U.S.S.R., which was granted. Their incorporation, completed on August 7th, was not recognized either by the United States or by the United Kingdom, but Russia doubtless considered the acquisition of a number of good Baltic ports more valuable.

M. Molotov had stated in March that Russia still claimed the return of Bessarabia, the Rumanian province between the Dneister and the Pruth, but that she did not propose to recover it by war. Statements of this kind by a totalitarian representative had come to bear a precisely opposite meaning to their wording, so that the announcement left the Balkans uneasy and Rumania particularly so. She had not long to wait. As soon as France had signed her armistice with Italy the U.S.S.R. issued an ultimatum to Rumania demanding not only the return of Bessarabia but also the cession of the Northern Bukovina. After some hesitation Rumania submitted and the districts were quickly occupied by Russian troops.

This was by no means the last act in the stripping of Rumania of the greater part of the vast acquisitions of terriory made in the First World War. Bulgaria put in a claim for the return of the Southern Dobruja, the Black Sea district immediately south of the Danube. Again the Rumanians did not resist, this time not because they feared the aggressor but because he was under the patronage of Germany, and agreement was reached on August 22nd.

Next came the turn of Hungary, who throughout the period between the two wars had bemoaned the loss of Transylvania. It appeared that hostilities might break out between Hungary and Rumania, but this Germany and Italy were determined to avoid. They wanted no fighting in Europe except in their own cause. At the end of August Hitler summoned the Foreign Ministers of the two states to Vienna, where Rumania was forced to accept Axis arbitration. Some two-thirds of Transylvania was awarded to Hungary. Rumanian indignation vented itself on King Carol, who had played a game of balances but could now do no more in that line. On September 6th the King abdicated and fled the country. His son Michael, who had as a child sat on the throne during his father's banishment, returned to it.

As regards south-east Europe the struggle had ended in Germany's favour. Russia had got Bessarabia and the Northern Bukovina, but she had lost her patronage of Bulgaria, which was entering Germany's sphere. Germany had also established effective control of Hungary and Rumania. In the war with Russia which broke out in the following summer Hungary and Rumania were to serve as Germany's subsidiary allies—to become her "satellites", as the phrase went—and to make heavy sacrifices for her. With Bulgaria the case was different. Germany never succeeded in leading her against Russia, and the operations which the Bulgarians did undertake, against Yugoslavia and Greece, were not costly and served their own interests. But Germany's strategic situation, apart altogether from the troops of the satellites, the oil resources of Rumania, the agricultural wealth of Hungary, was vastly improved. She controlled the Danube to its mouths and had a footing on the Black Sea. She had only to enter Greece in order to secure control of the eastern Mediterranean. She terrorized Turkey. Seldom have greater advantages been won without loss of blood. It was but a minor worry that her two new allies, Hungary and Rumania, detested one another and had to be watched as well as sternly admonished lest they should fall to fighting.

In August, acting apparently without consultation with his ally, the Italian dictator unleashed a press campaign against Greece, full of the vilest libels. On the 15th the little Greek cruiser *Helle*, which had visited the island of Tinos to celebrate the Feast of the Assumption, was sunk by a submarine. It was clear that the aggressor was Italian. Germany seemed to have attempted to restrain the Italians, perhaps because she did not desire them to divert their energies from North Africa, where their undistinguished performance even before the attack at Sidi

Barrani had suggested that they had plenty on their hands. Mussolini, however, was determined to assert himself, to raise Italian prestige by showing that he too could win a "lightning" war, to extend his power in the eastern Mediterranean, and to forestall Germany in case the latter intended to add Greece to the trophies already in the game-bag.

Like Italy, Greece was under the sway of a dictator who had retained the monarchy. General John Metaxas had been ruling without a parliament for four years. He was hated by the left-wing parties, but they were prepared to fight an invader under his leadership. He had improved the armament of the country's forces, though it was still light and primeval by comparison with that of the Italians. To oppose the 150,000 men whom the enemy had concentrated in Albania the Greeks had not half the number, though full mobilization, if time were afforded for it, would put them on much better terms numerically. In the air the Greeks were even more heavily at a disadvantage, but here the R.A.F. came to the rescue, establishing squadrons first in Crete and later on the mainland.

The Italian scheme was to pass a column, of which the core was a division of Alpini of the best quality available, up the valley of the Vojusa to the mountain town of Metsovo, thus cutting off the Greek forces in Thessaly and Macedonia from those in Epirus. How the expected victory was to be exploited is not clear, but that victory there would be the Italians had no doubt. Setting the ball rolling with the accepted formula, the presentation of an ulti-matum—in this case their ambassador did not even know the terms of which he demanded acceptance—they started to cross the frontier half an hour before it expired on the morning of October 28th.

The Italian column following the Vojusa made rapid progress against an unprepared defence. In the easy coast sector a subsidi-ary advance struggled forward to the Kalamas river, but was there held up. A consignment of anti-tank rifles, flown up by the R.A.F., wrecked nine of the Italian light tanks. Further north, opposite Koritza, the Greeks, quickly completing mobilization, crossed the frontier and surprised the enemy by themselves taking the offensive. The Italians were pushed back to the mountains above the town. Meanwhile the Greeks had sent all available reinforcements to the Pindus front. Suddenly they fell upon the flanks of the Vojusa column, destroyed a great part of it, and drove the rest back in flight. R.A.F. bombers now attacked Valona, the principal Italian port of entry into Albania, and raided Brindisi. In fighter actions the Italians also lost heavily.

On November 18th the Greeks, having drawn in the maximum Italian strength to defend Koritza, suddenly attacked further south. The Italian front collapsed. The retreat speedily became disorderly. Koritza was entered on the 22nd. In the space of little over three weeks the invasion had been repelled and the invaders pushed back all along the line with a loss of 7,000 prisoners and considerable quantities of transport and stores. It was a brilliant feat, which aroused admiration and enthusiasm all over the world.

The Greek counter-offensive continued in stormy weather with frequent showers of snow. By the beginning of 1941 the Greek advance in the Vojusa approached the strong Italian position at Klissura, 60 miles to the north-west of the original Italian objective at Metsovo, an objective which the enemy had come near to attaining less than two months before. This time the Italians, fearful of envelopment, lost their nerve and abandoned their fortifications, leaving behind them much material. If British attacks on Valona and Durazzo had been more frequent and heavier, the enemy might have suffered a complete disaster, but the R.A.F. had not the aircraft to enable it to seize this golden opportunity. And when the bombers were not upon the scene Italian vessels could make the short crossing in numbers sufficient to maintain the army in Albania.

As things were, the Greeks contrived to maintain their offensive in the depth of winter, but it was on a small scale. On January 29th General Metaxas died, probably not regretted by the majority of the people but a heavy loss none the less. On March 9th the Italians launched a powerful counter-offensive between the Vojusa and the mountains east of Berat. After overrunning the outpost positions it was completely defeated, while in the air British Hurricanes and Gladiators gave the enemy a thrashing. The fighting then died down. German intervention was looming nearer, forcing the Greeks to withdraw forces towards the Salonika and Struma fronts. The secret of the Greek success, which the world found astonishing, is to be found in the combination of superior leadership, superior courage, above all superior skill in mountain war. These more than counter-balanced Italian superiority in armament.

In the first days of March Germany put the screw on Bulgaria, obtained a pact of the usual pattern from that country, and then sent in troops across the Danube from Rumania. This was a serious matter for Greece. Hitherto she had been separated by buffers from German might; but it was drawing close. Yugoslavia also found herself in a deadly strategic situation, with German forces on all her frontiers except the southern, where she joined Greece. Immediately she too felt the pressure. Prince Paul, the young King's uncle and the Chief Regent, was all for capitulation, and advised the government in that sense. This time the pact was signed in Vienna, and it seemed that the affair would follow the usual course.

There was, however, unexpected spirit in Yugoslavia. A military *coup d'état* overthrew the government and was welcomed by the country. Yugoslavia decided not to abandon liberty and honour without a struggle. In the United Kingdom her action was greeted with natural pleasure, but this sentiment degenerated into exaggerated and unfounded optimism, even in the highest places. The "Jugs" were in! To unbiased observers it was apparent that they would soon be out.

The recalcitrance of Yugoslavia did, however, come as a surprise to Germany. She had to revise her plans, which had originally envisaged an offensive against Greece through Bulgaria alone. Now she decided to mount an operation which would overrun Yugoslavia and Greece in a single campaign, and this caused some delay. Meanwhile a British force had been landing in Greece, fulfilling British obligations of honour but, as has already been pointed out, weakening British strength in North Africa to a calamitous degree.

The German attack on Yugoslavia was launched on April 6th, 1940. The chances of the defence were in no case bright, but they were seriously weakened by the dispositions, which covered the Danubian territory acquired from Hungary in the last war, country wholly indefensible against troops with armament and mobility as superior as were those of the Germans. The bulk of the Yugoslav forces were spread out in a cordon along the German, Hungarian, Rumanian and Bulgarian frontiers, an army group on the north and north-west fronts, a second on the Hungarian border, a third—much the largest, three armies of some fifteen divisions—facing the Rumanian, Bulgarian, and Albanian fronts. Out of a total of 28 infantry and three cavalry divisions only a single division was held in strategic reserve.

The Germans had at their disposal some 33 divisions, including six armoured. They advanced in a series of six powerful columns, sweeping easily over the Yugoslav positions in the north-west and on the east breaking through the passes with but little more difficulty. The Yugoslav fortifications on the Hungarian front were turned and enveloped by a break-through from Bulgaria. Yugoslav towns, Belgrade in particular, were ruthlessly bombed, and the Italians, little as they did on the ground, contributed by heavy assaults from the air on Yugoslav communications. The defenders were split up into small parcels before a fraction of their forces had been directly engaged. Thus a great army of some of the best fighting men in Europe was smashed to pieces in the space of ten days. The Yugoslavs capitulated on April 17th.

The enemy crossed the Greek frontier on April 6th. The Greeks had prudently drawn in their horns, evacuating Western Thrace but for frontier posts. Three divisions held Salonika and the frontier from the Varda to the Mesta. Two more formed a link between the British force and the Greek force in Epirus. The British force under the command of Lieut.-General Wilson consisted of the 1st Armoured Brigade, the 2nd New Zealand Division, and the 6th Australian Division. The dispositions were better devised than those of the Yugoslavs, but nevertheless also faulty, because they had not taken into account the rapidity and completeness of the Yugoslav collapse and were only partially altered to do so. The vital gateway into Greece was the Monastir Gap, and this was not defended in sufficient strength.

The Germans quickly broke through the Monastir Gap. They entered Salonika, cutting off the Greeks east of the Vardar and forcing them to lay down their arms. General Wilson ordered a withdrawal to the Olympus line, round the flank of the mountain, through Servia, and round the bend of the Haliakmon river. This was completed by April 13th, but by this time the Greeks, pounded by bombers which they could not engage in return, were nearing the end of their powers of resistance. The British armoured brigade was no longer a fighting force. The new line was too long to hold with the available troops and the Germans were already feeling their way past Olympus and into the Peneios Gorge. It was therefore decided to fall back to the Thermopylæ pass, under cover of a small Australian and New Zealand rear guard. This put up a magnificent defence against two German divisions.

The Thermopylæ line was manned on April 20th, but that day also marked the last battle of the R.A.F. in Greece. The Germans could henceforth use the roads beyond the range of allied artillery as they pleased. They massed great forces with tanks in full view of the position, but beyond reach. At the same time other German divisions were racing down the west coast to cut the retreat at Corinth. The Greek army, fought to a finish after a heroic resistance against strength even greater than the British had to face, capitulated on April 21st. Evacuation was all that Lieut.-General Wilson could now hope to achieve, and that appeared doubtful, since ships could take off troops only at night and even then ran a heavy risk of being caught by aircraft at sea after dawn. His plan, worked out with the Navy, was to withdraw part of his force into the Peloponnese, where it would be taken off, and ship the remainder from Piræus and the smaller ports of Attica.

Despite lack of air cover, despite the energy and skill of the pursuing enemy, the evacuation was surprisingly successful. Out of nearly 58,000 troops landed nearly 48,000 were safely withdrawn. The majority of the Greek destroyers and all the submarines likewise escaped. The Kings of Yugoslavia and Greece, with their principal Ministers, had avoided capture, and King George of Greece, who had still island territories unviolated, set up his government in Crete.

The campaigns in Yugoslavia and Greece provide a striking example of the power of superior arms and mobility over the second or third best, even when handled by brave men. The strategic situation of Yugoslavia was in any case nearly hopeless, resembling somewhat that of Poland in 1939, but the Yugoslav command also played into German hands by its bad dispositions, inherited from the regime of Prince Paul. The Greeks were handicapped by continuous bombing and by their lack of anti-tank artillery, but their leadership by General Papagos was greatly superior to the Yugoslav. The campaign also proved, however, the wonderful tenacity of sea power in adversity. The with-drawal of the troops in the face of untrammelled air ascendancy and of hotly pursuing land forces was perhaps the most striking feature of all.

The final scene in the Greek tragedy was played in Crete. The 2nd New Zealand Division had been evacuated to the island and now provided its principal defence. Part of the Australian division was also retained there. Royal Marines held Suda Bay, and there were also two skeleton, half-armed Greek divisions. There were three airfields, but after heavy bombing by German aircraft the remaining R.A.F. fighters were withdrawn on May 19th. The German airborne invasion began next day.

The anti-aircraft artillery was for the most part quickly silenced. Then the enemy began dropping parachutists, and great numbers of troop-carrying gliders were released between Melame and Canea. A large proportion of the first waves were killed, but the Germans followed them up with some 3,000 more at Heraklion and Retimo. A firm foothold was gained, and the loss of Melame airfield on the 22nd proved fatal to the defence. A reckless attempt to support the air-borne operation by a landing from the sea was utterly defeated. A fleet of commandeered Greek caiques, escorted by an Italian destroyer, approached the island on the morning of the 22nd. By gun-fire and ramming, a British force of three cruisers and four destroyers sank the escort and nearly every vessel in the convoy. Later in the day a second convoy was attacked with great effect. But aircraft from the Dodecanese intervened, and the British suffered grievous loss, including the cruisers *Fiji* and *Gloucester*. The enemy, however, made no fur-ther attempt to land troops from the sea until the issue was de-cided.

By the 28th it was clear that Crete could no longer be held. Once again the evacuation was more successful than could have been expected, but the proportion saved was smaller than on the mainland. About 13,000 British and 5,000 Greeks troops were left behind. The Germans are believed to have suffered between twelve and fifteen thousand casualties.

Crete provided an ideal setting for the fullest exploitation of an airborne offensive. The enemy had airfields in Attica, in the Peloponnese, on the island of Melos, and in the Dodecanese. Having attained full air ascendancy, he was able to put the anti-aircraft defences out of action by bombing. Once the R.A.F. had abandoned its airfields in Crete, there were no other bases close enough to provide fighter cover. Yet it was a touch-and-go battle. The Germans gambled boldly, since success, though it assured them of possession of Crete, did not guarantee the destruction of the allied force, which in fact was not destroyed, whereas failure would have involved the destruction of their own force.

It was considered by calm observers, who had little criticism to make of the campaign on the Greek mainland, that there was a case to answer in Crete. Why had not the defence dug itself more thoroughly into the easily-worked limestone? Had aircraft been protected in pits with splinter-proof walls as at Malta? Was it humanly possible to arm more Greek troops with Italian weapons captured in North Africa? Did realization of the danger come only from the enemy's activity instead of from a strategic appreciation, which would have provided more time for preparation? These and other questions are as yet unanswered. There can be no doubt of the gallantry of the defence and little that the strength of the resistance and his own losses surprised the enemy and to a certain extent embarrassed him in working out his future programme.

An astonishing and ironic revelation regarding the campaign in Greece has been made since the war by the Greek Commander-in-Chief, General Papagos. The Greeks actually asked Britain not to send help, feeling that it would be too small to be effective but enough to attract the Germans like a magnet. Britain insisted in order not to lose face. The whole episode now appears a sorry tale of political and strategic frivolity, and the British Government did not deserve to get off as lightly as was the case.

CHAPTER X

Eighteen Months of the War at Sea

INCIDENTS of the war at sea have been recorded in relation to the developments of the war as a whole and the campaigns on land. It is now time to deal with the framework of the naval war and to describe its general nature. The primary task of the Navy was to keep open British maritime communications, particularly in the Atlantic. Its major resources were devoted to that end. As in the First World War, the enemy's principal weapon was the submarine. His object was to starve the United Kingdom of food and the other goods which it was compelled to import in order to live, let alone to fight.

It has been mentioned that at the outset the submarine attacks were not as heavy as had been generally expected. Hitler was to declare later on that he "was almost ashamed to recall" how few submarines had been at sea when war broke out. The Germans were, however, ready for the first blow, as they showed by the sinking of the *Athenia*, and they speedily increased the pressure. The first eighteen months of the war can be divided, from the point of view of hostile submarine activity, into two equal but distinct and sharply contrasted periods: that from the outbreak to the fall of France, and that from the fall of France and Italy's entry into the war to about the middle of March, 1941.

In the former of the two periods the chief targets of the U-boats were found in unescorted shipping in the South-Western approaches, the approaches to English ports round the south coast of Ireland. Here the British were hamstrung by the neutral-ity of the Irish Free State and the loss of the base of Queenstown, which had served them so well in the last war, so much so that they had to abandon these routes. After the German invasion of Norway and Denmark the attacks became heavier. In these ten months over two hundred merchantmen of a total of 800,000 tons were sunk. Twenty-three U-boats were sunk or believed to be sunk—on many occasions there was no absolute certainty about the matter, but it is unlikely that the verdict was often wrong. Thus we lost about nine merchantmen, to say nothing of naval shipping, for every U-boat sunk. It was a heavy price, but one which we could have afforded. Unfortunately the total tonnage lost was to be far exceeded in later phases of the same length and even much shorter. In one of these phases also the proportion of British merchantmen lost to U-boats sunk was to leap up by over 50 per cent.

In the second period the proportions were virtually the same, but the total of losses was more than doubled and that of "kills" almost exactly doubled. The circumstances were now greatly changed to the disadvantage of the British by a whole series of adverse factors. First, the Germans had carried out their training programme and accelerated their production of U-boats. Secondly, their acquisition of Scandinavian bases, which they could exploit only to a minor extent between the conquest of Norway and the fall of France, was now paying full dividends. Thirdly, we had lost the aid of the French fleet. Fourthly, the enemy had acquired new bases in the Channel and the Biscay ports. Fifthly, Italy, with her considerable submarine fleet, had entered the war, and was in future to show a good deal of activity in the Mediterranean, and on occasion outside it, notably along the coast of Portugal. And lastly, through Italy's action, Mediterranean submarine bases had been made available to the Germans, who were always more enterprising than their Italian allies.

It is thus no matter for astonishment that the sinkings rose. It is perhaps more remarkable that the increase was not even greater. We lost over 400 merchantmen of a gross tonnage of 2,000,000 tons, and 45 U-boats were sunk or probably sunk. The heaviest losses were now in the North-Western Approaches, the routes round the north coast of Ireland to the Clyde and Mersey. Here German "aces", commanders of exceptional skill and daring, operated with deadly effect. These men were the pride of Germany, and the country rang with tales of their exploits, which lost nothing in the telling. In fact, the tonnage sunk was always greatly exaggerated by the German publicity services, but it was in truth heavy enough.

But, as we too were to learn to our cost, pitchers of this sort go too often to the well. About March, 1941, three of the best U-boat commanders in the service were drowned or captured. They included Prien, responsible for one of the most daring and sensational deeds of the war, the sinking of the *Royal Oak* inside

Scapa Flow on October 14th, 1939. These losses counted, and the
toll taken of the most competent U-boat commanders was a
factor to be appreciated throughout the war and one which influenced future German strategy and tactics.

The best "killer" of U-boats, now as throughout the war, was
the surface ship, and the best weapon was the depth charge,
though gun-fire and even on occasion ramming also claimed their
victims. In both these periods more submarines were accounted
for by surface ships than by all other means, such as aircraft,
submarines, and mines, combined.

In view of the ubiquity of the aircraft and the immense scope
of its vision by comparison with the surface ships, this in itself was
proof that the Navy was starved of air cover. And starved it was
indeed. It had, after a great struggle, only recently established its
right to its own air force, the Fleet Air Arm, but the aircraft of
this force were already obsolescent when war broke out and there
was no chance of replacing them owing to the demand for
fighters. This demand was justified up to the hilt, since without
fighters the country was in peril, but it was to be long before the
Navy got its bare necessities in competition with the prestige
and power—to say nothing of the vast losses—of Bomber Command.

Again, though the Navy naturally had a close liaison with
Coastal Command, it could not supervise its training, which,
from the point of view of navigation, was deficient in those early
days. Nor was Coastal Command itself at this period equipped
with aircraft suitable for the work it had to perform.

What the Navy required was more modern aircraft carriers
—which were now under construction—small escort carriers,
especially for the smaller convoys not accompanied by the big
carriers and for which these could not be spared; improved types
of aircraft, fighters, bombers, and torpedo-carriers; more light
craft, from destroyers downwards, and escort craft of various
types; and a fuller say in the policy and construction programme
of Coastal Command. These were all to come, but tardily, and
in 1942 and early 1943 this country was to come perilously
close to losing the war through failure to strengthen its nautical
life-line and delay in providing scientific anti-submarine devices,
such as the "Asdic".

The U-boat was not by any means the only foe to the Navy

and the merchant shipping which it was its task to convoy. The Germans after the fall of France began to operate long-range bombers from the Biscay coast. The Condor was a formidable giant, with a high performance. These aircraft not only attacked shipping themselves but also acted as the eyes of submarines.

In the summer of 1940 the enemy also sent out commerce raiders, which added to the sinkings. These were for the most part fast ships, well equipped. The British on their side also employed armed merchant cruisers, but, since in this form of warfare the defensive required so many more vessels than the offensive, they were not, certainly to begin with, as well armed as their opponents, and this was proved in several engagements between vessels of this type. The German battleships *Scharnhorst* and *Gneisenau* put to sea in 1941 and at the end of the first week in March were reported in the Atlantic, where they did some damage. Finally, after badly mauling a convoy off the Azores, they eluded pursuit and put into Brest. Here they were constantly attacked by British bombers and it was hoped immobilized. They were afterwards to prove, however, that this was far from being the case.

One surface raider, the armed merchant cruiser *Narvik*, appeared first in the Indian Ocean and later in Australian waters, where she operated with two tenders with Japanese names and doubtless obtained with the connivance of the Japanese Government. In a successful cruise in waters which had hitherto been considered relatively safe she sank ten ships, British, Australian, Norwegian and French. This was a disquieting episode, but it had no successors of any importance. Germany never became a serious foe in the Indian Ocean or in the Pacific. With more enterprise the Italian submarines on the Red Sea coast might have proved troublesome, but they missed their chance and were finally eliminated by the capture of their bases.

On August 17th, 1940, German declared a "total blockade" of the United Kingdom. This was, however, little more than a phrase which did not seriously alter the position. The conquest of Norway, the Low Countries, and France, and the entry of Italy into the war, had brought to an end the shipping of goods to British ports from European neutrals. Once there had been heavy traffic of this sort, and as many as a score of Dutch ships had lain in the Downs at one time. Now all the shipping, which was considerable in quantity, of the conquered countries, including Poland, that had escaped the Germans passed over to Britain. It still flew its national flags and sailed for the account of the exiled Governments of Poland, Norway, Belgium and Holland, which, were all established in London, or that of the Free French organization of General de Gaulle; but for practical purposes it had become British, and was of course as much subject to attack by the enemy as British ships. The neutral shipping which now visited British ports was very small in quantity.

The British blockade of Germany was limited in its effects, first, because Germany had made careful preparations for war, including the construction of plants for the extraction of fuel oil from coal and for the manufacture of synthetic rubber; secondly, because Germany's conquests and later her peaceful absorptions, such as that of Rumania with her oilfields, had so greatly contributed to her resources; and thirdly because there was as yet no means of preventing neutrals such as Turkey, Spain, Portugal, Switzerland and Sweden from supplying Germany with their products. Some of these, as Turkey's chrome and Portugal's wolfram, were of immense value to her. Every one of these countries except Sweden could despatch goods to Germany overland, and Sweden had at her disposal a covered route through the Baltic which could not be interrupted. Russia, too, was making regular deliveries under a trade agreement which formed an appendix to the pact between the two countries.

Nevertheless, the British blockade was keeping out an appreciable quantity of goods whereof Germany was much in need, particularly copper, ferro-alloys, and rubber. For the most part the blockade was a silent watch for ships which never appeared, but they would have appeared if it had not been in force. The part played by the Navy, with both surface craft and submarines, and the R.A.F. in hampering and damaging coastwise traffic was even more important. The Germans could not get on without this, and were forced to persist in its use, even in the Straits of Dover, in face of steady losses. Norway, owing to the difficulty of landward communications, to which reference was made in the chapter on the German invasion, was an area in which the enemy made particularly large use of coast shipping and suffered heavy loss. On July 8th, 1940, H.M.S. *Snapper*, one of the most famous and successful of British submarines, obtained no less than five hits on a convoy off the Norwegian coast. That was a red-letter day, but there were numerous other successes. The other most fruitful target was Italian shipping in the Mediterranean conveying supplies to the army in North Africa. The losses inflicted never sufficed to immobilize those armies, but it did handicap them and keep their margin narrow, particularly in petrol.

Mining was carried out on a great scale. At the outbreak of the war a vast minefield had been laid by Vice-Admiral B. H. Ramsay from Dover, a barrage of mines laid at varying depths with the object of closing the Straits to U-boats and, incidentally, forcing them to use in coming out the longer passage round the north of Scotland. It had fulfilled its purpose. It was succeeded by a very extensive, though relatively thin, minefield from the Cornish coast to the Tuskar Rock off Wexford and by one stretching from the Orkneys to Iceland. Others were laid in the North Sea. What were called the "invasion ports", those from which German shipping was likely to sail for the invasion of the United Kingdom were continually blocked with mines. The Germans naturally swept their approaches as regularly, but the mines took their toll of vessels which did put out. Needless to say purely defensive mining of British ports was regularly carried out and in fact large flotillas, formed to a great extent at the expense of the fishing fleet and manned by its personnel, were continuously at work, laying mines in areas suitable for defence and sweeping those laid by hostile submarines or dropped by German aircraft in the fairways and buoyed channels.

The building programme, both for naval and merchant shipping, was satisfactory in so far as it was comparatively little interrupted by the enemy's bombing. Neither the yards of the Clyde nor those of Belfast Lough were ever seriously damaged; the attacks in the Tyne were heavier, but these yards too came off surprisingly well. For small craft new yards or slips were established in many parts of the country, and on occasion sleepy little West Country seaside places, famous for shipbuilding in the days of the Armada but since sunk into decay, were reborn and contributed to the defence of the United Kingdom by turning out modern small craft from launches upwards. Nevertheless, the sinkings were already substantially in excess of new construction, and this situation could not fail to create anxiety in view of the certainty, after the fall of France, that the war would be a long one. On the other hand, the United States had embarked upon a building programme on British account under which considerable deliveries were hoped for before the end of 1941.

The most deadly period of the Malta convoys had not yet arrived, but it was approaching, and it was already clear that a vast effort would have to be made and heavy sacrifices would have to be accepted, if the island were to be kept armed and victualled. One of the most unfavourable elements in the situation was the impossibility of keeping secret the start of convoys from Gibraltar. This invariably became known to the enemy, being immediately reported from La Linea, Algeciras, or Ceuta, so that it was possible for him to shadow the convoy from the first and attack it at whatever point best suited him. On the other hand the ships which survived to reach Malta, if they were not sunk in one of its harbours, commonly returned singly to Gibraltar and were on the whole remarkably successful in escaping damage or even attack.

There was always in the press and in public discussion a strong demand for fast freighters which, it was said, would do much to defeat the U-boat menace, but it is to be doubted whether the question was fully understood. Fast ships certainly avoided submarine attacks. They were invaluable for the purpose of carrying special cargoes, and the more Britain possessed of them the better. But, whatever was done in this respect. the principal convoys had to be made up of vessels built before the war, and the pace of such convoys was that of the slowest ship in them.

In general it may be said that the Admiralty suffered from frustration. The conditions under which the Atlantic routes could be kept open—not without heavy and damaging losses at the best, but in such a manner that a long war could be faced with some confidence—were becoming clear. On the other hand, the various forms of equipment required were not available, and it was obvious that their production would take a dangerously long time. Would it take too long? Could the traffic be maintained while waiting for the bare necessities, some only just on order, others not yet allotted their place in the programme of construction? These were sombre questions to have to ask. It was long before satisfactory replies could be given to them, and the general situation was to become worse before it improved. But the country was kept from hunger.

CHAPTER XI

The War in the Air: Second Phase

AFTER the German defeat in the Battle of Britain daylight air attacks on this country virtually ceased. They were not resumed by the *Luftwaffe* except in the form of small, brief raids, sometimes carried out by single aircraft, for the most part against coast towns. These raids extended as far north as Peterhead and as far west as Dartmouth, occasionally even further. Their probable object was to keep as many men as possible in the anti-aircraft units and to keep the Anti-Aircraft Command as dispersed as possible.

The night attacks on Britain continued through the winter and into the summer of 1941. London was the chief target, and after London the big ports, which were all constantly attacked, except that Glasgow got off relatively lightly and Belfast, a distant target, was attacked only on two successive nights, though it suffered a considerable amount of damage. Few were more hardly dealt with than Plymouth and Devonport, which were heavily attacked at the end of April five times in the course of nine nights. Merseyside was persistently assaulted. After mid-winter the bombing of London became less regular, but the capital benefited little from this change of method because attacks, if spaced out, were far heavier than before, and on several occasions the mass of incendiaries dropped was so great as to render it impossible for the fire-fighting machinery to deal with them. It is related that when Queen's Hall was set afire the first fire-engine to reach the scene was one which had come from Belvedere, far down the Thames. This process of overwhelming the defences by masses of incendiaries became known as "saturation", and the Germans were to find that others than themselves could practise it.

It was, however, devastating where London was concerned. Examination of all the damage done to the city from the late summer of 1940 to the early summer of 1941 reveals the fact that the greater part of it was done in the course of about a dozen nights. To begin with the losses of the enemy in these night attacks were trifling. He carried out many of them without having a single aircraft shot down. His terrific raid on Coventry on the night of November 14th cost him two. Throughout the whole month of December only ten were shot down over or near the British Isles. However, with the development of radio-location, matters began to improve in this respect. This is a system of emitting electro-magnetic waves unaffected by cloud or fog and which, when they strike a solid substance, such as an aircraft in the air or a ship at sea, send back a reflection. The effects of "radar", as it soon came to be called, combined with that of the more numerous and better-organized night-fighter squadrons with superior machines, was seen in the losses suffered by the enemy. During the month of May 143 night raiders were destroyed, and this despite the fact that the attacks began to tail off after one exceptionally heavy assault on London on May 10th, in the course of which no less than 33 were shot down. With the attack on Russia the night-bomber offensive ended. It is doubtful if more than fifty German aircraft crossed the coast on any night during the remainder of the year, and that number only on three or four occasions.

The effects upon production were rather more serious than was generally supposed, but they were by no means crippling. They would have been worse but for the fact that the expenditure of munitions by the Army was so small. During Wavell's campaign in North Africa only two divisions had been in action at any given moment, and the consumption of material in East Africa was at no stage considerable. The country had in fact budgeted for a greater expenditure of ammunition than had been required, so that it was not necessary to work the ammunition-filling factories at full pressure. A large proportion of British industrial capacity was at this period devoted to the Royal Air Force.

During the Battle of Britain the chief targets of British bombers had been the ports from which the invasion was to have been launched, and in which, between Amsterdam and Cherbourg, the enemy had collected some 3,000 barges and a large amount of shipping. Though the danger appeared to be over for the winter when the German daylight air attacks ceased, there seemed every prospect that it would be renewed in the spring, and the barge concentrations were not at once dispersed. Bomber Command's attacks on ports and shipping therefore continued. Attacks on

Germany increased, but they were on a small scale by comparison with those of the Germans on Great Britain.

A new policy was, however, at work. In order to compensate for the German advantage in possessing airfields close to Britain, whereas British aircraft had to make long flights to attack objectives in Germany, it was decided to concentrate on large, long-range night-bombers, relatively slow but carrying a great weight of bombs, and with them to keep under constant attack the cities, factories, docks, and communication centres of Germany, as far afield as Berlin. Though it may be said that the statements issued about the policy were propagandist in type, they appear to have reflected a genuine belief that the war could be won by methods such as these.

There was at least this much to be said for the policy, that it provided a means of striking at Germany from Britain at a period during which there was no other means of doing so. The other side of the picture was naturally not displayed, and there were comparatively few with eyes acute enough to read it. The Army was being starved for lack of air co-operation. The campaign in Greece had possibly, and that in Crete had certainly, been lost for this reason. Worse disasters still were in store for the end of the year, when Japan entered the war. The risks taken with the Navy were even sharper and less justified; for, if Britain could not hope for victory without a strong Army with adequate trained air support, she could not hope for survival unless the Navy was able to bear the strain of keeping open the cross-Atlantic routes. This problem, however, is so big that it must be more fully considered in dealing with the situation at a later period when British bombing attacks had reached their height. Up to the summer of 1941 they were on a relatively small scale, and it was not until 1943 that the tonnage of bombs dropped in the course of a month reached five figures.

After the fall of France the main task of Coastal Command became that of combating the German attacks on shipping. In the last chapter, dealing with the war at sea, it has already been pointed out that the acquisition by the enemy of the coasts of Norway, the Low Countries, and France had enormously increased his opportunities of attacking the British Atlantic convoys. To oppose this threat Coastal Command was strengthened. Airfields were established in Iceland, shortly after that island had been occupied by British troops in May, 1940. Early in 1941 the base-line of the Command was extended to West Africa, so that its length was now 3,500 miles; but in this base-line there was a vast gap caused by the coasts of France, Spain and Portugal, and French and Spanish West Africa, with only Gibraltar as a port of call in its midst. At the same time the bases of the Command on the west coast of Scotland and in Northern Ireland were increased, the better to cover the North Atlantic. Lough Erne, in County Fermanagh, became an important seaplane base, at which were stationed Catalinas, flying-boats recently provided by the United States and able to keep the air for eighteen hours in summer, and to a certain extent Sunderlands.

The equipment of the Command in shore-based aircraft had also improved, again with American aid, which had provided the long-range Liberator and the all-purpose Hudson. The Beaufort was now serving as a torpedo-carrier, and in another form, known as the Beaufighter, as a long-distance fighter. General reconnaissance, photographic, meteorological reconnaissance, were other tasks of the Command. Best of all, it was now providing direct cover to the North Atlantic convoys up to a distance of a thousand miles. This was the approximate patrolling range of the Catalina, which carried out the most distant escort duties; they were then taken over by other aircraft as the convoy approached the British Isles, the process being reversed in the case of out-going convoys. The machinery of the Command was improving, as was its efficiency, but the extent of the Atlantic which it was able to cover or ever could cover was limited. No adequate answer to the U-boat, with its superior range, would be possible until air cover could be provided on a similar scale on both sides of the Atlantic and the convoys could be provided with carriers which could adequately cover the gap still remaining in the centre of the ocean.

The Germans possessed in the Condor a land-based aircraft (not a flying-boat such as the Catalina and the Sunderland) with immense range. Flying from the Mérignac airfield near Bordeaux, it could make a great half-circle over the Atlantic to an airfield in southern Norway, and after refuelling and resting the crew make a similar flight back to Mérignac. It made constant attacks on British shipping. As the armament and skill of the gunners in the freighters increased and the volume of fire of the escorts became greater, the Condor achieved less success in its rôle of bomber and began to find its task in this capacity too dangerous and expensive. Yet it still represented a powerful threat. From the beginning of 1941 its most common tactics were to shadow the convoy and by use of its wireless call in any U-boats which might be in the neighbourhood to attack it.

The Condor was faster than the flying boats which provided the more distant cover to the convoys, yet Catalinas and Sunderlands frequently succeeded in driving it away from its prey and occasionally shot one down. And when the convoy was in the range of the British shore-based aircraft such as Hudsons, the boot was on the other foot and the chances of the Condor were poor unless it could escape into cloud. Closer to the British shores the Germans also employed aircraft of less range but better performance, such as the Junkers 88 and the Heinkel 111. The duel was fought on the well-established principle that, the longer the range of the aircraft, the less was its speed and its general capacity as a fighter.

The conditions of air warfare in the Mediterranean were altered by the arrival at the end of 1940 of a force of some 400 German aircraft in Sicily. The *Luftwaffe* at once showed its mettle by a strong and determined attack on the naval squadron which was escorting two convoys through the Sicilian Narrows. The cruiser *Southampton* was set on fire and had to be sunk. The aircraft-carrier *Illustrious* was severely damaged and had to put in to Malta. The enemy then launched some of his heaviest air assaults on Malta, obviously in the hope of destroying the ship. This they did not succeed in doing. They inflicted heavy damage on the cluster of little towns in the area of the docks, but the bombing was strictly directed against what were still called "military objectives", and, owing to the amount of underground protection in already existing cellars and caves and others hastily cut in the cheese-like limestone, civilian casualties were comparatively few. The enemy's own losses were considerable; for example, on January 19th, when he made five attacks, 17 German aircraft were shot down for the loss of one British fighter; on March 6th, when he put upwards of one hundred aircraft into the attack, he lost 16 of them, the British loss again being one. By the end of February Malta had endured its three hundredth attack. The damage done to the dockyard was such that it was not possible to complete the repairs to the *Illustrious*, but she made her way out to Alexandria, round the Cape, and across the Atlantic, to be made battle-worthy again in an American shipyard.

The chief task of the R.A.F. and of British naval aircraft in the Mediterranean was attack on the enemy's communications with North Africa and on his transport columns in Cyrenaica and Tripolitania. These operations were carried out in conjunction with the Mediterranean Fleet, based on Alexandria. On April 21st aircraft supported a naval raid on the port of Tripoli, in which two transports were observed to have been sunk and others were hit. Benghazi was heavily attacked by the R.A.F. on the night of the 22nd. On May 8th and 10th that port, which played so big a part in the maintenance of the Axis advanced force in North Africa, was again attacked, aircraft in this instance playing only a covering rôle. This operation was carried out in concert with the passing of a convoy through the Sicilian Narrows by the fleet based on Gibraltar. On June 26th the Fleet Air Arm intercepted an Italian convoy Africa-bound, hitting two of the largest ships with torpedoes, though the fall of darkness made it impossible to observe their final fate.

The people of this country and the world in general were disposed to question the effectiveness of the air attack, and indeed of the submarine as well, on the Italian convoys crossing the Mediterranean and in harbour because it was apparent that the Axis force in North Africa was maintained and in fact steadily increased in strength. It is true that the commentaries put out, in particular by the Air Ministry, gave an exaggerated impression of the damage that was inflicted. The amount varied with the success or failure of the land forces based on Egypt because, the further advanced their front, the more conveniently situated were the British airfields. In unfavourable circumstances the toll taken of the convoys might be as low as five per cent. In better times it might be several times as big. It did not, as was to become all too apparent, prevent the enemy from carrying out operations over a considerable period and involving a large consumption of fuel.

There is nevertheless evidence to-day that these attacks on the sea communications of the Axis in North Africa, added to the frequent bombing of road transport in the country, constituted a sharp brake upon the activities of the force. It was compelled to exercise the utmost economy. At certain periods it had to lie up and remain almost entirely inactive until it had filled up its dumps. It had to base its operational schemes, not always to their advantage, upon the capture of British petrol. It is probable also that its retreat in the second desert campaign, to be recorded in a later chapter, was due at least in part to administrative difficulties. The air operations should have been more effective than they were, but they were none the less a most important factor in the campaigns in Libya and the Western Desert of Egypt.

CHAPTER XII

Hitler turns against Russia

THE Soviet Union had viewed with disquietude the German march into the Balkans. There had been no comment from Russia when Hitler carried out a military occupation of Rumania, but the Kremlin expressed disapproval when he subjected Bulgaria to the same process. It also pledged itself not to embarrass Turkey if she should be driven to fight for the defence of her territory. On the very day of the German attack on Yugoslavia the Soviet Union signed a pact of friendship and non-aggression with that country, This was at least an expression of a diplomatic policy opposed to that of Germany. Yet the Soviet Union appears to have been slower than outside observers in divining that Germany was preparing to turn east. It gave Turkey, now in imminent danger of attack, no promise of support. It recognized Rashid Ali, the puppet of the Axis in Iraq, which might have been construed as a taunt to Britain. It withdrew recognition from the Belgian, Norwegian, and Yugoslav Legations in Moscow after Yugoslavia had been overthrown.

On June 18th, 1941, Turkey, in hopes of avoiding destruction, signed a treaty with Germany pledging the two countries to respect each other's territory. At the same time notes were exchanged with a view to negotiations on economic subjects. The Turks refused to denounce their treaty of alliance with the United Kingdom and kept the British Foreign Office informed of the conversations. The incident naturally caused displeasure in Whitehall, though it was impossible not to feel some sympathy with Turkey's plight or indeed not to recognize that she was making some attempt to fulfil her obligations. It was believed that she would still fight to oppose any attempt on the part of Hitler to pass through her territory in order to attack Britain in the Middle East.

Hitler did not intend to attack Turkey, at least not at this stage. After long discussions with his advisers, but in the teeth of all the soundest German military opinion, he had decided to postpone his attempt to subdue Britain and to strike at Russia before she became more powerful. That was the primary consideration, to rid himself of the one strong rival now remaining on the European continent. It was, however, complicated by territorial, ethnic, and above all economic ambitions, by the search for that *Lebensraum* which was considered essential to the German race. The Nazis, in throwing Europe into war, had been fired by ambition: first, to unite with themselves the colonies of Germanic race outside their present frontiers; secondly, to bring within their control races, such as the Dutch and Scandinavians, which they were pleased to consider as akin to themselves; thirdly, to seek near their frontiers rich agricultural land in the hands of races which they ranked as inferior and in these territories plant settlements of their own people; and, fourthly, to seize some of the sources of the primary raw materials which they themselves lacked or did not possess in adequate quantities.

The first and second aims had now been reached. Some progress had been made towards the third by clearing of its inhabitants territory in western Poland, attaching it to the Reich, and opening it up to German farmers and artisans. The acquisition of Polish Silesia and the virtual acquisition of the Rumanian oilfields contributed to the realization of the fourth. But there remained much to be accomplished in the latter half of the programme, the chief items of which were, under the third heading, the corn-lands of the Western Ukraine, and, under the fourth, the mineral wealth of the Eastern Ukraine and the Don basin. Behind these motives there was the desire to penetrate to the oilfields of the Caucasus and into the Middle East.

The risks were great—hence the warnings of the pessimists in Hitler's camp. The enormous size of Russia and her terrible winter climate made her a nightmare for the invader. Where was he to stop? How much would he have to accomplish before crippling his opponent? What would Russia have to endure before she owned herself conquered? Hard questions to answer. In fact, it was better not to ask them. It would certainly be worth while to capture Moscow, though that had been done before by an invader to whom it had brought no good, and its very name was of ill omen to a dictator. The one sure method was to destroy the Russian armies in the field, draw in the reserves which would flock forward from the deep rear and the steppes of Siberia and destroy them too, and then to occupy the capital and the chief centres of population, industry, agricultural and mineral wealth, and communications—all of which might for practical purposes be considered as lying to the west of a line from the mouth of the Volga to Leningrad—and leave the Russians, with the remnant of their military power, helpless in the vast undeveloped areas to the east. It was with these objects that the Germans attacked on June 22nd.

British reaction was immediate and decisive. Mr. Churchill that evening broadcast a declaration of policy, in which he stated that he had sent clear warnings to Premier Stalin of what was coming. He went on to say that "we shall give whatever help we can to Russia and to the Russian people. We shall appeal to all our friends and allies in every part of the world to take the same course." Britain played a big part in persuading allied powers, unfortunate Poland in particular, to improve or recreate relations with the Soviet. On July 13th Great Britain and the U.S.S.R. announced that a pact of mutual assistance—in fact an alliance—had been signed the previous day in Moscow. Military Missions had already been exchanged between the two countries. On July 18th an agreement between the Soviet and Poland was signed in the British Foreign Office whereby diplomatic relations were restored, the Soviet-German treaties of 1939 were declared invalid, and a Polish Army under a commander appointed by the Polish Government was to be formed to operate under the Soviet Supreme Command from the troops taken prisoner in 1939. In this happy accommodation, unfortunately not destined to endure, the personality of General Sikorski, the Polish Prime Minister and Commander-in-Chief, played a great part. The Polish Commander chosen in Russia was that General Anders who had distinguished himself in 1939 and had since been in solitary confinement in Russia.

The Germans started the campaign with some 150 divisions of which about twenty were armoured, not including a dozen or so Rumanian and soon afterwards ten Finnish. The Russians opposed the attack with about 158 divisions in the frontier regions and 180 divisions in all, plus 55 tank brigades. The Germans had the advantage in experience and armament, though the Russians were better armed foes than any they had yet encountered. The northern army group (Field-Marshal von Leeb) and the southern (Field-Marshal von Rundstedt) had in each case

THE
RUSSIAN FRONT
June 1941 – March 1943

Line Dec. 1941 ▬▬▬
" Nov. 1942 ▬ ▬ ▬
" Mar. 1943 ●●●●●

Miles
0   100   200   300

FINLAND

L. Onega

L. Ladoga

LENINGRAD

L. Peipus

L. Ilmen

Novgorod

VALDAI HILLS

ESTONIA

LATVIA

POLAND

Kalinin

Volokolamsk

MOSCOW

Volga

Gorki

Kazan

Oka

Smolensk

Vyazma

Penza

Bryansk

Tula

Volga

Minsk

Orel

Kursk

Voronezh

Don

Serafimovich

KIEV

KHARKOV

Izyum

STALINGRAD

Dnieper

Voroshilovgrad

Donetz

Dnepropetrovsk

Bug

Dniester

Rostov

Elista

Kherson

Sea of Azov

Krasnodar

Kuban

Mozdok

RUMANIA

ODESSA

Crimea

Maikop

Pruth

Sevastopol

Kerch Str.

Novorossiisk

CAUCASUS MTS.

Nalchik

BUCHAREST

Danube

B L A C K   S E A

Batum

BULGARIA

TURKEY

one, and the central (Field-Marshal von Bock) had two of a new type of formation called then or a little later a "Panzer Army", of armoured and "light" or completely mechanized, divisions, invaluable for an offensive in open country. In the air the Germans, each army group backed by a complete air fleet, were the better equipped and probably the more numerous. Each side could call upon large reserves, but, while in man-power those of the Russians were several times more numerous, in engines and material of war, always excepting oil, those of Germany would be superior for a considerable time to come.

Making consummate use of their well-trained armoured and motorized divisions, the Germans strode through the Russian array in the old style. The pace of their advance was a rapid as in their previous campaigns, and though they were embarrassed as they had not been in France by the dour resistance of Russian formations outflanked or even completely enveloped, they made vast hauls of prisoners and killed vast numbers of their opponents. Russia was preserved from collapse by her spirit, her refusal to accept defeat; but she owed an almost equal debt to her size because the depth of the German penetration would have overwhelmed any other country in Europe.

The main axes of the German advance were through Southern Poland into the Ukraine on Kiev; through White Russia on Minsk in the general direction of Smolensk and Moscow; and through the Baltic States, which were quickly overrun, northeastwards towards Lake Ladoga and Leningrad. Here the Finns collaborated from the north against Leningrad and by pressing eastward on Russian communications with Murmansk. The right-wing army and the Rumanians did not make a serious advance until the first week in July. Then, taking advantage of the turning of the Russian river defences, the Prut, Dniester, and Bug, by the successful Ukraine drive, this wing too advanced swiftly through Bessarabia and along the Black Sea towards Odessa and Kherson.

By August 12th the German right was nearing Odessa; Kiev was menaced; the centre was at Smolensk; the left, pushing towards Leningrad, was round Lake Peipus. The latter part of the month witnessed something approaching deadlock in the centre on what may be called the "Moscow front"—though it was 250 miles wide—a relatively slow German advance on the northern front towards Novgorod and Leningrad, and in the Southern Ukraine a disastrous Russian collapse, which permitted the invader to reach the great bend of the Dnieper. A great enveloping movement against the salient held by the Russians round Kiev, carried out by the armies of Bock from the north and those of Rundstedt from the south cornered the armies of Budyonny, who is believed to have lost over half a million men.

The Soviet armies astride the roads to Moscow were without doubt better equipped and led than those in the south, but at the same time the Germans were now resigned to a pause for preparation before the final thrusts for Moscow. Vast and skilful work under the control of the Todt labour organization was applied to the communications. Hitler himself proclaimed when the need for secrecy was past that some 16,000 miles of Russian railways had been reconstructed and some 10,000 miles altered to the German gauge and that vast depots had been established behind the Moscow front. The Russians had been dealt terrible blows and seriously weakened, but it is certain that the German's underestimated their resiliency and the speed with which they could put reinforcements, including new formations, into the line. Nevertheless the German offensive launched against Moscow on October 1st was promising and well justified.

The right wing was on Orel, 200 miles south of the capital, thrusting north-eastward by way of Tula; the left just south of the Valdai Hills. The force of the blow made the Soviet forces reel. Between Briansk and Vyasma large bodies of them were annihilated, and the Germans claimed 350,000 prisoners in this region alone. They reached Tula to the south and Volokolamsk, 60 miles north-west of Moscow. In southern Russia their progress continued beyond the Dnieper bend. They entered the densely industrialized area of the eastern Ukraine and approached Rostov-on-Don. But in front of Moscow the Soviet troops under a new commander, the best the Russians ever produced, General Zhukov, were fighting stubbornly. A state of siege was proclaimed in Moscow. The embassies, a number of government departments, and a proportion of women and children were withdrawn. The world held its breath.

Once more, however, the offensive began to run down. Winter was coming on and some snow had fallen. In the south, where the Russians had made no partial recovery similar to that of their central front and where they were in all probability seriously outnumbered, the Germans gained one more brilliant and unexpectedly easy success. After being held up for only a few days in the Perekop isthmus, which joins the Crimea to the mainland, they broke through on October 28th and speedily overran the whole peninsula with the exception of Sebastopol.

Early in November, determined to have the capital and its shelter before the worst of the winter, the Germans launched yet another offensive on Moscow. If the last offensive had been justified, this was not by military considerations. It would have been wiser to draw back and await the spring. Yet for several days the fate of Moscow seemed to hang by a thread. From the north-west the enemy got to within thirty miles of the suburbs—and he had come 700 miles from central Poland to get there! One more push, and it would be over.

It could not be done. The limit of force had been reached. Human endeavour could achieve no more. On December 7th the Germans announced that operations would be closed down for the winter. There they deceived themselves. They might in effect have closed down operations if they had gone back only fifty miles or so, to Vyasma and Rzhev. Now the Russians passed to the offensive. They retook Kaluga and Kalinin. They gradually extended the front of attack opposite Moscow to 400 miles.

They operated in columns, generally headed by troops on skis dragging their baggage on sleighs. They cut off German garrisons, destroying the small ones and beleaguering those which they found too powerful to overrun. The Germans, short of winter clothing owing to a gross miscalculation, suffered terrible hardships. Apart from their battle losses they lost many men with frost-bitten limbs. Acute anxiety reigned in Germany.

Yet the troops stood up to the strain as few would have. Ever in danger of attack from Russian columns suddenly appearing out of the snow, continually harried deep in the rear and on the lines of communication by partisans who dwelt in bands in the forests and marshes, they faced and overcame a peril which at times came near to causing a collapse. The Commander-in-Chief, Field-Marshal von Brauchitsch, was dismissed, and Hitler himself assumed supreme command, with results which, to begin with, were satisfactory. Gradually the front solidified, and it became evident that, not only was the danger to the Germans at an end, but they were left in a favourable situation for an offensive in the spring or summer of 1942. On the other hand, their war machine had been seriously weakened. The damage suffered by the Russians had, however, been infinitely greater. Their best corn-lands in the Ukraine and some of their best industrial plants had been overrun. Obviously the main factor in the renewed struggle would be the extent to which they could recover from these terrific blows. The German strength and the magnitude of the German effort could be estimated; those of the Soviet could not be as yet.

At this point it may be well to discuss the question of the relative numerical strength of the combatants, one which has been the subject of much disagreement. Soviet spokesmen have always resented the statements made in allied circles which attributed to their side an enormous preponderance. So far as can be ascertained they have been justified in this. Russian preponderance was never as great as has been stated, and for a considerable period there was in fact an inferiority.

At the outset there was approximately a parity between the two sides or at most a small Russian superiority. Then, however, the first enormous hauls of prisoners taken by the Germans; the vast excess of Russian slain over German; the intervention of Germany's allies, Hungary and Italy, who followed Rumania and Finland into her camp and sent strong contingents into the field; the creation of new German formations gave Germany the lead. In early 1942 the Russians were definitely inferior in strength. By the end of that year something like parity had again been reached. From that time forward the relative strengths of the combatants became more and more favourable to the Russians. Even then, however, their numerical superority does not appear to have grown as rapidly or ever to have become as great as has commonly been supposed in this country. In November, 1943, the Germans estimated it to be one and a half to one. At some period in 1944, probably not until towards the end of the year, it amounted to about two to one. Its maximum in early 1945 was probably not much above two and a half to one. It must of course be realized that over-all superiority of one and a half or two to one renders local superiority of three to one—still the accepted formula for success—easy to attain.

The western world was deceived in this matter by the rapid growth in numbers of Russian formations. It is true that the number of Russian divisions was multiplied nearly three times between 1941 and 1945. But in these same four years the establishment was reduced to approximately one-third. The original Russian infantry division had an establishment of about 17,000. By the winter of 1941 it had been reduced to 13,000. A year later it stood at 9,500. The final establishment was about 6,000. The Soviet command doubtless found the smaller divisions handier for manœuvre, though to British eyes the final establishment appears unduly low. But the final total of divisions, which may have approached five hundred, did not produce a greater numerical strength from the actual divisions—though corps and army troops must have greatly increased—than the 165 divisions of 1941. If these figures, which are based on authority as good as is available, are correct, the Russian achievement is even greater than the people of Britain and the United States supposed.

On the industrial side it was equally impressive. The vast industrial losses in southern Russia were in large degree balanced by great expansions in the east and even beyond the Urals. Machinery, in some cases even whole factories with their work-people, were removed from the threatened areas and transferred to sites beyond reach of the enemy's land forces and in the main even of his bombers. Only an extremely tough people could have stood the strain of such an exodus, of the primitive accommodation of the new quarters, and all the hardships of the new life. Fortunately, the Russian factory worker was in general separated by only one generation from the Russian peasant, and his endurance was altogether superior to that of the western European. The policy of withdrawing the industrial centre to the deep rear was expensive in transport—and Russian railways were few—but there is little doubt that it constituted a major factor in the prolongation of resistance.

On September 29th, 1941, a conference of Three Powers, the U.S.S.R., Britain, and the United States, opened in Moscow. America was not a belligerent, but President Roosevelt was determined to support the U.S.S.R. to the limit of his power. The British representative, Lord Beaverbrook, and the American, Mr. Averell Harriman, pledged themselves to meet practically every Russian demand for food and war material, causing some subsequent anxiety to the military authorities of their respective countries but taking the wisest as well as the boldest course. The delegates gained the impression that the Russians were by no means pessimistic about the outcome, and this was confirmed by an optimistic speech delivered by Premier Stalin on December 6th. To western observers the Soviet leader appeared unduly sanguine. He proved to be the best judge of the resources and the spirit of his people.

CHAPTER XIII

North Africa to the Summer of 1942

THE British had considered the possibility of clearing North Africa of the enemy and using it as a base from which to attack him in Europe. In the first half of 1941, however, such a goal was still manifestly distant. The urgent matter was to establish a secure grip upon the whole of Cyrenaica, bringing its ports and airfields into use, relieve the strain upon Malta, and with Malta's aid break the enemy's domination of the Sicilian Narrows. This would not in itself make the Mediterranean safe for traffic, but it would go a long way towards reopening it. The Greek episode had been a diversion, perhaps unavoidably, but an interruption of a military policy which it was necessary to maintain steadily. Others were to come, which certainly could not have been avoided, but they were fortunately less expensive and more successful.

On April 3rd a group of officers overthrew the Government and seized power in Iraq. The new Prime Minister whom they set up, Sayid Rashid Ali el-Gailani, stated that he would fulfil Iraqi obligations under the treaty with Britain, which, among other things permitted the maintenance of British troops in the country in time of war or threat of war. When, however, a few days after his installation, the British landed a brigade group at Basra on April 18th, as they could with fullest right, he became perturbed, and when this first detachment was reinforced threw off the mask of friendliness. On May 2nd Iraqi artillery began a bombardment of the British airfield and cantonment of Habbaniya, west of Baghdad.

War notoriously involves distortion of political affairs, and it is seldom in one of this sort that the alleged aggressor is in a position to play the rôle of injured innocent in a spirit of such unquestionable honesty as could Britain in this case. She was on firm ground and acting incontestibly within her treaty rights. The German attack on Russia had not yet taken place—in fact, the Soviet Union, as already mentioned, established diplomatic relations with the Government of Rashid Ali, which it would scarcely have done had it expected to require British assistance in the near future—though the possibility was already much in the mind of Whitehall. The first consideration was the safety of the oilfields and pipe-lines; the second was determination to prevent the Germans from establishing themselves on the eastern flank of the Middle East position. The campaign proved neither difficult nor costly, though the British community in Baghdad had to endure a hard and trying time in its refuge in the British Embassy and United States Legation. The Regent, who had been absent from the capital at the time of the *coup d'état*, returned, and all speedily became quiet again.

This brought up a new problem. During the fighting German and Italian aircraft had appeared in Syria, had bombed Habbaniya, and had been attacked on the airfields of Damascus, Rayak and Palmyra, which they were using. The French High Commissioner, General Dentz, had also forwarded arms to the Iraqis. With the approval of General de Gaulle, Britain decided to enter Syria and Lebanon by force of arms, unwillingly enough, since she did not desire to stir up further trouble with the present French Government, and was at the time short of troops and material in the Middle East Command after the reverses in Greece and Crete.

This was a much more difficult campaign than that of Iraq, and the French troops, especially the Senegalese, well commanded, put up a stiff resistance. The hope, which appeared to have some foundation, that the French would not do more than fight for form's sake, was disappointed. Allied forces, consisting of the 7th Australian Division (less a brigade in Tobruk), an Indian brigade, and a Free French contingent, under the orders of General Wilson, crossed the frontier on June 8th, and later in the month a small force from Iraq intervened from the east; but it was not until July 14th that an armistice convention was signed at Acre. This gave the Allies the right to occupy all Syria and Lebanon.

In Iraq Britain's case had been clear as crystal; in Syria and Lebanon there was justification for her action in the circumstances of war; in Persia there was more than a hint of what is called "power politics". There had been some German penetration into Persia, and this constituted a certain danger, but that cannot disguise the fact that the principal motive of the action now taken was to open an avenue to Russia's back door, that is, to the Caspian ports and the Trans-Caucasian Republics, by which Britain and the United States could send in the supplies she so sorely needed. An almost bloodless campaign in late August ended in a joint Russo-British occupation of the country, and vast efforts to improve its communications were at once set in hand. This action was of vital consequence to the Soviet Union, and together with the Arctic convoys probably made just the difference between its power to fight on and its complete defeat for lack of supplies, above all of transport.

These expeditions made a call on considerable resources at a time when the Middle East had not recovered from the campaigns in Greece and Crete. It might have been wiser to await recovery before taking further action in the Western Desert. However, after a small attack at Sollum on May 15th, which proved abortive, a more ambitious venture was begun by General Wavell on June 15th, with the object of seizing the Halfaya defences and exploiting success in the direction of Tobruk, with which General Wavell was anxious to re-establish land communications. The operation began well, but the enemy's armour counter-attacked and drove back the covering force of the 7th Armoured Division at Sidi Omar. On the night of the 17th Wavell withdrew. The decisive element was the new 50 mm. gun with which the enemy's tanks were equipped, and in a secondary degree the 88 mm. anti-aircraft gun which he was using as an anti-tank gun and which was to be one of his most formidable weapons until the end of the war.

It was now decided that new blood was required in the Middle East. The command was entrusted to General Sir C. J. Auchinleck, who was then Commander-in-Chief in India, and General Wavell took his place at Delhi. During the remainder of the summer a strong force, known as the Eighth Army, under the command of Lieut.-General Sir Alan Cunningham, was formed in the Western Desert. It consisted of the XIII and XXX Corps, the former of two infantry divisions with a tank brigade, the latter of the 7th Armoured Division with an extra armoured brigade, making three in all, an infantry division, and a brigade. In Tobruk there were a division, a depleted tank brigade, and a Polish detachment. The strength of the R.A.F. had now risen to 12 fighter and 15 bomber squadrons.

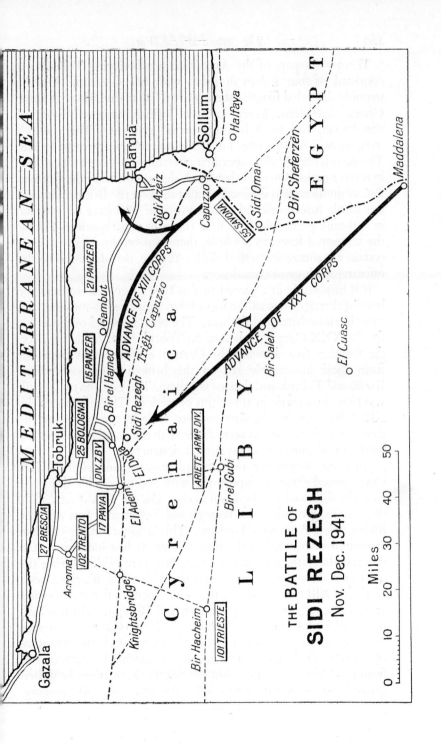

THE BATTLE OF
SIDI REZEGH
Nov. Dec. 1941

Miles

0   10   20   30   40   50

MEDITERRANEAN SEA

Gazala

Tobruk

Acroma

Knightsbridge

Bir Hacheim

Bir el Gubi

27 BRESCIA
102 TRENTO
17 PAVIA
101 TRIESTE
ARIETE ARM.ᴰ DIV.
25 BOLOGNA
DIV. Z.BV.
El Adem
Sidi Rezegh
Bir el Hamed
El Duda
Gambut
15 PANZER
21 PANZER

C y r e n a i c a

L I B Y A

ADVANCE OF XIII CORPS

Trigh Capuzzo

ADVANCE OF XXX CORPS

Bir Saleh

El Cuasc

Sidi Azeiz

Bardia

Sollum

Capuzzo

Halfaya

Sidi Omar

Bir Sheferzen

55 SAVONA

E G Y P T

Maddalena

The greater part of the Axis force was besieging Tobruk. It consisted of four Italian divisions with one German. On the strongly defended frontier there was an Italian division with some German battalions. In rear lay two German armoured divisions, one Italian, and an Italian motorized division. The enemy's strength was far superior, but it was for the greater part Italian. The British had a slight superiority in tanks and a large superiority in reserve tanks. On the other hand, the armament of the German *Panzer* divisions was distinctly better than on the British side, and the whole force possessed a superiority of well over two to one in anti-tank guns, which were at the same time heavier. Taking the armoured forces as a whole, there was on the enemy's side a certain advantage in tactical skill. Yet the British passed to the offensive with great confidence.

It is impossible in a record of this type to give more than the briefest sketch of one of the most interesting, fastest-moving, and most intricate battles of the war. The plan, in broad outline, was for the XXX Corps to advance on Tobruk from Maddalena, on the frontier, first drawing the German armoured divisions out from their inaccessible lair in the broken country between Bardia and Tobruk and destroying them. The garrison of Tobruk was to make a sortie in aid of this operation. The infantry of the XIII Corps was in the first instance to hold the enemy on its front, and afterwards, in accordance with the development of the battle, to advance and complete his destruction.

Early on November 18th the advanced guard of the XXX Corps passed through gaps in the wire and minefields along the frontier, followed by the main body. On the 19th it seized the dominating ground at Sidi Rezegh and fought an action with the Italian Ariete Armoured Division. This brought out the German armoured divisions, but the fighting was at first indecisive. On the 21st they attacked Sidi Rezegh, but were held. During the next two days a fierce and complicated battle took place here, while the XIII Corps worked round the enemy's frontier position at Sidi Omar. In the end we lost Sidi Rezegh. On the 24th Rommel made a sensational drive with his two German armoured divisions across the frontier at Bir Sheferzen, with the intention of getting astride the British communications. He caused confusion and loss to transport, but the fighting formations held their ground and his own transport suffered heavily from air bombing.

Then he turned and made his way back. Meanwhile the New Zealanders of the XIII Corps had retaken Sidi Rezegh. Lieut.-General Willoughby Norrie, commanding the XXX Corps, having partially reorganized his depleted armoured forces, attacked the German armoured divisions as they returned. After fierce fighting the enemy broke through to his bases west of Bardia. He nearly cut off the New Zealand Division as he passed through and forced it south of Sidi Rezegh.

Then the British attacked again, but Rommel had had enough. He began to pull out under cover of a strong flank guard. He got away, but left his force on the frontier to be mopped up, and, moreover, left some 400 tanks on the battlefield. We took between ten and eleven thousand German prisoners and 26,000 Italians, our own losses being 18,000. It was a victory of courage and endurance against superior weight of metal, though Rommel contributed to it by his error—like that of Marmont at Salamanca —in attempting to envelop the British before pinning them down.

The whole of Cyrenaica had now been cleared, but at this moment General Auchinleck was hit by the Japanese attack in the Far East just as General Wavell had been by the call to support Greece. Rommel, considerably reinforced, struck back in January, 1942, from Agheila, and forced the Eighth Army back to a line from Gazala to Bir Hacheim. This was a disappointment, but even then we had no reason to be disappointed by the balance of the operations. A lull followed, during which the opponents built up their strength. On our side the railway was pushed on to the neighbourhood of Tobruk. General Auchinleck was hoping to receive tanks armed with the new 6-pdr. gun as some counter to the superior 75 mm. and 50 mm. guns of the German tanks. None had yet arrived, though he had received some 6-pdr. anti-tank guns and also enough American General Grant tanks, armed with a 75 mm., partially to equip his regiments with them. The Eighth Army's front had been fortified with deep minefields. Some of the formations which had taken part in the last offensive had been withdrawn, to refit or to move to other theatres, but it had been reinforced by the 2nd South African Division, now in Tobruk. Two divisions and a French brigade held the Gazala-Bir Hacheim line. In rear was the XXX Corps with five armoured brigades, two motor brigades, and two infantry brigades, one of Guards, the other Indian. Facing this force was the now famous

German Africa Corps of two armoured and one motor divisions, part of a third German armoured division, and four of the best Italian divisions, one of them armoured.

On May 27th Rommel led off with an assault on the British southern flank with the main weight of his armour, drove back the force covering it, passed round, and pushed north towards the fortified position held by the Guards at a point known as Knightsbridge. A fierce armoured battle developed in this region. The enemy had meanwhile cut gaps through the minefields of the main position, overwhelmed a section of the troops holding it, and thus provided himself with a shorter supply line than that round Bir Hacheim. The Army Commander conceived that he was trying to retreat through this corridor, but Lieutenant.- General Norrie, the first British commander to grip the tactics of armoured warfare in this country, came to the true conclusion, that he was building up strength in his "bridgehead" east of the main position and would try to smash a way out if he could first wear down the opposition sufficiently. This was, indeed, typical German tactics, already fully described in a book, *Blitzkrieg*, published in England by a Czech student of war, Captain Mikche, and therefore should have been recognized for what it was.

After a long series of duels with heavy losses on both sides, a determined attack was launched by the British on the night of June 4th to crush the bridgehead, or the "Cauldron", as it had been named. This attack failed in face of the enemy's powerful array of anti-tank artillery. There was insufficient infantry at the disposal of the Eighth Army to drive it home. Bir Hacheim had to be evacuated to avoid the complete destruction of the French brigade holding it. After a short lull the fighting round Knightsbridge reached new fury. The Guards had withstood attack after attack, but the armour was now too depleted to support them and on the 14th they were withdrawn to avoid annihilation. General Auchinleck rightly decided to retire to the frontier, but, much more questionably, to hold Tobruk, as General Wavell had done. The withdrawal of the troops in the main position was a masterly performance, the 50th Division in the centre actually moving west in the first instance, then south and round Bir Hacheim, under the direction of Lieut.-General Gott, commanding the XIII Corps. But at Tobruk there was a terrible disaster. Covered by bombers using airfields captured from us, the enemy crashed through the perimeter defences, breaking up the Indian brigade on which the assault fell. The German armour then swept in, beat off a counter-attack, and played havoc with the parked transport. A few small parties fought their way out, but the bulk of the troops which tried to do so were headed off. Over 20,000 fell into the hands of the enemy, together with great quantities of supplies, including food, which was valuable to him at this moment. The moral effect all over the world was calamitous.

Doubtful of being able to hold the frontier position for long, General Auchinleck decided to fall back to Matruh, to the position held by General Wavell before his offensive against the Italians eighteen months earlier. But even that could not be held. Orders were therefore issued for withdrawal to El Alamein, where there existed a relatively narrow front of about thirty-five miles, which could not be turned, since it lay between the sea and the vast salt-pan known as the Qattara Depression. The defence was organized here with what resources were available, battalions being represented by companies or even platoons, and amalgamated wholesale. On July 1st, Rommel, who had covered nearly thirty miles a day and now believed he had Egypt in his grasp, launched his first attack. He was sharply repulsed. Other attacks followed, but no real impression was made on the position. Then the British began to strike back. The position was, however, as cramped from the point of view of attack as it was strong from that of defence, and the Eighth Army did not make much progress with costly frontal assaults. However, the position was stabilized and the enemy was halted, though only 70 miles from Alexandria. Reinforcements and fresh material began to reach the scene.

Great and brilliant deeds were accomplished in the defence of the Gazala Line and in the fierce battles round Knightsbridge, yet, compared with the engagements of the previous winter, this phase was bitterly disappointing to the Army, to public opinion, and to all the friends of Britain. Though we had been again heavily out-gunned, we had been less at a disadvantage in this respect than at Sidi Rezegh. General Auchinleck had been most unfortunate in his arrangements for command. He had superseded Lieut.-General Cunningham in the midst of the first battle, replacing him by Lieut.-General N. M. Ritchie from his own staff. In the second battle he removed Ritchie from his post and himself took over direct control of the Army. As a personality, he showed himself one of the finest the British had produced in modern times, and it seems likely that his influence and inspiration made all the difference beween the holding and the loss of the Alamein Line.

Auchinleck and his Eighth Army saved Egypt. Auchinleck also planned a new offensive with certain of the characteristics of that which was actually launched later in the year. But, apart from the trouble and muddle of the command, it seemed that a change was needed. If we did not do away with the tactics of dispersion and learn to keep our formations in mutually support-ing positions, however fast they were moving, and so balanced that they could always concentrate speedily, then, even if we improved our armament, there was always a chance that Rommel might defeat us again when he got us into the open. Great man and fine soldier as Auchinleck was, there was no mere whim or choler in the decision to send new men to the Middle East.

CHAPTER XIV

At Home and Abroad

DESPITE the losses and dislocation caused by the German air attacks, Britain was in most respects stronger by the time the heaviest bombing ceased in the summer of 1941 than she had been when they started. New factories were coming into production, and adequate labour was made available for them. The Government possessed the confidence of the country, and one disquieting element, the number of votes cast at by-elections for independent candidates, some not of the highest credit, appeared to be due to impatience with real or imagined short-comings in the conduct of the war rather than to any weakening of national resolution. There were fairly frequent changes of office, but the character of the Government remained unaltered. The most important change was that at the end of 1940, when Mr. Anthony Eden left the War Office to become Secretary of State for Foreign Affairs in the room of Lord Halifax, who became Ambassador to the United States on the death of the Marquess of Lothian.

In April, 1941, the Chancellor of the Exchequer, Sir Kingsley Wood, introduced a war budget of £4,000,000,000. Taxation was greatly increased, but a new expedient, that of post-war credits, for a small proportion of the tax paid, was devised to soften the blow. Rather less than half the total was to be met by taxation, the rest being covered by internal loans and borrowing from balances accumulated abroad. Subscriptions to loans were at that time bringing in £1,500,000,000. The Government continued and stepped up its policy of resisting inflation by subsidies —though without acknowledgment of the elementary economic truth that subsidies must themselves in the long run involve inflation. Yet, if it had a taxation policy, a food subsidy policy, and a limitation of profits policy, all of which were sound enough in themselves, it had no wages policy, and in this respect the structure of war finance was lopsided. The Minister of Labour, Mr. Ernest Bevin, strong and even ruthless on the subject of man-power, put no limit to the rise of wages. So far this had not been excessive, but in trades such as engineering, ship-building and metallurgy the percentage of increase above the pre-war level was 43 by the end of 1940, and the curve continued to rise fairly sharply.

The age liability to service for men was raised to 51 years from 41 and lowered to 18½, but a large proportion of the older men were in fact never called up. Service became compulsory in the women's services attached to the Navy, Army and Air Force for women between the ages of 20 and 30, but again large numbers between these ages were directed to industries considered to be essential or to the bureaucracy, which in its own eyes was the most essential of all. Rations decreased somewhat in 1941, but considering the dangers of the Atlantic passage and the vastness of the sources of supply on the European continent which had been cut off, they were remarkably well maintained with the aid of more intensive agriculture and the increased proportion of land put under the plough.

As has already been pointed out, the Royal Air Force was from many points of view the most favoured of the three services. Apart from the concentration of the Ministry of Aircraft Production on heavy bombers, which has already been mentioned, good work was being done on the improvement of fighters. The Spitfire of the Battle of Britain was being transformed, and it may be said that it maintained its lead in the type of screw-driven fighter throughout, though it was later to be threatened by the Focke-Wolf 190, which was at certain altitudes its superior. The jet-propelled aircraft, on which both Britain and Germany were at work, was still in the experimental stage. Co-operation with the other services was also becoming closer.

All that it is possible to say in so brief a record about the Navy and its problems is said in the chapters specifically dealing with the war at sea. The Army training at home had made rapid strides in rearmament and in training since the withdrawal from the Continent. It had in particular been concentrating upon building up its armoured divisions. A special command had been created for this purpose under a highly-experienced general officer, Lieut.-General G. le Q. Martel. The lessons of the African testing-ground were absorbed. On the material side there was improvement, but there were also serious delays and false starts, which resulted in various types of tanks becoming obsolete before they had reached the stage of mass production. Much impatience has been expressed over the delays in tank design and production, and a good deal of it has been fully justified. It is, however, doubtful whether the full extent of the handicap under which this country laboured has even yet been realized.

The lead which the Germans had gained in time of peace had been a very long one. The Mark III German tank, which the enemy was to find useful up to the very end of the war, had been in production at the outbreak, and the Mark IV, which also endured throughout the war, followed close upon it. The British were thus handicapped in respect of time in tank design and compelled to go into full production with designs which it was fully realized were not satisfactory because it was necessary to give the troops something to fight with. In the same way they lagged behind in the development of guns to be used in the tank and as anti-tank artillery because they were competing against a country which had been steadily working up to production on a war scale in time of peace. They were handicapped also by the nature of their motor industry, which did not in general produce engines suitable for tanks, even with considerable modification. It would appear that they relied too much on this industry, which lacked the necessary experience and which was largely captained by men who were financiers and dealers rather than engineers. As a result, whereas British tank production was enormous quantitatively, it was qualitatively inferior. A German tank industry, almost ludicrously small by comparison, taking into account the relative strength of the armies, kept its fighting forces on the whole adequately provided with good tanks, whereas thousands of British tanks came from the factories to be dumped and never used.

Yet even with these grave weaknesses there was a great and swift improvement in British fighting capacity in armoured warfare. Much care was devoted to the selection of officers, training of mechanics, administration and signal communication. The air superiority which was gained in one theatre of the war after another covered up many deficiencies and enabled British armoured divisions to defeat foes which might otherwise have proved too hard-hitting for them. And in respect of mobility—which is in a tank a combination of speed and reliability, and, to a lesser extent long mileage without refuelling—the situation was satisfactory all through the war.

The United States of America had all along taken the deepest interest in the war. Even the uninstructed were now beginning to realize that America was no longer as remote from European conflict as in the past. The possibility of German penetration of South America across the South Atlantic from West Africa, which had hardly been considered before the outbreak of war, had now become very real. For a brief period in late 1940 the people of the United States turned their back upon Europe while they prepared for the presidential election, but as soon as that was over and Mr. Roosevelt had been granted his third term on November 5th they once more became absorbed in the war and its possible effects upon themselves. The President was determined that they should not forget it.

Even before the elections a transaction had been carried out which brought Britain and the United States to a condition of partial alliance. The American Government provided this country with fifty destroyers, old vessels which had been laid up, but still highly serviceable and invaluable in view of the losses we had suffered and the demands of the submarine war. In return it was given the lease of a number of bases, mostly in the Carribean, which it had long desired in order to have the opportunity of meeting German aggression, if this should come, at some distance from the shores of the American mainland.

On January 10th, 1941, occurred an event of vital importance to the relationship between the two countries and to the future course of the war. On that day the Senate and House of Representatives received the draft of what was described as an "Act to promote the Defence of the United States". It was almost immediately to become known as the "Lease-and-lend" Act, soon shortened to "Lease-lend". It permitted the President to manufacture any weapon for the Government of any country whose defence he deemed vital to the defence of the United States; to "sell, transfer, exchange, lease, lend, or otherwise dispose of to any such Government any defence articles"; to repair equipment for any such Government; to communicate to any such Government information about any equipment supplied to it; and to release for export to any such Government any defence article whatever." The Bill was amended in some respects, as regards the total value which might be disposed of without authorization of Congress, and without consultation with the chiefs of the forces before parting with any equipment belonging to them to a foreign Government; but on the other hand it was strengthened from the British point of view by permission to include agricultural commodities.

The Act became law on March 11th. It relieved Britain of financial anxieties about her orders in the United States which might soon have become overwhelming. It led to enormous additions to the extent of those orders, which was invaluable to this country and at the same time not disagreeable to the American military and naval authorities because it brought American war production into operation and provided a reserve of weapons and equipment which they could lay their hands upon should their own danger become greater. And one of the most remarkable features of the whole war is the efficiency and strength of the armament of the United States when brought into the conflict by a sudden surprise attack, by comparison with that of the last war, which the nation entered of its own volition, deliberately and after prolonged consideration. In this respect the country owes a deep debt of gratitude to its administration.

On April 11th, 1941, the United States took a further important step. The President issued a proclamation opening the Gulf of Aden and the Red Sea to American shipping. The effect of this was to enable shipment of war material to be sent direct to the British forces in the Middle East without transhipment to British freighters and without infringing the Neutrality Act which had hitherto prevented American ships from entering certain danger zones. On April 25th the President informed journalists that measures would be taken to protect American shipping carrying goods across the Atlantic on British account by extending patrols deep into the Atlantic. By these and other measures, including a conference at Washington of the naval authorities of the Latin-American countries, the United States made preparations for the protection of the Western Hemisphere and its shipping, increased its support of Britain and the British Commonwealth, and showed itself more and more wholeheartedly opposed to the aims of the Axis.

Then, in August, these material measures were confirmed by one which set on record "certain common principles in the national policies" of the two countries. Mr. Roosevelt and the British Prime Minister, Mr. Churchill, met at sea and drew up a joint declaration, the Atlantic Charter, on which, they declared, they based "their hopes for a better future for the world." The following is a summary of the eight clauses.

1. The two countries sought no aggrandizement.
2. They desired no territorial changes which did not accord with the wishes of the peoples concerned.
3. They respected the right of peoples to choose their form of Government and wished to see sovereign rights restored to those forcibly deprived of them.
4. They were pledged to further enjoyment by all States, great or small, victor or vanquished, of access to trade and the raw materials of the world.
5. They sought collaboration between all nations to secure improved labour standards and social security.
6. After the destruction of Nazi tyranny, they hoped for a peace which would afford all nations the means of dwelling in safety within their boundaries, and assurance that all men might live out their lives in freedom from fear and freedom from want.
7. Such a peace should enable all men to traverse the seas without hindrance.
8. They believed that all nations must come to the abandonment of the use of force. Since no future peace could be attained while armaments continued to be employed by nations which threatened aggression, they believed that, pending the establishment of "a wider and permanent system of general security", the disarmament of such nations to be essential.

The state of the world to-day is a melancholy commentary upon these pronouncements. It should not for that reason cause the Atlantic Charter to be viewed with the eye of cynicism. It was a noble declaration of faith. It was also in the psychological field the first effective counter to the programme of the Nazi New Order.

Early in 1941 Japan intervened in a dispute between Siam and the French authorities in Indo-China as a self-appointed arbiter. In this role she handed over a considerable slice of French territory to the Thais. Having thus established ascendancy over the helpless colony and its officials, she approached the French Government with a demand for bases in it. An agreement came into force on July 29th, providing for "the joint defence of Indo-China", and immediately afterwards Japanese forces began to land in the country and the airfields were taken over. This was one of the cleverest moves in the whole of Japan's politico-strategic game. As Siam scarcely counted, could easily be overawed, and had indeed virtually become a satellite of Japan, the acquisition of Indo-China placed the Japanese in a first-class position for offensives against Burma and Malaya. It also added to their power to strike at China, the Netherlands East Indies, and the Philippines. It was upon this Japanese aggression and this new French surrender that the future campaigns in south-east Asia were to be based.

Germany had been consolidating her grip upon north-western Europe by a policy of Nazification in Norway, Denmark, Holland and Belgium. In all these countries she had found men who were prepared to profess the Nazi creed—some of them, indeed, had become its followers before the war—and ready to pursue this Nazification in the governments, administrations, police and press, and seats of education of the occupied countries. In general they made relatively little impression on the bulk of the population. On the other hand, it is clear that the orderliness of the occupation and the high standard of correctitude and discipline of the German garrisons had made themselves felt. This was perhaps particularly the case in Belgium, the only one of these countries to have been occupied by Germany in the last war. The people at large could not but contrast the present good behaviour of the Germans with the brutality, drunkenness and plunder of the period from 1914 to 1918.

Yet, in Belgium as in the other countries concerned, reaction was beginning and was to grow rapidly. If the garrisons were well behaved, the various types of police forces were cruel with a cold and diabolical refinement of cruelty. The forced labour and deportations, the deliberate soul-killing tyranny, ate into the hearts of the people. The German policy was stupid as well as savage, for it sacrificed initial advantages so great that they are seldom even now admitted in these countries, still less in our own.

In France the situation was rather different, but the reaction was similar. The Germans were putting heavier pressure on the

Vichy Government to accept ministers suitable to their own ends, in particularly the intensely unpopular Pierre Laval. Vichy was being thrown more into opposition with Britain. On the other hand, the propaganda which had sought to vilify Britain, to decry her part in resistance to Germany, and to pretend that she had betrayed France, was beginning to wear thin. Germany was finding in France one of her most difficult problems. Nor should it be forgotten, though it generally is, that the resistance to German designs in and on France came largely from elements which had no particular sympathy for General de Gaulle and his Free French movement, and extended even to Government circles. The intense suspicion with which all negotiations with Vichy were regarded in the United Kingdom may well have prevented this country from establishing better relations with Unoccupied France, in which, despite its weakness, not one man in ten desired German success.

CHAPTER XV

The Russian Campaigns to Stalingrad

AS the spring thaw of 1942 came to an end in Russia, it was clear that the Germans, despite their rough handling during the winter, were in a position to strike further deadly blows. Even where the Russian light forces had flowed beyond the important road and rail junctions west of the main front, these were in practically every case still held by the Germans. In May they launched a local offensive in the Crimea and drove the Russians from their small holding in the Kerch peninsula. Early in June they set about the reduction of Sevastopol, which they carried after four weeks' heroic defence, thus clearing their southern flank and depriving the Russians of their best naval base in the Black Sea. Their main offensive did not come as soon as was generally expected, but it was certain that there would be one.

Meanwhile, however, on or about May 12th, the Soviet forces on the south-central front under the command of Marshal Timoshenko had launched an offensive south of Kharkov with the object of anticipating the enemy and throwing him off his balance. This thrust penetrated ten miles or more on a fifty-mile front. It was brought to an end within about a week by stiffening resistance and a brilliant riposte by the German commander, Field-Marshal von Bock (transferred from the central to the southern front) who crossed the Donetz at Izyum on the southern flank of the Russian salient. Fighting continued until the end of the month. The offensive may have in some degree upset German preparations, but not seriously.

On May 26th a formal treaty of alliance between the United Kingdom and the U.S.S.R. was signed in London. Discussions took place later on with the object of accelerating the supply of war material to the Soviet forces. The Soviet Foreign Minister, M. Molotov, immediately visited the United States, where he took part in conversations with the same end in view. On his return to Moscow he announced a large increase in American credits already promised to Russia and agreement about the need for creating a second front in Europe in 1942—which was, in point of fact, wholly beyond American and British power. Convoys to Northern Russian ports by the Arctic route were, however, increased. They constituted a heavy strain, not only by reason of the severity of the northern weather, but also because the proportion of losses on this route was always higher than on any other. Supplies through Persia were now flowing in at a good rate, despite the demands of the war against Japan.

The offensive of 1942 was in its preliminary stages better contrived, more practical, and more in accordance with well-founded German principles than that of 1941, successful though the latter had been. It was confined to the southern front instead of being spread over the whole, but the first blows were struck on a frontage of 150 miles at most, from the neighbourhood of Kursk to south of Kharkov. In this sector Field-Marshal von Bock had massed three army groups, each consisting of an infantry and a "Panzer" army, and enormous striking-power in armoured and motorized divisions, artillery, ammunition and stores, supported by one of Germany's air fleets and the Richthofen Assault Corps. He had in all some 45 infantry or motorized divisions, 16 armoured divisions, and 15 to 20 divisions of the "satellites". Manstein was still engaged in the Crimea, but would soon be free. He possessed complete command of the air. The country was well suited to rapid movement and armoured manœuvre in the open, though the heat and dust were trying to the troops. The Russians, though they had achieved successes in the winter, had not recovered from the effects of their earlier defeats. The German commander had almost everything in his favour. His aim was to smash to pieces the Soviet forces on the southern front, capture the remaining southern industrial area still in Russian hands, cut the routes by which the Caucasian oil reached the main Soviet armies—including the Volga, which carried a fleet of small tankers in summer—and seize at least the nearer of the oilfields. If he could succeeed in these tasks, the final operations for the reduction of Russian power might perhaps stand over until the following spring, with every hope that they would then be put through, though Marshal Stalin afterwards declared that the enemy meant to end the war that year. The Japanese war made it clear to the Germans, whatever might be agreed between M.

Molotov and the British and United States Governments, that they need not worry seriously about diversions in the European continent in 1942.

Bock led off with a fierce thrust south of Kharkov on June 10th. On the 28th he launched a more powerful attack from Kursk. On July 2nd he struck again north-west of Kharkov. In this area the Germans claimed 240,000 prisoners. Then the front was extended southward. The Russians were in full retreat. Heavily as they had lost, they seem to have avoided letting their main body be pinched between the armoured fingers stretching out from Kharkov and Kursk and to have withdrawn a considerable proportion across the Don. Their armies, battered and depleted, were still in being. At Voronezh, on the Don, they resisted fiercely, and the Germans could not take it for all their endeavours. Henceforth this place was to be the northern hinge of the German offensive, which swung forward from it. For 300 miles to the south-east Bock reached the Don, and at many places passed it, by mid-August, and at the same time his right was well into the foothills of the Caucasus. By the 17th he had in his hands the first of the oilfields, that of Maikop, and the refinery of Krasnodar.

A few days later the Germans closed upon what had always been one of their main objectives, the elbow bend of the Volga at Stalingrad. At the approaches to this modern industrial city there began one of the dourest, bloodiest, and most prolonged battles of the war. Slowly and in face of the most bitter opposition the Germans fought their way to Stalingrad. They entered the town, but the Russians would not give in. The city crumbled, but the vast concrete factories and assembly shops, however shattered they might be, still provided cover, and their underground compartments were scarcely affected. The struggle went on in the streets, from house to house, and sometimes in the same building. As week succeeded week the German press began to betray some anxiety. It seemed incredible that no decision should have been reached. The Germans continued to make progress, but it grew ever slower and more costly. The Russians, who included workers from the factories equipped with rifles and light machine-guns or anti-tank rifles, refused to give in.

In order to make a deep invasion of the Caucasus a militarily sound undertaking the Germans needed to inflict a crushing defeat upon the Soviet armies from Voronezh down to a point on the Volga considerably south of Stalingrad and to secure a firm hold upon that river. Neither of these conditions had been really fulfilled. The Russians were standing firm, and everything pointed to their having been reinforced. The German hold on the Volga was but slight, though a small bridgehead north of Stalingrad had been secured. In plunging deep into the Caucasus, therefore, the enemy was taking heavy risks. These he accepted, and for a time it seemed with justification. His southern army group, commanded by Field-Marshal von List, no mean expert in mountain warfare, made good progress. The Germans crippled the Russians at sea by the capture of the great port of Novorossisk. They passed the outlet of the pass road leading to the port of Sukhum, but did not attempt to venture far down it. They reached the gates of Mozdok, and the entrance to the two more important passes, the Ossetin and Georgian Military Roads, the latter of which led to Tiflis. On November 2nd they captured Nalchik. Now, even if they were baulked at Stalingrad, they seemed well placed for their part in a great two-pronged offensive in the Middle East, which would not only give them the Caucasus and bring them to the shores of the Caspian but also link their forces in Russia with those in North Africa, destroy the British forces, and perhaps even establish contact with the Japanese. But though his lieutenant, List, had been doing his part, Hitler was not destined to become the modern Alexander. List was presently held on the Terek, where the Russians fought heroic battles. In Africa Alamein had been fought and won, and Rommel was in retreat. The British-American allies had landed in French territory. And at Stalingrad—at Stalingrad disaster was looming.

Suddenly, on November 19th, the Russians went over to the offensive under the supreme command of Zhukov, who had been sent down from the Moscow front. One thrust under Rokossovsky crossed the Don at Serafimovich; a second struck the Don bend just north-west of Stalingrad; a third was delivered south of Stalingrad. The first fell upon "satellite" forces, which were completely disrupted. But a far worse disaster than this fell upon the enemy when the pincers closed on the remains of some 18 German and Rumanian divisions round Stalingrad itself. Having isolated this force, the Russians proceeded to push away from it the main body, so as to ensure that it should not be relieved. The Germans did make one determined effort under Manstein's command to relieve it, but were driven back after initial progress. To prevent reinforcements moving south, the Russians followed up their success by secondary offensives west of Moscow.

By the last day of 1942 there were no German troops within a hundred miles of the doomed Sixth Army penned in just west of Stalingrad. It resisted stoutly, but on January 31st, 1943, Field-Marshal von Paulus, with fifteen general officers and all that was left of the battered force, surrendered. It was the greatest disaster that Germany had undergone in the course of the war. By glorification of the heroism of the Sixth Army everything possible was done by the Nazis to obscure the fact that it had been wantonly sacrificed to rash ambition and an unsound strategic plan. Yet the incident is known to have caused the gravest anxiety in all circles, military, official, and civilian. Even they, however, can scarcely have realized that Germany's strategic offensive was over or that she was to fight a losing battle, broken only by occasional local and temporary successes, from now to the end of the war.

Meanwhile the Russians had gained another success. In mid-January the enemy was driven back from the shore of Lake Ladoga, so that a corridor was opened to Leningrad and the investment was broken. The city had endured frightful sufferings, especially during the previous winter, during which many of the windows had been deprived of their glass. Thousands had died of starvation. Yet some factories had remained at work and had supplied material and munitions to the garrison.

In the south the most serious anxiety for the Germans was the vast gap in their array caused by the destruction of so many divisions and the reduction of others to such a point that they were of no military value. The most urgent necessity was to shorten the front and provide new reserves by withdrawal from the Caucasus. This they accomplished with skill and tenacity, one half of the force retreating through Rostov before the Russians could reach that point and so close the last land route of escape, the other withdrawing into the Kuban peninsula, where it could assemble its transport and gradually transfer all but a minimum to the Crimea. The fourth disaster which many had foretold, a second great Russian trap south of the Don, was thus avoided. A certain number of divisions were re-organized, re-equipped, and assembled on the Donetz under General von Manstein, in some German professional eyes the most capable soldier produced by the German Army in the course of the war.

During the early part of February the Russians continued to press forward steadily, but their advance began to slow down as the Germans exerted all their efforts to prevent the door at Rostov from closing on their columns withdrawing from the Caucasus. They kept it open long enough. In the latter part of February the Germans began to strike back on the Donetz. At first they made little progress, but an early thaw, which affected the Russians advancing over ruined country more than it affected the Germans with their intact communications behind them, altered the situation. The Russians were forced back from the considerable amount of ground which they had gained in the Donetz valley. This cleared the way for the Germans to strike northward at Kharkov, which the Russians had recently taken. Gathering up the bulk of his armoured strength, Manstein boldly thrust his way into the Russian lines actually far east of the city, then turned in upon it and retook it on March 15th. The Russian offensive was halted. Fighting continued until the end of the month, but with relatively little change in the situation.

When the conditions of spring brought it completely to an end, just as they had in the previous year, the southern front ran from 275 miles west of Moscow—where the Russians had also gained ground—generally south-east, to pass in a semi-circle east of Orel, formed a square Russian salient west of Kursk, bent east of Kharkov, and then ran down to the Don estuary near Taganrog. Despite the check they had suffered at the end of their offensive, the Russian advance from Stalingrad to the Donetz at Voroshilovgrad measured about 225 miles. The whole of the Caucasus had been regained except for a German bridgehead only some 40 miles across, but including the port of Novorossisk.

But the victory cannot be measured wholly or even mainly in terms of ground. In the moral sphere it was far more important still. The watching world had admitted the stubborn courage of the Russian resistance but had been doubtful of the Russian ability to turn to the counter-offensive on a large scale and to maintain an advance over a long period. It could conceive of the Germans being checked, but not of their being flung back in rout. Now this had happened. The Germans had been heavily defeated—that was not to be denied.

Yet not even in the moral sphere is to be found the true importance of the Russian victory, especially since there is evidence that Manstein's success at Kharkov, his paralysing of the whole Russian front by dealing one section of it a crippling blow, so typical of German theory and practice, had brought a fair amount of comfort to the Germans and led them to hope that if they did not repeat the madness of 1942 they might not have much to fear. "We have space enough left for fighting," said General Dietmar, the foremost German military broadcaster. No, it was the human and purely material damage which she had suffered that Germany was now to find so embarrassing. The "satellite" armies of the Don were cut to ribbons; the remnant of the Italian component in fact shortly afterwards went home. Scores of German divisions had been reduced to shadows, and hundreds of thousands of the finest troops, who had been victorious all over Europe, had been killed or captured. Somehow or another all these men would be replaced, but the quality would not be quite the same. Huge quantities of material and equipment of every sort had also fallen into Russian hands or been destroyed in the retreat.

At some moment within the same period the Soviet forces appear to have gained at least parity in the air, and in the early summer of 1943 they possessed superiority. This meant all the more to them because the roads of Russia are few and far between, so that transport was an easy target from the air. Hitherto no movement by day had been safe behind the Russian front. Now all that was changing, and in the later campaigns it was possible to move big columns by daylight. The operations of the R.A.F. in the west contributed in great degree to this transformation by tying down an increasing proportion of German fighter aircraft to airfields in France, western Germany, and the neighbourhood of the cities most in danger of attack. The advent of the United States Army Air Force and the capture of airfields in Italy were to increase this diversion.

In every respect the Battle of Stalingrad and its exploitation must be considered one of the most important victories of the war, if not the most decisive of all.

CHAPTER XVI

Japan Attacks

THE United States had viewed with profound disquietude as well as profound distaste the aggressive acts and attitude of Japan. Government and people had for long been uneasy in their consciences on the subject of the yoke which the Japanese had imposed upon the richest areas of China. They had been critical of the British action in temporarily closing the Burma Road by which supplies were transported—though in trifling quantity in proportion to needs—to the Chungking Government, considering that it smacked of the appeasement which had previously been practised with regard to Germany and Italy. The administration fully appreciated the threat constituted by Japanese penetration into Indo-China and by the manifest pressure being exercised against the Netherlands East Indies. It realized that danger to Holland and to Great Britain in her Indian Empire must also involve danger to the United States.

Yet the anxiety went deeper than this. The possibility of direct aggression on the part of Japan against the United States had been present in the minds of Americans long before they gave a thought to any such risk from Germany. To many of them, including high-ranking military and naval officers, Japan was the natural potential enemy to a far greater extent than Germany. They were nervous because so large a proportion of the American output of munitions of war, using the term in its broadest sense, was being shipped across the Atlantic to aid Britain in her struggle against Germany. The conception of eastern Asia welded together into a single economic and political sphere under the domination of Japan threatened not only American trade interests but also foreshadowed an attempt to expel American power and influence from the whole Pacific area. And they were right in supposing that Japan would realize the opportunity she now possessed of fulfilling her widest ambitions and the impossibility of its ever recurring.

In early October, 1941, the Japanese were in full possession of French Indo-China. On the 16th occurred an ominous event in their home politics. The Cabinet headed by Prince Konoe, which favoured agreement with the United States, resigned, to be succeeded by one headed by General Tojo. This was followed by bellicose announcements to the effect that Japan was more than ever determined to settle the China affair and to establish a "Greater East Asia Co-prosperity Sphere." The Japanese Government proposed that the United States should supply Japan with oil and discontinue financial aid to China, but offered no assurances to balance such concessions. On November 5th there was a slight *détente* in Japanese-American relations, when a special Japanese envoy, Saburo Kurusu, was sent to Washington to assist the Japanese Ambassador who was engaged in negotiations with the United States Government. Against the will of the American military authorities, who would have preferred to spar for time, the Secretary of State, Mr. Cordell Hull, presented to the Japanese delegates a somewhat stiff document outlining the American attitude and insisting that aggression in China and Indo-China must cease.

Meanwhile there were some signs of Japanese naval and military movements, including the arrival in Indo-China of forces in excess of those provided for in the convention on the subject between France and Japan. In China the Japanese carried out some offensive moves in the province of Honan, but these ended with retreat from the railway junction of Chengchow. The Japanese had in mind ventures beside which their campaigns in China were of secondary importance.

Early in the morning of December 7th waves of Japanese aircraft flown from carriers appeared over the Hawaiian island of Oahu, where the American Pacific Fleet lay in Pearl Harbour. It was a complete surprise. Fleet, airfields, troops, all alike were caught off their guard. Within a matter of minutes virtually the whole fleet was out of action, sunk or incapacitated for a considerable period, for the loss of 29 Japanese pilots.

Oceans of ink have been spilt already over the disaster of Pearl Harbour, and despite one investigation after another it is possible that there will always remain certain unanswered questions. The main facts, however, are reasonably clear. American military opinion in the first place thought it probable that the Japanese would begin by attacking the British and Dutch, which, it reasoned, would be good policy as well as good strategy because this course might be expected to split American opinion on the subject of intervention. Yet it did envisage the possibility of attack on American stations likewise, and as time passed it considered this more and more probable. Even then, however, the American authorities thought that Japan would not strike so far afield as Hawaii; it seemed much more likely that the blow would be dealt at the Philippines. The warnings issued to the naval and military commanders at Pearl Harbour were therefore not as insistent as they might have been, though it is common ground that they were not listened to and acted upon as they ought to have been.

The effects of the blow were far-reaching. For a long period to come the United States was almost helpless in the Pacific, or at least in a great proportion of its vast waters. Her own continent appeared to be endangered, and the first counter-measure taken was the reinforcement of the garrisons of the west coast, Panama, Hawaii, and Alaska. She could not support her outposts; still less could she afford aid to the British and Dutch in their even more desperate straits. She had to resign herself to a policy of waiting, to a slow building up of strength and repair of shattered resources and severed communications, when every instinct urged her to go out and meet the foe before he had consolidated his gains.

The Japanese followed up their success at Pearl Harbour by the capture of the islands of Wake and Guam in the central Pacific, the defence of the former by a handful of American Marines being a particularly heroic incident. They also immediately struck at the Philippines. These islands, wrested from Spain by the United States, were now on the high road to complete independence, and the last of the American garrison was due to be withdrawn in 1945. The President, Manuel Quezon, had obtained from the United States the services of an American general, a former Chief of the U.S. Army Staff who possessed intimate knowledge of the Philippines, General Douglas MacArthur, to organize a defence force. Seeing the danger of Japanese aggression even more clearly than his countrymen at home, MacArthur had made the utmost efforts to put at least the main island of Luzon into a state of preparedness sufficient to hold off an attack until reinforcements could reach the scene. He had not been accorded nearly all that he demanded, but he had nevertheless

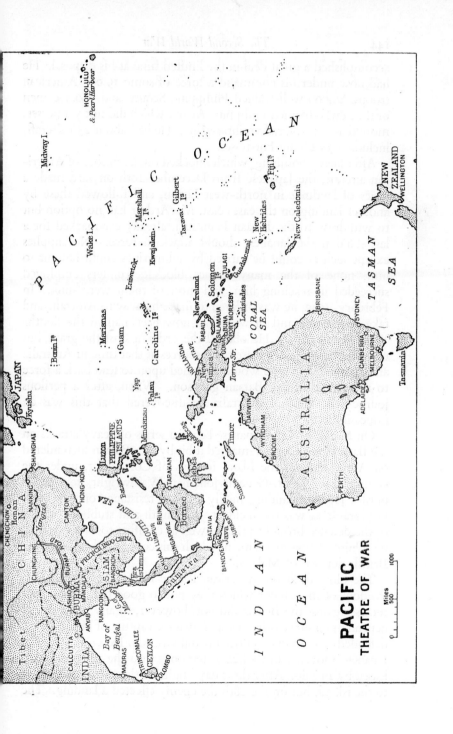

PACIFIC
THEATRE OF WAR

Miles
500   1000

accomplished a great deal in the limited time at his disposal. He had now under his command a force of some 19,000 American troops, 12,000 well-trained Philippine Scouts, and 100,000 men of the newly-formed Philippine Army, which did not yet possess more than a low-grade militia-value. He had about 250 aircraft, including 35 Flying Fortresses.

After heavy bombing, which knocked out a number of American aircraft, the Japanese from December 10th onward made a series of landings in north-west Luzon, and followed these by another landing on the east coast. MacArthur had no option but to withdraw to the Bataan Peninsula, already ear-marked for a last stand if the Japanese should attack in force. No supplies except such as could be carried by submarines could be sent to him; none of the many surface blockade-runners employed succeeded in reaching him, and most of them were sunk. In February, 1942, he was ordered to make his way to Australia and take over command of what had now been named the South-West Pacific Area. He obeyed the order against the grain, but unaware how slender were the resources at that time in Australia and convinced that he would be called upon to lead back a force to the rescue of the Bataan garrison. When, after a perilous journey, he reached Australia he discovered that this was an impossibility.

On March 31st the Japanese began a series of heavy attacks on the Bataan position and smashed it bit by bit. Bataan surrendered on April 9th, but the island fortress of Corregidor, under the command of Lieut.-General Jonathan Wainwright, fought on until a Japanese landing finally crushed resistance on May 6th. Deplorable as was the incident, the length and stubborn valour of the defence brought pride as well as comfort to the people of the United States in a sense in which this could not be said of the British defence of Malaya.

The blow dealt the American Pacific Fleet gave the Japanese freedom of movement which they put to good use. Their first success against the British did not, however, to any great extent depend upon superiority at sea. It was the capture of Hong Kong, defended only by half a dozen battalions. On December 8th the Japanese moved from Chinese territory into the mainland area leased by Britain. After three days' fighting the British withdrew to the island, but on the 18th the enemy effected a landing. The garrison put up a stout defence and prolonged the struggle until Christmas Day.

Meanwhile the Japanese had on December 7th crossed the frontier of occupied French Indo-China into Siam, or Thailand, where they encountered no resistance to speak of. On the 21st Siam concluded an alliance with Japan. The Japanese were now seated upon the narrow isthmus of Kra and in an excellent position to attack the richest tropical possession of the British Empire, the Malay Peninsula, the world's chief source of rubber and one of its best sources of tin. At the southern end, on an island joined by a causeway to the mainland, lay the great port and commercial centre of Singapore and the naval base which had been created at a cost of 60 millions.

The quickest way for the Japanese to make their way down the peninsula to Singapore would be by means of combined operations along the coasts. In this respect a fearful disaster which befell the defence on December 10th played into their hands. The new battleship *Prince of Wales* and the battle-cruiser or light battleship *Repulse*, which had been despatched to the Far East in view of the growing tension, were sunk by shore-based aircraft off eastern Malaya. The skill of the Japanese pilots was superior to any disclosed by the Germans. There was a general sentiment that a sortie without fighter protection, such as that on which the British ships were engaged, was exceedingly imprudent, and from the strategic point of view it appeared that, since it had obviously been impossible to send an aircraft-carrier in their company to the Far East, it would have been wiser not to have sent these two capital ships at all. However, such arguments must be expected after a disaster, and if the *Prince of Wales* and *Repulse* had met and sunk a large, lightly-protected Japanese troop convoy, as might easily have happened, the effect upon the campaign would have been great and there would have been world-wide praise of British prescience in getting them to the scene of action in time.

In the advance down Malaya the Japanese were henceforth able to make considerable use of captured shipping for a succession of landings behind the flanks of the defence. Their other great advantages were air superiority—they speedily put out of action a large proportion of the generally obsolescent British aircraft— the collapse of the timorous labour in the towns under relatively light bombing, their own great enterprise and skill in the tactics of jungle warfare, and their ability to march light on an emergency rice ration. The British forces consisted in the first instance of the 9th and 11th Indian Divisions and two Malay infantry brigades. They were later joined by the 8th Australian Division, with two brigades. On the mainland the Japanese possessed no great numerical superiority, but their progress was never held up for long and they moved south at the rate of some ten miles a day.

By the first days of January, 1942, the enemy was approaching Kuala Lumpur. Here there was a short stand, but the imperial forces abandoned the town on the 10th, after destroying the machinery of the tin mines and some stocks of rubber. By the end of the month the Japanese were in Johore, and it was considered advisable to breach the causeway to Singapore island over a distance of 60 yards. A fair proportion of the troops cut off in Johore were evacuated by sea, but the Japanese claimed the capture of 8,000 since they had crossed the Siamese frontier. In addition to the remnants of the formations already mentioned, the garrison contained the 18th (British) Division, which had been moving towards the Middle East and had been diverted. There were also garrison troops and a number of airmen and sailors.

It now began to appear that Singapore was doomed. With the eclipse of American and British sea power, it would be impossible to aid or supply it for some time to come. The fortifications were designed to defend the base against seaborne attack, and though the statement put about at the time and since that the shore batteries would fire only out to sea was nonsensical, they could find few good targets in the present circumstances. The size of the city and the tendency of its inhabitants to panic constituted a heavy handicap to the defence. Nevertheless, there seemed some prospect of prolonged resistance, and the more prolonged it could be made the better would be the chance of a rescue, though this was slight at best.

It was not to be. After a four days' bombardment the Japanese effected a landing to the west on the night of February 8th. They rapidly extended their bridgehead, despite a counter-attack which achieved a partial success. By the middle of the month they were in possession of the reservoirs in the centre of the island which supplied the city with water. On February 15th the British commander, Lieut.-General A. E. Percival, surrendered to Lieut.-

General Yamashita. This was one of the heaviest and most humiliating disasters ever suffered by British arms. Numerically, the Japanese forces on the island were markedly inferior to the British. The latter were worn out and dispirited by their long retreat. Troops long in the station appeared to be enervated by the climate, while new arrivals had not accustomed themselves to the conditions. The tactical leadership was pedestrian by comparison with the dash and daring of the Japanese.

The effects were almost as far-reaching as those of the blow struck at Pearl Harbour. The first and most obvious was that of laying bare the rich Netherlands East Indies. General Wavell had in December left his post as Commander-in-Chief in India to exercise the supreme command in Malaya, Burma, the Netherlands East Indies, and the British islands of the archipelago. The latter were almost defenceless, but the Dutch had at their disposal about 120,000 troops, European and Indonesian, of fair quality. Yet even if they had been equal in quality and numbers to the Japanese land forces available, which they were not, the inferiority at sea and in the air would have been a crippling handicap.

The Japanese began by securing positions in the islands which constituted the outer defences to Java, the most important and most strongly defended. Early in January they obtained a footing in Borneo at Brunei and Tarakan, where the Dutch set fire to the rich oil wells and destroyed the pumping machinery. The enemy also landed on Celebes, where he secured an airfield. By now he was in possession of the Malay Peninsula and in a position to attack Java and Sumatra simultaneously with Singapore. British, American and Dutch aircraft struck back gallantly and effectively, sinking or damaging a number of Japanese warships and transports, but without checking the offensive.

The fate of Java was decided at sea. The Allies had got together a squadron consisting of five cruisers—Dutch, American, British and Australian—with four destroyers. On the afternoon of February 27th, when it was returning to Sourabaya after a sweep, a Japanese fleet of at least six warships and a multitude of transports was reported 50 miles to the north. The Allies at once moved to the attack. When action was joined it was discovered that the enemy had at his disposal more cruisers, including two heavy, than had been previously observed and some 13 destroyers. Yet the first part of the action, which ended in darkness,

6

was not unfavourable to the Allies. The Japanese turned away, one of their 8-inch cruisers afire, but touch with them was soon lost. After dark Rear-Admiral K. Doorman, the Dutch commander of the allied squadron, started a sweep in the hope of intercepting the convoys, but one of his ships after another was destroyed by under-water explosions, almost certainly torpedoes fired from submarines. The famous *Exeter*, heroine of the River Plate action, which had been crippled early in the fight and returned to Sourabaya for such a refit as was possible, came out on March 1st, but was engaged by three Japanese cruisers and sunk, fighting gallantly. Virtually all allied warships in Javan waters were eventually sunk. The Japanese also lost heavily, but their superiority was so great that this had no effect upon their purpose.

During the night after the naval battle the Japanese began landing at three points on the north coast of Java. The Dutch forces, with small British and American contingents, put up a stout resistance for a few days, but all was virtually over by March 8th, the enemy reporting that 90,000 troops had surrendered at Bandoeng. The calamity was made more bitter for the Dutch because they had generously expended their aircraft in the defence of Malaya. The remainder of the islands were conquered, as far as was necessary, at the leisure of the Japanese. In several of them, especially Sumatra, allied detachments held out in the hills and forests, as was also the case in the Philippines.

This, however, represented an irritation rather than a menace to the enemy. He had now flung out to the southward a great defensive net, completely unassailable while he maintained naval and air superiority—Malaya, Sumatra, Java, Bali, Sumba and Timor. Behind this barrier the South China Sea was his lake. Through it he could issue forth by half a dozen channels into the Indian Ocean. He had acquired first-class bases and supplies of many of the commodities of which he was most in need, especially oil, rubber, and tin. The only question seemed to be which way he would next strike, towards India or Australia, if indeed his strength and resources were not such as to permit him to do both simultaneously.

Yet he had done one thing which he was afterwards to regret: he had brought the United States of America into the war. Germany and Italy made sure of full American co-operation with

the Allies by declaring war on the United States on December
11th. They also entered into a full military alliance with Japan
to prosecute the war until victory had been achieved. Japan had
made no move against Russia, and Russia did not declare war
against Japan.

On December 22nd Mr. Churchill arrived in the United States,
accompanied by his service advisers. On January 1st, 1942,
representatives of the United States, Great Britain, the U.S.S.R.,
the British Commonwealth, China, the Governments of the
nations over-run by Germany, and some of the smaller American
nations, signed a joint declaration which they described as that
of "the United Nations", a phrase destined to become familiar.
In this they pledged themselves to employ their full resources
against those members of the Tripartite Pact (Germany, Italy
and Japan) with which they were at war and to make no separate
peace. The concluding clause left it open for other nations rendering material aid in the struggle to adhere to the declaration later
on. There was set up in Washington a body known as the Combined Chiefs of Staffs Committee, consisting of three American
Chiefs of Staff and British officers representing the British Chiefs
of Staff Committee in London.

To return to the strategic plan of the enemy, it is now pretty
well established that it did not envisage invasion of either India
or Australia at this stage, and did not in fact aim at any immediate
conclusive result. The Japanese sought to establish the perimeter
Burma-Siam-Malaya, Netherlands East Indies—New Guinea (a
footing only) to link with their own mandates in the Central
Pacific. They estimated that Russia was doomed, Britain hopelessly on the defensive, and the United States incapable after Pearl
Harbour of decisive action for eighteen months. Meanwhile
they would consolidate the perimeter and exploit their gains, and
eventually the United States, whose democratic constitution they
despised, would come to an understanding. It was only because
their success had been unexpectedly swift and easy that they afterwards decided to go into the Solomons—and eventually to New
Caledonia and the Fiji Islands—in order to cut communications
between the United States and Australia.

CHAPTER XVII

Japanese Offensives in Burma
and in Australian Waters

THE situation of the British in Burma at the outbreak of war with Japan was weak. The natural communications between the country and India were by sea, and the Japanese secured command of the sea at once. There were no roads from the great plain of the Ganges or the valley of the Brahmaputra across the mountain chain—in effect an outlying spur of the Himalayas—into the Chindwin, Irrawaddy and Sittang valleys which constitute the heart of Burma. The resources of the country for the purpose of maintaining an army were of the slightest; nor was the aid to be expected of the inhabitants, certainly not that of the true Burmese as apart from the Chin, Kachin and Karen tribes, likely to be of much account.

The Japanese communications were also sketchy, but better by far than the British. For the time being Bangkok provided the enemy with his principal invasion port and advanced base, but if he could obtain possession of Rangoon he would be excellently placed to drive the British out of Burma and establish touch with his forces in China. Apart from his plans against India he had the incentive that the conquest of Burma would give him possession of the road from Lashio into the Yun-nan province of China, the famous "Burma Road" by which supplies were sent to free China.

The British had at their disposal two Indian divisions and some native troops. China agreed to send what aid she could, and two so-called "armies", of about the strength of our divisions, under the command of Lieut.-General Joseph W. Stilwell, American Chief of Staff to Generalissimo Chiang Kai-Shek, were set in movement soon after the first Japanese attacks. The handicap experienced in Malaya had to be faced in Burma also. Under the influence of bombing, which occurred in January, the population of Rangoon became panic-stricken, left its work, and took to looting.

The Japanese quickly reached the shore of the Gulf of Martaban. In mid-February, despite a strong defence which inflicted several checks upon them, they reached the Sittang, cutting off a considerable proportion of the 17th Indian Division which opposed them. The British made an attempt to cover Rangoon at Pegu, but the pressure became so heavy that it was decided on March 7th to abandon the port. This decision might have been taken earlier but for delay caused in waiting for the arrival of a new British commander, Lieut.-General the Hon. Sir Harold Alexander. This might well have proved fatal, since the Japanese cut the Pegu road while simultaneously they landed troops south of Rangoon. A most gallant assault broke through the enemy and cleared the road to the north, but only just in time.

After the fall of Rangoon the British forces withdrew up the parallel valleys of the Irrawaddy and the Sittang, each of which carried a road and railway. It was, however, with the Chinese, who had advanced as far south as Toungoo, on the Sittang, that the first heavy fighting since the actions north of Rangoon developed on March 23rd. The Chinese held firm for the space of three or four days, but were then forced back, and meanwhile, at roughly the same level on the Irrawaddy, the British were compelled to abandon Prome. By the middle of April the Japanese were closing upon the oilfields of Yenanyaung, where very heavy pressure on the defence was partially relieved by the arrival of a Chinese force from the Sittang to its aid.

There had at the outset been some hope of holding northern Burma, but that was fading now. The Japanese did not seem to know fatigue, whereas the retreating British and Indian troops were becoming worn out. The oil installations were destroyed, and a further withdrawal carried out, but the weight of the Japanese attack was now transferred to the Chinese front. Hitherto the Chinese had fought steadily, but now there occurred a collapse. A mobile Japanese force from Siam suddenly crushed the extreme Chinese left in the Shan States. This wing of the Chinese dissolved, and the Japanese made at top speed for the Burma Road at Lashio. They reached it at the end of April, thus cutting off the Chinese troops in Burma. They then pushed rapidly up it, meeting with no resistance to speak of, and crossed the Chinese frontier on May 5th.

General Alexander continued his retreat with the sole object of extricating his forces and leading them back to India. On May 10th the enemy made an attempt to trap troops still east of the Chindwin by an attack on a ferry with the aid of craft seized on the Irrawaddy. He was, however, beaten off. The Chindwin was crossed, but little in the way of artillery and transport could be brought over the river. In addition to the troops, large bodies of civilian refugees, for the most part Indian but including also a few British, Burmans, and Chinese, were making their way afoot through the jungle and over the mountains towards India. It need hardly be said that their sufferings were terrible. Supplies for them were dropped by the R.A.F. at certain points upon their route. But it was a melancholy retreat. The little army had almost ceased to be such, since the troops seldom possessed any weapons but those which they carried. The one bright spot was to be found in the fact that General Alexander succeeded in saving the bulk of his valuable man-power.

By the end of May the force was out of danger. The Japanese had seized Akyab on the Bay of Bengal at the beginning of the month, but the immediate invasion of India, which some had expected, did not follow. Even the Japanese must have been tired by now. The bursting of the monsoon upon their strung-out communications made a further great effort impossible. Though a Japanese squadron had entered the Indian Ocean at the end of March and had, as will presently be recorded, inflicted grievous loss upon the British in those waters, it had not remained there, and the enemy was never in a position to carry out large-scale combined operations. The heavy defeat inflicted upon him by the United States naval forces in the Battle of the Coral Sea between May 4th and 11th, followed by the second defeat off Midway Island in early June, coupled with the demands upon shipping of all natures brought about by his expeditions to the Solomons and New Guinea, prevented him from entering the Indian Ocean in great strength and certainly from remaining there.

The conduct of the campaign in Burma by the Japanese was brilliant. They made the fullest possible use of their air ascendancy and their superiority in jungle warfare. They took big risks, but these were always justifiable because the worst failure could scarcely bring about a disaster whereas success meant triumph. Their timing was remarkable. They just contrived to do all they set out to do, drive out the British, seize Mandalay, capture Lashio, and gain possession of the Burma Road, before the breaking of the monsoon. It could not then be realized that they were lacking in the finer points of strategy and tactics because there had been as yet nothing to test them fully, so that only their more formidable side had been displayed. And it was formidable enough. We had indeed, as the American General Stilwell remarked, taken "the hell of a beating". There was little cause to feel optimistic about the future, especially since there was a great deal of disaffection in India, and the Congress Party, which had just rejected a British suggestion for a constitutional settlement carried by Sir Stafford Cripps, was prepared to give no aid in defence of the country and in fact had links with men who were actively aiding Japan.

The Japanese naval incursion into the Indian Ocean, brief as it was, cost the British much of what little remained of their naval strength. It began with a strong attack by carrier-borne aircraft —five aircraft carriers were observed—on Colombo and Trincomalee, which did a great deal of damage, though 25 aircraft were reported to have been shot down by the defences. Admiral Somerville, who had been transferred from Gibraltar to Ceylon, put out with his weaker squadron, and thus baulked the enemy's hope of bringing off another "Pearl Harbour", but the Japanese, turning away, destroyed a whole convoy. The 8-inch gun cruisers *Dorsetshire* and *Cornwall* and the old aircraft carrier *Hermes* were also sunk at sea. The manner in which the *Hermes* was accounted for furnished fresh proof of the extreme efficiency of the Japanese naval aircraft pilots. They simply blew the bottom out of her with bomb after bomb, so that the tail aircraft of the attacking squadron did not even require to waste bombs upon her but turned away to attack another target. If the Germans or Italians had bombed in this fashion not a ship would have reached Malta and the island would have been lost ere this. The British suffered other naval losses at sea, and merchant shipping in the Bay of Bengal was sunk. Our affairs were indeed at a low ebb in these regions, and we should certainly have been hard put to it to defend Ceylon had the enemy had a landing force and sufficient craft ready for an attempt to take it. It was indeed surprising that he did not improvise an attempt to seize so great a strategic prize.

There seemed reason to fear that the Japanese would spread

further west, and soon the eyes of all who possessed any strategic sense were fixed upon Madagascar. This would have furnished an ideal base for the enemy and a deadly menace to the shipping routes round the Cape to the Gulf of Aden, India and Australasia. The British had, however, taken quick action. A force was on its way to the island, consisting in the main of the 5th Division, originally intended to reinforce India. It arrived on May 5th. On that day it was made clear to the French authorities and to the French Ambassador at Washington that there was no intention on the part of the British of interfering with the French status of Madagascar, which would remain part of the French Empire. There was fairly strong resistance to the first landing, but little thereafter. At least one dangerous Japanese move had been anticipated.

The Japanese had meanwhile been spreading out their power to the south-east, basing themselves upon their mandated territory in the Caroline Islands and later also on Mindanao in the Philippines, when that had been secured. They used each capture as a stepping-stone to the next, quickly establishing air and naval bases in expanding rings. They had everything in their favour because the Allies did not possess the strength to stand up to them. Even so, their combined operations must be considered bold, skilful, and speedy. Yet they proved to be not quite speedy enough. The Australian 6th and 7th Divisions were hurried home from the Middle East and arrived just in time to face the danger when it had reached its worse. The Australian Government, under Mr. Curtin, resisted the British plea that these divisions should be sent to Singapore or Rangoon, in addition to the 8th, which was lost in Malaya.

The immediate Japanese aim was to cut off Australia from American aid by seizing positions in New Guinea and the islands to the east and south-east. A footing on the Australian mainland, once the Torres Strait had been secured, would follow, and the country would then be at Japan's mercy. In January, 1942, the enemy secured Rabaul, at the northern end of New Britain, after a resolute defence by the little Australian garrison. This afforded him both a harbour and an airfield. Simultaneously he landed in New Ireland. The Australian Air Force, later on aided by American bombers, began to strike back, and the damage which it inflicted upon shipping and aircraft at Rabaul may have somewhat delayed the Japanese advance. If this was so it was highly fortunate, since the Japanese, had they landed in New Guinea by mid-February, would probably have secured Port Moresby, overlooking the Torres Strait, with incalculable consequences. As it was they bombed grounded aircraft with effect at Wyndham and Broome—apparently from Timor—and began a series of damaging air attacks on Darwin.

On March 7th they landed at Salamaua and Lae, in New Guinea, and thus gained two more airfields. Then ensued a series of air attacks on both sides, each combatant striking at the bases of his foe. In these the Australians and Americans, whose aircraft were arriving in increasing numbers, had the better of it, and inflicted sharp loss on Japanese shipping as well as damaging ground installations at Salamaua and Lae. The small Australian garrisons on this part of the coast had withdrawn into the interior, but the Japanese advance was held up by floods in the Markham Valley.

Meanwhile the United States forces were coming upon the scene. The Americans realized that they could not now save the Philippines or the Dutch East Indies. There was, however, just time to halt the Japanese advance on Australia and prevent the cutting of the sea routes to it from the American ports, and this would provide new bases for subsequent aggression. The first troop convoys had already arrived. More than that, the covering forces under Vice-Admiral Halsey made surprise attacks on Japanese naval air bases in the Marshall Islands and the Gilberts, the latter group a British mandate which had been occupied by the enemy. The chief attack was made against the anchorage at Kwajalein, where heavy loss was inflicted on Japanese shipping. By now, too, garrisons had been provided for islands hitherto undefended. In particular a large force had been landed in New Caledonia, which was to become an important American base.

But the enemy, exploiting his success, continued to extend his holdings in the Solomons and the Louisiade Archipelago, and it was clear that he intended to occupy the remaining islands in these groups and perhaps also to strike at New Caledonia, if not, as the Americans were inclined to believe, directly at Australia. On May 4th he seized the harbour of Tulagi in the central Solomons. Then the Americans struck back. In a battle fought by the air forces of both sides, the Japanese fleet was decisively defeated in the Coral Sea. This victory, followed a month later by a second off Midway—both are briefly described in Chapter XXII, dealing with the war at sea—completely altered the balance in the South-west Pacific. They brought the worst danger to an end and provided the opportunity for land counterstrokes, which were soon to begin.

That delivered in the southern Solomons was to exercise a notable effect upon future operations. A hastily prepared expedition—very different in this respect from others which succeeded it—resulted in landings on Guadalcanal and Florida Island by a force of Marines. A naval battle in two stages, against American naval forces covering from the south-east and north-east the area in which the transports lay, went all in favour of the Japanese, who sank three American cruisers and one Australian, but they did not press home their attack on the transports and supply ships. The landing proceeded. Then began one of the fiercest struggles of the war. It was not until early 1943 that the Americans, who had been strongly reinforced, finally cleared Guadalcanal. It was a magnificent campaign on their part, but one feels that a little more resolution and persistence on the part of the Japanese might have led to a disaster. But it was the loss which they had suffered in the Coral Sea and off Midway which tamed their ardour.

The Japanese suffered another check at Milne Bay, at the south-eastern end of New Guinea. On August 25th they landed from barges, and gained initial successes owing to superior equipment. Later on, however, they lost the aid of their tanks, bogged in the mud. The Australian garrison then took the offensive and kept up the pressure, though Japanese warships once more entered the bay on September 3rd. The enemy's resistance ceased on the 7th, though he withdrew some of his troops by sea. This was a great Australian achievement and the cause of natural pride and relief in the Commonwealth.

The Japanese had not, however, abandoned their designs against Australia. Having landed fresh forces at Buna and Gona in late July, they began an advance across the Owen Stanley mountains towards Port Moresby. They were opposed only by small rear guards until troops from the Middle East reached the scene. The Australians went into action carrying loads of from 60 to 90 pounds. Finally, on the last defensible ridge short of Port

Moresby, they held the Japanese, and almost immediately started to drive them back, with the aid of supplies dropped from the air. Kokoda fell on November 2nd, and the advance northward went on steadily, the Japanese suffering heavy loss. The last survivors of the expedition fled back to Buna. Things were looking up.

It required, however, a prolonged and difficult operation to clear the Japanese from the Gona-Buna area, which they had fortified strongly and which they could still precariously supply by sea. First of all a half-way point between it and Milne Bay was secured on the coast at Wanigela by an Australian battalion transported by air. An improved air-strip was then made, and by October 17th American troops had been brought in by air. The main assault began on November 19th, the Australians being allotted the task of taking Gona and then pushing on to Sanananda, while the Americans dealt with Buna, farther to the east. Major-General George C. Kenney, the able and energetic commander of the American Army Air Forces in the theatre, had instituted a vigorous air offensive which destroyed a great proportion of the Japanese shipping used to supply the position and compelled the enemy to use parachutes and submarines for the purpose, but a certain number of barges still managed to slip along the coast. Gona fell on December 1st and Buna on the 28th, but organized resistance at Sanananda did not cease until January 23rd, 1943, after the place had been enveloped by Australians on one flank and Americans on the other. It was estimated that a force of 16,000 of the enemy had been destroyed. The way was now cleared for operations against the even more important Japanese holdings at Lae and Salamaua, some 150 miles north-west along the coast.

By the opening of the year 1943, therefore, the Japanese expansion had been brought to a halt. A few slices had been taken off the structure of Japanese defence so speedily erected in the Pacific. They were, however, so far insufficient to weaken the structure seriously, though the success achieved in cutting them off had brought new confidence to the Allies. The heavy losses inflicted upon the enemy's shipping and aircraft had already produced hampering effects upon his mobility and power to support his outlying garrisons. It had begun to appear that, good as his first-line aircraft pilots were, the reserves to replace casualties were in many instances far from formidable, which pointed

to some deficiencies in his training organization. His best fighter
aircraft, known as the O, and named by the Americans "Zero",
while faster, more manœuvrable, and possessing a longer range
than the American machines employed against it, afforded the
pilot no armoured protection and was apt to break up in the air
as the result of a burst of fire. It was the ideal aircraft for a belligerent completely "on top", but by no means so once he met stiff
opposition in the air.

Even more important than these considerations was the realization in the minds of the Americans, especially in that of the extremely capable and far-seeing General MacArthur, that there
existed a technique by which the enemy could be beaten. It was
in brief: the use of air power to attack and neutralize the strength
of a strategic base held by the enemy and possessing an anchorage
and landing ground; a forward bound by seaborne or in rarer
cases airborne forces to seize this strategic point; swift development of the new holding as an advanced base from which to
repeat the process against the next strategic point which it was
desired to possess; the by-passing of Japanese forces situated
between two such points or driven into the interior of the large
islands after the bounds have been successfully carried out. As to
the direction in which the advance should be pursued, General
MacArthur was clear in his mind; his eyes were on the Philippines,
his old command, though not all observers were convinced that
he was right on this point.

There existed two other island chains across the Pacific by
which it might also be hoped to carry out a movement of a
similar nature. That of the Central Pacific ran through Hawaii
and the Japanese mandated islands, particularly the Marianas, to
the Bonin Islands and Kyushu, the southernmost island of Japan
itself. It would be more difficult than General MacArthur's
route because there was so much less land upon it, the islands
being small and separated by vast distances. Then in the far north
lay the chain of the Aleutians—in which the Japanese had early
established themselves—and the Kuriles. This appeared on the
map to be the best route of all, being by far the shortest, but the
climatic conditions and the prevalence of fog proved an insuperable handicap to its employment. Eventually the Americans
were to make use of both the central and southern land-chains.
Yet it could not be a quick process. The immense distances—for

instance, 28 sailing days in convoy from San Francisco to Sydney, 26 days to Guadalcanal—made very heavy demands on shipping at a time when it was needed also in great quantities on the routes direct to the United Kingdom and to the Middle East, including the Persian Gulf for Russian supplies. The general strategic principles adopted by the United States could command success, and no others would have done so. But not even they could in the circumstances command quick success against the deep and powerful network of defence established by the Japanese at the height of their power. There was a road to victory, but no easy road.

CHAPTER XVIII

The End in North Africa

THE most obvious difficulty in North Africa, that of expelling the enemy from the Continent in order, in the phrase of General Marshall, the United States Chief of Staff, to "facilitate allied global operations", by attacking from one end of the coast only, had been discussed as early as January, 1942, when the Prime Minister was in Washington. In July it was decided to launch an expedition into French North Africa in conjunction with a westward advance by the British Eighth Army from El Alamein, where a victory was expected with undiminished confidence. Landings were to be made simultaneously at Casablanca, Oran and Algiers. The advantages of landing also at Bône, and perhaps even Tunis, were not overlooked, but the danger of pushing convoys so deep and the lack of shipping, including aircraft carriers, made this appear virtually impossible, or at least unduly rash.

The problem was as much political as it was military. How would it be possible to take in advance measures to avoid heavy fighting with the French garrison, known to contain sympathetic elements, without the risk of giving the secret away? Some delicate preliminary soundings were made, but in the main reliance had to be placed upon last-minute broadcast announcements by President Roosevelt, General de Gaulle, and General Giraud, a distinguished French soldier who had escaped from captivity in Germany, that the Allies sought no French territory and appealed for French co-operation. The command was entrusted to the American General Eisenhower, who created a combined staff in London for the purpose. He was a man of remarkable personality, a brilliant organizer rather than a strategist or tactician. His greatest quality, however, was his genius for building up international team-work. In this he was supreme, and his success in it was to exercise an important influence in the latter half of the war in North Africa, Italy, and North-west Europe. He took over command of the American forces in the United Kingdom

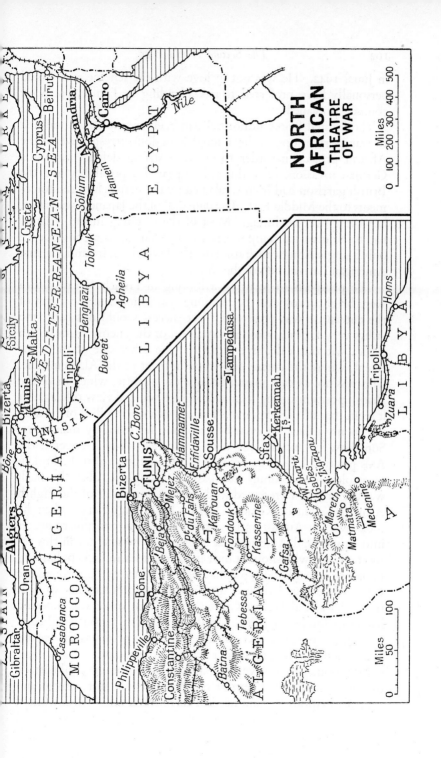

NORTH AFRICAN
THEATRE OF WAR

Miles
0 100 200 300 400 500

in June, 1942. He was not in love with the scheme and would personally have preferred to risk a landing in France, but wiser counsels prevailed.

The United States authorities had been anxious from the first to transport troops to the United Kingdom, irrespective of the African project, in order to assure a strong defence against a German invasion, since this still appeared a possibility and the British garrison had been weakened by the despatch of reinforcements to the Middle East. The demands of the Japanese war were, however, overwhelming. Most of the shipping in the Atlantic had to be diverted temporarily to the Pacific. As a consequence only a single American division reached Northern Ireland, the first American station, before the summer.

The prospects of securing a footing in French North Africa were bright, provided the planning was sound and the secret of the enterprise was preserved. Yet success would not carry the Allies very far or assure the expulsion of the enemy from North Africa without a decisive victory at the other side of the Continent, where the enemy still stood in front of the Alamein Line. This was not an easy matter because the qualities which made the British position strong from a defensive point of view told against it from that of the offensive. There was no possibility of turning the enemy's flank or even of stretching his front by manœuvre. Somehow or another the deep mine-fields which covered the Axis position had to be breached and his front had to be broken by a column or columns after passing through the obstacle. Such was the problem presented to the new commander of the Eighth Army, Lieutenant.-General Sir B. L. Montgomery, when he took over on August 13th. Britain was now pouring resources into Egypt, and America was affording powerful aid in this respect. Those who thought only in terms of sea miles kept harping upon our heavy handicap in having to send everything round the Cape while the Axis got supplies and reinforcements straight from Sicily, Calabria or Greece. The Cape route was indeed a handicap, but port facilities and above all berths far outweighed it. We must have possessed ten times as many berths as the enemy even when we could no longer berth at Alexandria.

Montgomery, however, had a lot to do before he could attack the enemy. The last reinforcements had only just arrived and some formations were in need of further training. Meanwhile it was clear that the enemy was prepared to attack him, and it could be concluded that he would do so at the time of the full moon, which he would require for illumination while breaching the British mine-fields. And in fact Rommel, after announcing to his troops that they would find themselves in Alexandria within two or three days, launched his assault just after midnight on the morning of August 31st. The main attack was in the south, on a sector relatively lightly held. The enemy penetrated deeply, 15 miles by ten o'clock that morning, and then wheeled north-ward to roll up the British front. But his every move had been anticipated, and he found himself blocked by the British armour and artillery on the Alam Halfa ridge. In the end Rommel suffered a sharp though by no means decisive defeat, which had an invigorating effect upon the Eighth Army and brought it confidence in its new commander.

Like Rommel, Montgomery needed a full moon; he might have been able to use the next but for the delay caused by the Battle of Alam Halfa, but he had to miss it and did not launch his attack until the night of October 23rd. His plan embodied two main features: first, as to aim, he intended to destroy methodically the enemy's infantry divisions, while holding off his armour to be dealt with later; secondly, as to method, the main thrust was to be carried out in the north by four divisions, which had the task of forcing two corridors through the minefields, and the armoured X Corps was to be passed through, in the first instance to meet, on ground of its own choice, the enemy's armoured counter-attack.

Counting by divisions, the enemy would appear slightly superior in strength, but this was far from being the case. In tanks the British had a numerical superiority of two to one, but about half were armed with the obsolete 2-pdr. gun. In field artillery the British superiority was about the same, but in medium the odds were the other way. In the air the British were domin-ant. Finally, though some of the Italian divisions in the Axis ranks were of good quality, they were not in general in the same class as the British and German. Montgomery had at his disposal six armoured brigades—his strength is given in this form because his three armoured divisions were not all on the same establish-ment and some of his armoured brigades were independent—and seven infantry divisions; Rommel possessed two German and two Italian armoured divisions, two German and six Italian infantry divisions.

The first attack was a success. It was made under cover of an artillery bombardment in which some 800 guns took part and preceded by parties of engineers who made gaps through the mine-fields. But a hard, lengthy, and complex battle followed, during which the British armour got stuck between two belts in the enemy's mine-fields and some of its formations suffered heavy loss. Montgomery coolly switched his attacks, counter-manding those which did not pay a dividend. He smashed a final counter-attack by the German armour on November 2nd and finally broke through on the northern part of the front the following day. Rommel promptly abandoned the Italian divisions in his centre and on his right wing and concentrated on saving his German Afrika Korps and above all its personnel. The tanks he might hope to replace, but he would never get the equivalent of the officers and men, among the best-trained and most skilful in the world, if he should lose them now. Montgomery, hindered by heavy rains, which for a brief but vital moment bogged his pursuit, could not cut them off, but he took 30,000 prisoners, and it was estimated that up to November 11th the Axis forces suffered nearly 60,000 casualties. The vast majority of the tanks with which the enemy had started the battle were destroyed or abandoned. The British lost as many tanks as he did, but the majority of them were recoverable; British casualties in men were about 13,500. It was a great victory, if its results fell short of the annihilation at which Montgomery had aimed.

Rommel had gone back to his old position at Agheila. Montgomery had a difficult administrative problem until the captured port of Benghazi had been restored. He could not at first risk a heavy battle. However, with the aid of an outflanking movement, he pushed the enemy out of his strong position and resumed the pursuit. The next stand was at Buerat, 250 miles further west. Again, on January 15th, 1943, Montgomery combined an out-flanking movement on the enemy's right with frontal pressure and heavy air bombardment, which forced him back. Yet it was only just in time. The Eighth Army was, in fact, in an awkward situation, since if it did not reach Tripoli within the ten days' limit imposed by administrative exigencies it would have to halt or even fall back. The advanced guard forced its way into Tripoli on January 23rd. From there the Eighth Army pressed on quickly to cross the Tunisian frontier.

The landings in French North Africa took place in the early hours of November 8th, 1942. Two huge convoys, with powerful British naval escorts under the command of Admiral Sir Andrew Cunningham, sailed on October 25th from British ports with British and American forces. A third, destined for Casablanca on the Atlantic coast, was wholly American in composition. Eisenhower established an advanced headquarters at Gibraltar, and it is worthy of note, as indicative of the confidence and comradeship existing between the two nations, that while he was there he commanded the fortress. The convoys could not be concealed, but their destination was not generally suspected, and the landings came as a surprise. Resistance was brief in Algeria, but more prolonged and sterner in Morocco. It was fortunate that opposition was not stronger, since there were many mistakes due to inexperience. There was a political hitch. It was desired to secure French co-operation at the earliest possible moment, but it was found that was no enthusiasm for the de Gaullist movement and that General Giraud could at first command no great following. The Allies therefore made use of the Vichy ex-Minister, Admiral Jean Darlan, who was visiting Algiers. He assumed authority in the name of Maréchal Pétain, and though repudiated by the latter, was able to exercise and maintain it. General Eisenhower was bitterly criticized on ideological grounds for his action in this matter. Darlan was later on assassinated, but he had served his turn and was peacefully succeeded in his authority by Giraud, only for the latter to be eventually elbowed out by the masterful and persistent de Gaulle.

The immediate German reaction to the landing was the occupation of "Vichy France", the southern half of the country which had not hitherto been occupied by the German armies. It was carried out swiftly and met with no opposition. Hitler announced that its object was to prevent an allied landing in Corsica or on the south coast of France. The occupation did not include Toulon, where the French fleet lay. It was stated that the Germans had received a solemn assurance that the fleet and the forts would defend themselves against any attack by the Allies. On November 27th, however, the Germans entered Toulon to seize the fleet, whereupon it was scuttled by the order of Admiral de Laborde. It included the fine battle-cruisers or light battle-ships *Dunkerque* and *Strasbourg*.

As speedily as possible after the capture of Algiers leading elements of the British First Army, under the command of Lieut.-General K. A. Anderson, secured the port of Bône and pushed eastward in an endeavour to overrun Tunisia before the Axis could transport to the scene sufficient troops to defend it. Had the French put up even as strong a resistance to the Germans in Tunisia as they had to the Allies in Morocco this might have been achieved, but they did not. And had the Allies possessed a strong parachute force they could have prevented the enemy landing by air at Tunis, but there was only a single British brigade, of which one battalion landed at Bône and the other two near Souk el Arba and Pont du Fahs. By November 18th there were 18,000 Axis troops with some tanks in northern Tunisia. The Allies, in three columns, made a great deal of ground and nearly brought off the coup, but by the end of November were held up well short of Tunis and Bizerta, though they had their grip on the vital area of Mejez-el-Bab. They now had to build up their strength and improve their communications.

In early December the enemy struck back and regained some ground. Lieut.-General Anderson drew back from certain ex-posed positions in order to reorganize for another offensive, but this was forestalled by rain. Unfortunately, the delay gave the Axis time to reinforce, and by the end of the year there were 40,000 troops, two-thirds Germans, and 150 tanks in the coun-try. On the other hand, French troops under the orders of General Giraud were moving up from Algiers to cover the right flank of the British and American forces. The allied achievement was all the more creditable because the enemy possessed air ascendancy in the early stages and British fighters could not reach the front, while even on the lines of communication there was heavy Ger-man bombing. This, however, was gradually being rectified as more advanced airfields were established. Round about the New Year there was sharp but indecisive fighting, but the front was more or less stabilized on a north-south line through Mejez, Bou Arada, and Fondouk. By February, the First Army consisted of a British armoured division with two infantry divisions and a similar American contingent, but some of the troops were strung out and had not yet reached the front. Many more American troops would have been available, but the communications would not support them.

On February 14th the enemy struck back, using some of his new Tiger tanks which mounted an 88 mm. gun. He broke through the Kasserine Pass and inflicted very heavy losses on the Americans, including about 100 tanks and 90 guns. He was, however, halted, and then driven back, finally drawing off after giving the Allies a scare, but teaching them some useful lessons.

The ability of the Germans to launch this secondary counter-offensive had been due to the junction of the forces led back by Rommel from Alamein with those landed in Tunisia. Rommel might well have shown more determination and pursued his advantage against the First Army, since he had for the moment nothing to fear from the Eighth. Montgomery had only two divisions facing the Mareth Line, the French defence system covering Tunisia from the west, and was in a somewhat anxious situation. Rommel at once swung his armour against the Eighth, but when he did strike back Montgomery had a third division on the scene. Rommel's attack, known as the Battle of Medinine, on March 6th, was made in haste and without proper reconnaissance. The British defensive position was admirable and the anti-tank artillery was served with skill and coolness. The hostile armoured divisions lost 52 tanks and drew off at night. It was a sharp check.

Meanwhile General Alexander, who had taken over the Middle East Command at the same time as Montgomery had assumed that of the Eighth Army, had been appointed to the operational command of all land forces engaged in the campaign, that is, the British First and Eighth Armies, the United States II Corps, and the French forces. The first results did not appear promising, since the German Kasserine offensive immediately followed his appointment. Alexander, however, proceeded to rectify the dispositions in Tunisia, which were marred by dispersion, absence of striking power at any point, and lack of reserves. In the air the Allies now possessed complete ascendancy, and the airfields behind Montgomery's front were particularly valuable.

On the night of March 20th, the Eighth Army attacked the Mareth Line. The bridgehead secured beyond the precipitous and muddy Wadi Zigzaou, which was embodied in the defences, could not be maintained, but this attack drew in the Axis reserves as to a magnet, so that a flanking attack west and north of the Matmata Hills—to which the Mareth Line was anchored—proved a complete success. It was one of Montgomery's finest victories, though he did not succeed in cutting off the retreating enemy as the latter passed between marshes and sea through the "Gabes Gap". The Eighth Army followed up its success by smashing the next line of defence on the Wadi Akarit on the night of April 6th. American troops of the II Corps, moving down from Gafsa, made contact with the Eighth Army next day. The enemy fell back towards Enfidaville. Capturing the ports of Sfax and Sousse, the Eighth Army pressed on upon his heels.

Throughout April the allied forces in Tunisia based on Algeria, that is, the First Army, Americans and French, were engaged in hard slogging, which appeared disappointing to the outside observer but was in fact leading rapidly to a crisis for the enemy. In the north an Axis pocket near Beja was squeezed out after stiff resistance. The Fondouk pass was opened on April 9th. In the Mejez sector the fighting was fierce and bloody, as the British struggled for the heights which prevented them from obtaining a clear run towards Tunis. On April 20th the Eighth Army attacked the strong Enfidaville position and made some vauable ground, but it was clear that a further advance through the hills on this flank would be very costly.

General Alexander had decided to strike his main blow towards Tunis, with a second blow towards Bizerta, the latter to be dealt by the American II Corps, which was rapidly transferred to the coast sector after the Battle of Enfidaville. The Eighth Army was called upon only to keep up the pressure. One armoured and one infantry division were withdrawn from it and transferred to the area of Mejez, for the main thrust.

The enemy possessed eleven German divisions (including three armoured), six Italian, not counting the remnants of two Blackshirt, but none of these were at full strength, and he was probably outnumbered by three to two, 300,000 men to 200,000, though again it must be noted that the French divisions on the allied side were ill armed. In tanks the odds against him were by now something like ten to one. He had, however, plenty of anti-tank artillery, and it looked as though his final defence might be pro-

longed. That was all Hitler asked for now. It was clear to him
that the Axis forces in North Africa were doomed, but he hoped
they would afford him time to prepare his European defences and
deal satisfactorily with Russia. Escape was impossible owing
the tightness of the allied naval and air blockade. The Axis air
strength had been virtually destroyed, and the transport service,
which had been active, was now at an end. The allied air forces
had awaited a good opportunity to strike when the maximum
numbers of transport aircraft were on the ground in Tunisia and
Sicily, had found it on April 5th, and had carried out devastating
attacks in which the destruction of 200 aircraft was claimed. In
addition, the final land offensive was heralded by the heaviest air
offensive yet launched.

The final advance began on the night of May 5th. On the
following day the British infantry broke through the defences in
the Mejerda corridor, and the armour passed through. Tunis was
seized by one armoured division while another wheeled east,
broke through an apparently impregnable position at Hamma-
met, and reached the Cap Bon Peninsula, where the enemy had
intended to make his last stand. This action may have shortened
the campaign by a month. The Americans smashed their way
into Bizerta. The enemy now possessed no intact forces except
those facing the Eighth Army, and they were taken in rear. One
by one formations surrendered, until on May 13th the Italian
Commander-in-Chief, Marshal Messe, ordered the whole force
to lay down its arms. The total of prisoners taken in the whole
Tunisian campaign numbered a quarter of a million and included some of the finest troops Germany ever put into the
field.

If we had to do it all over again we might save a valuable
month in the process, but then, if imagination is to allow us to
correct our mistakes, it cannot deny the enemy the right to correct his. Taking a broad view, it was a brilliant performance. The
numbers engaged were small by comparison with the vast armies
on the Russian front, but the campaign subjected the Axis to a
far greater strain than was immediately realized. The fighting in
North Africa had in fact broken the spirit and the power of Italy.
On Germany the effect was less strong, but it was considerable.
On the allied side a technique had been perfected which was to be
of the greatest service in the future, particularly so to the Ameri-

cans, who were not enthusiastic about taking lessons from the British, but who learned from their own experiences and errors with astonishing speed and promulgated the lessons with their characteristic thoroughness.

CHAPTER XIX

Plans and Counter-Plans

THE disasters suffered in the Far East were critically received in the United Kingdom, much more so in fact than in the United States. Accounts of atrocities committed by the Japanese against prisoners of war had increased the public disquietude and dismay. In a debate in the House of Commons in January, 1942, Mr. Churchill received a vote of confidence by 464 votes to one, the biggest majority he had ever obtained, but had to listen to severe animadversions on the conduct of the war. The line he took was unanswerable: there had undoubtedly been shortcomings in the Far East, but if every conceivable mistake had been avoided the results would not have been different. "There never has been a moment, there never could have been a moment, when Great Britain or the British Empire, single-handed, could fight Germany and Italy, could wage the Battle of Britain, the Battle of the Atlantic, and the Battle of the Middle East, and at the same time stand thoroughly prepared in Burma, the Malay Peninsula, and generally in the Far East against the impact of a vast military empire like Japan, with more than 70 mobile divisions, the third navy in the world, a great air force, and the thrust of 80 or 90 millions of hardy, warlike Asiatics."

The Prime Minister could not speak then, though he did afterwards in secret session, of crippling losses suffered at sea which had hampered the nation's arms at a most critical moment. They included the sinking—fortunately in very shallow water, so that the loss could not even be observed from the air—of warships in Alexandria Harbour by daring Italian swimmers who affixed "limpet" bombs to their bottoms.

The fall of Singapore had not then taken place, but it came almost immediately afterwards, to increase the public discontent. Curiously enough, the country was even more deeply shocked by the escape of the German battleships *Scharnhorst* and *Gneisenau* and the cruiser *Prinz Eugen*, which, after lying in Brest under constant bombing by the R.A.F., sailed out on the night of February 11th and made their way to safety by passing through the Straits of Dover. This was an episode of minor significance compared with that of Singapore, but it struck the nation a blow in the face. And perhaps it was a sound instinct which aroused the country's anger; for it revealed the deficiencies of a system of control which allowed Bomber Command, while making enormous demands upon the productive capacity and man-power of the United Kingdom, to fight what amounted almost to a private war with Germany, irrespective of the circumstances, of the needs of the moment, and of the principles of co-operation.

Mr. Churchill carried out a reconstruction of his War Cabinet and Ministry which was on the whole well received. Yet the by-elections continued to reveal dissatisfaction, and the independent candidates who challenged Conservative candidates received an increasing support, largely made up of the Labour vote. Though Labour Party leaders filled half the Government offices and parliamentary representatives for the most part honoured the political truce, other elements contrived to father upon "the Tory Party" whatever was weak or unpopular in the Government as well as the blame for misfortunes in the conduct of hostilities. This policy was to become more successful in the second half of the war.

The Government had to face an even more bitter debate, beginning on June 25th, after the defeat on the Gazala Line and the fall of Tobruk. If the earlier criticism had been mainly directed against the conduct of the war, it was in this case rather turned against the equipment of the forces. Mr. Churchill, who returned from Washington in the midst of the debate, affirmed that, despite the disasters, the general prospects of the United Nations were on the upward grade. The motion in favour of "no confidence in the central direction of the war" was defeated by 476 votes to 25.

The Prime Minister had spoken even more truly than he can then have known. Alamein, the landings in French North Africa, Stalingrad, the victories in New Guinea, were close at hand, and even Mr. Churchill's optimism cannot have foreseen the full improvement ahead. The British Government was to have hardly any further serious criticism to answer regarding the conduct of the war, the strongest being directed against a failure in the Dodecanese and alleged slackness in seizing opportunities in Italy. At Christmas, 1941, General Sir Alan Brooke had been moved by the Prime Minister from the command of the Home

Forces to the War Office as Chief of the Imperial General Staff in succession to General Sir John Dill, who was promoted Field-Marshal and sent to Washington as the chief British military representative. There was general regret at his departure, not only on the score of his own merits but also because his successor appeared to be by far the greatest living British soldier and the destined commander-in-chief if a great British or allied army should return to the Continent.

This disappointment was unjustified. In the first place, Sir John Dill was exhausted by never-ceasing work, whereas at Washington, where he had less to do, he recovered and proved himself invaluable. He gained the friendship of the President and the chief service authorities and showed masterly skill and patience in composing such differences as appeared. And the hope that General Brooke might serve as allied generalissimo was far-fetched. The United Kingdom was not destined to put into the field in Europe a vast army of sixty divisions or more as in the previous world war. The claims of the Far East, the vastly increased manpower demanded by industry, the enormous shore and ground establishments of the Navy and the R.A.F., the needs of civil defence, and the Army's own increased establishment of virtual non-combatants combined to render this impossible. The United States would supply the chief army in western Europe and would demand the right to appoint the supreme commander. At the same time General Brooke was to prove himself an even greater C.I.G.S. than his predecessor. His strategic grasp was firmer, his temperament more equable. He was more at home in the political world, which was of the highest importance, especially when the Prime Minister was also Minister of Defence and was so brilliant but also so impulsive a man as Mr. Churchill.

After the Russian victories in late 1941 and early 1942 the British and American allies began to see their way clear in Europe. They had no more serious anxiety of Russia being driven out of the war, though some of Russia's strongest friends in their own countries were whispering blackmail and suggesting that, in default of a speedy invasion of western Europe, she might conclude a separate peace with Germany. They could reckon on upwards of two hundred German divisions being contained in the east. They could put into the air fleets of aircraft many times greater than those of the enemy, and with their aid they could hope to destroy a high percentage of Germany industry and to cripple German communications. Air power would also afford them the great advantage of fighting with their own lines of communication relatively safe, whereas those of the enemy would be placed under the continual threat of attack, so that he could probably not move his transport by day. The landings in French North Africa had proved that it was possible to protect great troop and supply convoys at sea, despite the submarines. They had therefore decided that an invasion of the Continent was not only possible but would lead to a victorious decision within a relatively short time.

The vital question was how soon it should be attempted, and where. The American authorities were inclined to take a more optimistic view of the possibilities than the British. It seemed that after the occupation of the North African seaboard the next step should be the conquest of Sicily; that was more or less common ground. The Mediterranean would then be clear enough for practical purposes. But what next? The Americans were inclined to favour an immediate invasion of Western France. The British preferred to cross the Straits of Messina, invade Italy, drive the Italian nation out of the war, possess themselves if possible of the Italian fleet, establish airfields in Italy from which the bombing offensive could be extended to those regions, such as Upper Silesia, to which Germany was gradually transferring war industries, and which it was not easy or economical to attack from British airfields. The Americans were doubtful of this strategy; to them it seemed unduly timid. Where would a campaign in Italy lead except to the Alps, where the Germans might well hope to block armies of superior strength? Some of them who were less charitably minded than others probably considered—it has at least been said since—that the British were influenced by their interest in the Mediterranean and by a desire to be well established in its waters when hostilities came to an end.

The Americans possessed a great aptitude for modern warfare. They analysed it scientifically. In some respects their minds moved more quickly to their objectives than did those of the British because they were rather more imaginative and more at home in the realm of industrial mechanics which afforded many short cuts to success. Yet at this period they were still feeling their way. The British were—though only for the time being—equipped with professional training and experience which they could not match. The British military leaders came to conferences, notably that held at Casablanca after its capture, better grounded, better "briefed". And when it came to thrashing the matter out round the council table and assessing the chances objectively the Americans were compelled to admit that, whatever the demerits of a campaign in Italy, the Allies were not yet ready for one in France, where the Germans could probably maintain an army thrice as great as any that they could maintain in Italy.

The training programme of the United States Staff was on a par with all its conceptions. It put American resources and capacity for swift construction to the best use. The splendidly-equipped camps grew like mushrooms. Yet, for all the speed with which the work was done, it could hardly be fast enough to carry out the invasion of France in 1943. Then there was the question of equipment. A new factor had been introduced into combined operations, the specially designed landing craft, first used by the Japanese in the invasion of China, but in later forms the result of research and experiment carried out by the British Combined Operations Command. This Command had been instituted under a veteran of the last war, Admiral of the Fleet Sir Roger Keyes, who was succeeded in October, 1941, by Captain Lord Louis Mountbatten. Its functions included research, training, planning, and the direct command of a special force, known as the Commandos, at this period consisting of a single brigade, formed with the purpose of striking back at the Germans on the Continent at a time when no other land forces could do so. In March, 1942, they were employed in a brilliant raid on St. Nazaire. In August they took part in a far bigger raid on Dieppe, though on this occasion the main force consisted of normal infantry drawn from the Canadian contingent in the United Kingdom. The Dieppe raid was costly and in many respects disappointing, but it provided a large fund of experience, and all subsequent British landings were to a greater or less degree based upon its lessons.

One of the major contributions of Combined Operations Command was the landing craft. When the Germans had made preparations to invade England they had relied upon the big barges used on the Dutch and Belgian canals and in some cases for open-sea work. A large proportion of these were power-driven and some of them were armoured in rudimentary fashion by the Germans. But they did not compare in efficiency with the special craft built in the United Kingdom. These took a number of forms, which were gradually added to as experience suggested. There were assault craft for infantry and tanks, larger supporting craft to carry stronger contingents in the second wave, and several other types. For a time Combined Operations Command controlled all the rapidly increasing personnel of the landing craft, so that there were in effect two navies. It was afterwards taken over by the Admiralty. At the peak, in the summer of 1944, the personnel of landing craft and landing ships exceeded in numbers that of the whole Royal Navy in time of peace. At the same time the British were experimenting with amphibious tanks, waterproofing of normal tanks—which had been done in time of peace as a test—and amphibious troop-carrying vehicles, though in the last it was the United States which took the lead.

The lessons of Dieppe and of experiments at home combined with close and dispassionate study of the various problems to be faced in a major invasion showed that it could hope to succeed only as the result of the most meticulous planning. Nothing could be left to chance. In particular, it would succeed or fail according to the adequacy and suitability of the material provided, chief among which would be the various forms of landing craft. But these craft did not exist in sufficient numbers. They were, in fact, barely prepared in time for invasion of Western France in the summer of 1944, and even then enough were made available only at the expense of cutting out a projected simultaneous landing in the south of France and depriving the forces in Burma of the landing craft which they would have needed in order to reconquer the country from the south, through Rangoon.

It therefore appeared inevitable that the only continental invasion which would be carried out in 1943 would be that of Italy, though Russia would certainly not consider this an adequate "second front". Meanwhile the United States air forces would be transferred to England as fast as possible and later based also on Italy, and would attack Germany from these bases. This would introduce a new element into the air attacks, since, whereas the British heavy bombers were designed for night work, the

American were built for daylight flying, and were therefore faster and more heavily armed, but carried a smaller bomb load. The invasion of Western France would follow as early as possible in 1944.

The U.S.S.R. did not enter deeply into the plans of the British Empire and the United States, since Russian suspicion was too deep for full and frank exchanges. The most that could be obtained was a general understanding. The Russians demanded from the Allies the maximum quantity of material and supplies, above all aircraft, tanks, transport vehicles, and food—and a "second front", by which was meant an invasion of Western Europe. After that they were confident of managing their own affairs successfully, expelling the Germans from their soil, recovering the accretions of territory they had previously acquired in Poland, the Baltic States, and Bessarabia, and finally invading Germany.

Though the British had despatched a Military Mission to Russia, there had been little serious discussion of affairs, except as regards supplies, between it and the Russian General Staff until General Martel, the former Commander of the Royal Armoured Corps, was appointed chief of this mission in April, 1943. He, and he alone, and that for only a brief period, was able to carry out a genuine liaison with the Russian General Staff, including its able head, Marshal Vassilievski. He discussed German strategy and tactics and was left with the impression that his views had had some influence, especially as regards the method of holding an armoured assault by sealing the flanks of the breach. Whether or not this was the case, the Russians decided that they would not repeat the strategy of 1942 by anticipating the next German offensive. This time they would sit tight, contain the offensive when it came, and then launch a counter-offensive when the enemy was fully committed. Beyond this it is difficult to decide what were their immediate plans, but there could be no doubt of their confidence, despite the losses they had suffered in their industries and their best corn-lands, which had hampered output and reduced their people to hunger.

After the loss of the North African coast and the defeats suffered in Russia in late 1942 and early 1943, some of the best instructed German commanders and staff officers began to speculate whether the war were not already as good as lost. The professional elements were, however, in the grip of Hitler and his Nazi organization, to whom they had sold themselves. They had by now abandoned the hope of conquering Russia or of over-whelming Britain by invasion, though they had not altogether ceased to play with the prospect, unpromising though it might be, of detaching one or other from the alliance. There were plenty of matters of discord, and these they worked upon through their propaganda machine. They still thought it might be possible to defeat an invasion of the Continent and that if this were effected the discouragement and distress of Great Britain would be such that the attempt would not be repeated. The submarine battle was still going well for them; in fact, the entry of the United States into the war was followed by outstanding successes in the Western Atlantic. Even now they might hope to deal Russia so hard a blow that, if she could not be conquered, her aggressive power might be restricted. Finally, they were pushing forward a number of long-range weapons which they hoped would pound London and other British cities into ashes. One of these was a big flying bomb; a second was a huge rocket-propelled bomb; and there were various variations on these two main themes, some of which had to be discarded but others of which proved promising. They were experimenting with the still more deadly weapon of atomic energy. The majority of the General Staff decided that it was well worth while to fight on because the result of defeat or surrender would be so grim.

As regards the war against Japan, the United Kingdom and the United States had come to an agreement that, while it should be vigorously prosecuted, it must take second place to the war against Germany. The British Government recognized, however, that the Americans must be their own interpreters of this formula in the zones which affected them, even if their interpretation should not exactly accord with the British. Another great disaster in the Pacific might so affect Congress and public that the hands of the military and naval authorities would be forced and they would be driven to divert resources from Europe to the Far East. It sometimes did appear to British observers that the Commander-in-Chief of the United States Navy, Admiral King, a man of great energy and deeply in the confidence of the President, turned his eyes more frequently to the Pacific than to the Atlantic, and certain of them afterwards considered that the war against

Germany might have been ended sooner had America devoted a slightly larger proportion of her energies and power to it. But perhaps this was an excessively critical attitude. It did nothing to disturb the excellent relations which prevailed between Britain and America from first to last on the subject of the conduct of the war.

In the Pacific the Americans saw their way clearly. They were confident that their strategy of advancing in bounds under cover of their predominant air force and seizing one valuable island base after another would eventually enable them to crush Japan by air bombardment and invade her territories when she had been sufficiently weakened. But the main Japanese fleet was still in being. Though it was becoming unbalanced by the loss of cruisers and destroyers, it was strong in capital ships. The moment must come when the Japanese would decide to risk the fleet in a decisive action to prevent the Americans closing on the homeland. It was impossible to say how long they would hold back, but it seemed probable that they would not allow the Americans to occupy the Philippines without picking up the glove. The results of the Coral Sea and Midway battles promised well, but there had been ugly moments at Guadalcanal, and no risks could be taken.

The Americans were also extremely anxious to do their utmost for China. There was in their country a sentiment of friendliness, admiration, and pity for the struggling Chinese which transcended strategic considerations. Months before the United States had entered the war American aircraft had been sent to China, where they were flown by American volunteers. When the Japanese closed the Burma Road the American General, Joseph W. Stilwell, who had commanded the Chinese army in Burma, organized an air ferry service over the Himalayas in order to maintain the supply of essentials to China. Later on America put at British disposal a considerable force of transport aircraft for the supply of the Burma front. She was anxious to provide the British with all possible aid for the purpose of ejecting the Japanese from Burma, and, even if she looked upon the reconquest of that country from the point of view of aid to China rather more than from that of aid to Britain in India, the results were satisfactory and the British had no cause to grumble.

The British themselves had not to the same extent a free hand

7

in the Far East. For them it was not simply a matter of policy but one of the hardest necessity that the German war should come first. The Burmese war had for the time being to be waged, so far as material was concerned, with the scrapings of the European dish. In fighting man-power the situation was by the late summer not unfavourable, though it had seemed desperate earlier in the year. New divisions had been formed in India and would shortly be available. Reinforcements in the air arm could also be provided; there was a good prospect of snatching from the Japanese in Burma the mastery of the air much sooner than it would be possible to defeat them on land, and this in fact occurred. But they were in possession of the Andaman and Nicobar Islands and they were maintaining a powerful naval force at Singapore, so that the eastern waters of the Indian Ocean were closed to British shipping. In any case there was a grave shortage of British shipping. There could be no hope of reconquering Burma by the obvious method of first retaking Rangoon. On the other hand, the land communications between India and Burma were of the worst. They could be improved, but they could never become easy owing to the nature of the mountain barrier between the valley of the Brahmaputra and that of the Chindwin.

The immediate aims on the Burma front had therefore to be limited to an advance in the coast strip known as the Arakan and to opening up a new route to China, from the railhead of Ledo in Assam, to replace the Burma road. It was not until the autumn —the beginning of the operational season after the monsoon—of 1943 that more ambitious plans could be set in train, and even then they were confined to the reoccupation of northern Burma as far south as Myitkyina with the primary object of supporting China.

Japan had been checked, though not as yet heavily, in the Pacific, but in Burma her advance had been brought to an end, not by opposition, but simply as the result of the strain upon her communications. In the Pacific it would appear that she was constrained to stand upon the defensive. She intended, in fact, to carry out an invasion of India. No strength which she was capable of maintaining in Burma would suffice for the conquest of India purely by force of arms, but the Japanese hoped they would be able to use another method in addition, that of raising a general revolt. They were aware that the extremists of the

Congress were little more favourable to the British than to themselves; they were at best neutral in the struggle, and certain of them had become active Japanese supporters. This did not imply that the Indian Army would take the same line, yet from their prisoners of war and Indians recruited in the territories which they had overrun the Japanese had created a corps which they named the "Indian National Army", and counted upon increasing it. In order to enter India they required a decisive military victory in Assam, but the next stage they hoped would be carried out with the aid of propaganda and heralded by the war-cry of "Asia for the Asiatics".

The foregoing represents the broad features of the plans and counter-plans of the chief belligerents early in 1943. Japan's designs upon India apart, those of the Axis were in the main defensive, whereas those of the United Nations were offensive. Their passage to victory seemed clear. In fact there were hidden snags sharp enough to wreck their prospects, and the time factor, which appeared to be completely in their favour, was in some respects against them.

CHAPTER XX

Sicily conquered: Italy invaded

THE conquest of Sicily at the earliest possible date after the conclusion of the African campaign had been agreed upon at the Casablanca Conference. The allied hierarchy of command was: supreme commander, General Eisenhower; naval commander-in-chief, Admiral Sir Andrew Cunningham; land commander-in-chief, General Alexander; air commander-in-chief, Air Marshal Tedder. The forces were divided into Eastern (British) and Western (United States) Naval and Military Task Forces, the air forces being centralized. The British Eighth Army, under the command of General Montgomery, was to land on the right, the American Seventh Army, commanded by General George Patton, on the left. A total of 2,500 craft of all kinds—warships, assault craft, transports, and supply ships—was required for the operation.

The planning had been in progress ever since the Casablanca Conference, but when General Montgomery found himself free from his work in Tunisia and had time to study the scheme he disagreed with it. It proposed that Sicily should be invaded simultaneously by the Americans in the north-west and the British in the south-east on wide frontages. This sort of dispersion was anathema to the commander of the Eighth Army. Eventually General Eisenhower altered the plan. It was now decided that the two task forces should land almost side by side, the British in the south-east corner of the island, the Americans in the Gulf of Gela. In mid-June the strongly-defended islands of Pantellaria and Lampedusa were taken. Pantellaria surrendered after terrific bombing, but in neither case did the garrisons await an assault. These islands made a certain contribution to the invasion, but nothing to that made by Malta. Its airfields were invaluable and it afforded an ideal station for headquarters. One of its infantry brigades was to take part. The heroic island was given the fullest opportunity of avenging its former sufferings and making, in attack, a further contribution to the cause which it had served so magnificently in defence.

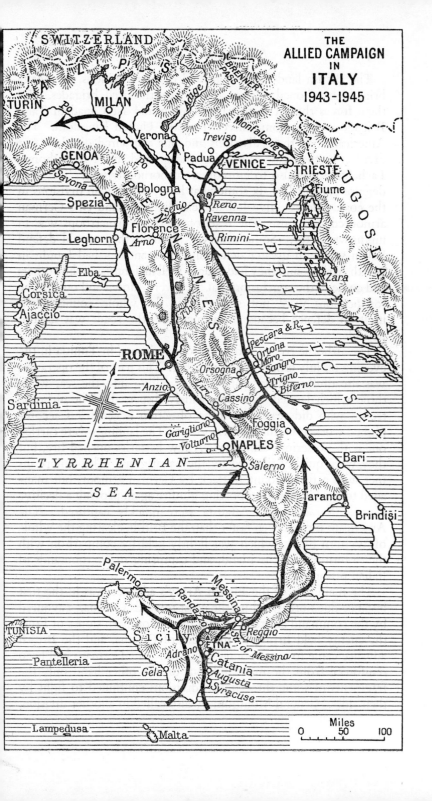

THE
ALLIED CAMPAIGN
IN
ITALY
1943-1945

The British land forces consisted of four divisions, the Malta brigade mentioned above, and three armoured brigades. Of these forces the 1st Canadian Division and 1st Canadian Tank Brigade were to come direct from the United Kingdom. The Americans had three divisions and one armoured division, one division in their case also being transported direct from home. Each force was also to employ an airborne division. The Axis defence consisted of six somewhat low-grade Italian divisions in the coast defences, five Italian field divisions, and two German armoured divisions. The reaction of the Italian troops was an unknown factor. Some observers thought they would defend Italian soil with greater determination than they had fought in North Africa—and they had fought well in Tunisia—while others had come to the conclusion that they were "down and out". The fortifications were not strong, but the whole country lent itself to defence because movement off the roads was seldom possible.

The airborne troops took off from Kairouan in Tunisia in the evening on July 9th, in rough weather. This part of the operation was dreadfully costly, many gliders falling into the sea, while those which landed were too widely dispersed. The airborne troops who did reach the scene of action nevertheless accomplished work as useful as it was gllant. The landings were carried out with no serious difficulty. A few batteries opened fire, but they were quickly silenced by the naval guns. The Americans met with a fierce counter-attack by German armour, but managed to hold it, naval supporting gunfire again proving a decisive factor. Syracuse and Augusta were quickly captured. The Americans moved even faster than the British, clearing the whole of Western Sicily, which was lightly held by comparison with the eastern half of the island, and capturing many thousands of Italian prisoners.

The main axis of the Eighth Army's advance was in the first instance due northward up the coast towards Catania. Favoured by the command afforded to him by the southern slopes of Etna, the enemy held firmly to the plain of Catania, and the British advance came to a temporary standstill. The Germans had been reinforced from the mainland, but on the other hand only the fragments of some three Italian divisions continued to fight by their sides. General Montgomery also called in another division, which was rapidly transported from Sousse. He then switched his main thrust from the coast to the western flank of Etna, aiming for the key point of Adrano on its slopes. Then, finding that the American advance eastward, in touch with his left flank, was being slowed down by stubborn resistance, he turned on the pressure along the coast once again, so that he was attacking with equal strength on either side of the great mountain mass. The heaviest and most costly fighting of the short campaign took place upon its lower slopes. However, Adrano was occupied on the night of August 6th, and on the 13th the Americans captured Randazzo. The whole system of defence based upon Etna had been broken up.

The Germans were now intent only upon getting their troops out of Sicily, and they succeded to an extent which surprised observers. The Americans, in addition to their advance on the Eighth Army's immediate flank, were moving eastward along the main road which follows the northern coast, making small landings behind the enemy when held up, It began to look as though the remainder of the Axis forces would be trapped just as they had been in Tunisia. But the conditions were very different. The Straits of Messina were so narrow that several crossings could be made under cover of darkness, and a smoke cloud by day had almost the same effect. Again, the daunting effect of a sufficient concentration of artillery upon naval and air forces was proved. The Germans are believed to have mounted 500 anti-aircraft guns astride the straits, and they had coast-defence batteries as well. With searchlights and mines added, they made the crossing virtually unassailable, though a certain number of craft were sunk. There was something of a race for Messina, which was won by the Americans; they entered the town on the night of August 16th, but the evacuation was then complete. The Germans transported to the mainland 60,000 men, two-thirds of their total force, and lost only 7000 prisoners, a disappointing result. A certain number of Italians reached Italy, but nearly half their total force was captured and many thousands more simply put on civilian clothes and disappeared.

The Germans had been unduly dispersed to begin with, and had been completely surprised. Yet both command and troops emerged from the campaign with the highest credit. They were heavily outnumbered, there being never more than four divisions in the country, besides auxiliary troops and airfield staffs, and only a few of the Italian troops put up any fight at all.

The collapse of Italy was in fact complete. Mussolini had been arrested on July 26th, and Marshal Badoglio had formed a government with the object of seeking peace, though he had to keep his intentions secret from the Germans. In August Italian emissaries met British and American representatives at Lisbon, where the allied terms were revealed. An armistice convention was signed at Syracuse on September 3rd, and the programme of invasion of Italy put forward. But the Germans, realizing what was happening, closed on Rome, from which the King and Badoglio had trouble in escaping. The Italian fleet escaped and sailed to Malta to surrender to the British on September 11th. It included four battleships—a fifth arrived later—and six cruisers. This was a great success, but most of the provisions of the armistice remained inoperative owing to Italian weakness.

On September 3rd—16 days after the end in Sicily and just about as soon as any military operation of the sort should have been launched—British troops landed on the mainland north of Reggio, virtually without opposition. On the 9th the American Fifth Army, under General Mark Clark, consisting of one American and one British army corps, landed in the Gulf of Salerno, south of Naples. There has been endless controversy as to whether or not this represented a timid piece of strategy, whether or not the landing should not have taken place considerably further north. It is no easy matter to decide, but the fact that some fighter cover, even though individual aircraft could give it only for brief periods, was provided for the troops landed at Salerno may well have made the difference between their holding on and their being driven back into the sea. It had been hoped to land an American airborne division on the airfield outside Rome at the same time, but the Italians were unable to maintain their hold upon it, so the scheme had to be cancelled. The Allies have been strongly condemned for failing to seize the advantages with which they were presented by the Italian surrender, but when one comes to analyse the situation one fails to observe any advantages, except the acquisition of the fleet, which made it possible to seize Taranto, undefended by the Germans. After what had happened in Sicily, it was clear that the Italians would not fight seriously. The Germans at once overawed and disarmed the Italian divisions, though there were about 18 Italian to 15 German in the country, and thenceforth had little more trouble. The civil population was delighted to see the Allies in the areas which they reached, but it did nothing to hinder the Germans in the areas to which they managed to cling. The Italians became hewers of wood and drawers of water for the opposing armies, especially for the Germans, who transported tens of thousands to Germany as labourers. From the moral point of view the fact that the king broke with the Fascists and set up a government in the south under the allied banner may have had a certain value; from the military it does not appear that Italian action or failure to take action had any effect worth mentioning.

This, however, is to look a little way ahead. The Fifth Army on the beaches of Salerno had an ugly time before its situation was secure, and at one moment it looked as though the whole force would be driven back into the sea. The Germans had concentrated five divisions quickly against it, and they hit hard. By September 14th the German counter-offensive had been fought down, and two days later the advanced guard of the Eighth Army made contact with the right of the Fifth. It had pushed along the "toe" of Italy, with a division on each coast road. There was practically no opposition from the retreating Germans, but mine-fields and demolitions on the winding roads slowed down the advance to some extent. Nevertheless, the army covered not far short of 200 miles in 13 days.

It was now called upon to switch to the eastern flank of the Apennines and transfer its lines of communication from Calabria to the eastern ports of Brindisi, Taranto, and Bari, where the head of another division landed on September 22nd. And, if the Allies can be accused of lack of foresight, it is not on the political side but on the purely administrative. This move of the administrative axis to the "heel" ports of Italy had not been thought out in advance. The shipping was not loaded exclusively with the material most in demand. Altogether there were serious delays which, far more than any alleged failure "to take advantage of the Italian armistice", killed the hope of seizing Rome and Pescara before the winter.

However, for the time being all seemed to be going well. The Eighth Army swept over the plain of Foggia, capturing the network of airfields. (This, though invaluable in the long run, constituted for the moment another handicap to the Eighth Army, since the shipping became occupied and the ports became congested with the vast supplies of material, including enormous quantities of metal "carpets" for landing strips, required by the allied air forces in order to make the speediest use of the airfields.) From Foggia Montgomery brilliantly rushed the passage of the Biferno, with the aid of landings from the sea. That, however, was to be his last rush in the Italian campaign. The enemy reacted quickly, counter-attacked fiercely, and broke off the action only to withdraw to the next river, the Trigno. Henceforward the Eighth Army was to be confronted with one river after another, running down from the spine of the Apennines into the Adriatic. They were at all seasons formidable obstacles, since the gorges in which they ran were immense by comparison with the flow of water. But, when swollen by rain or snow, they became very much more difficult, especially as the approaches became simultaneously water-logged. In the bed itself the water would rise many feet in a few hours, often thus dislocating pontoon bridges and exposing troops who had secured a footing on the far bank to acute peril.

The Fifth Army also pushed on at a good speed after the defeat of the enemy's attempt to drive it back into the sea and his withdrawal to the mountain passes north of Salerno. It forced those passes, debouched into the next plain, and entered Naples on October 1st. It also had administrative difficulties. Its supplies had to be landed over the open beaches at Salerno, and it was some time before even the brilliant American engineers could clear the port of Naples, where ships had been sunk across the entrance to the harbour and alongside the quays.

It was still hoped to reach the main road across the country from Pescara to Rome before the winter. Grimly the Eighth Army forced the Trigno and by November 8th was over-looking the most formidable barrier it had yet encountered in Italy, that of the Sangro. Montgomery expressed full confidence and called upon his troops to hit the enemy "a colossal crack". The Sangro was forced; the Moro followed. In one of the bloodiest battles of the war British, Canadian, New Zealand and Indian troops fought their way by the end of the year to the line Ortona-Orsogna in terrible weather. But that was virtually the end. They were bogged down. Meanwhile by great exertions the

Fifth Army had forced the passage of the Volturno and pushed up towards the even more formidable Garigliano.

By this time the allied forces in Italy (15th Army Group, commanded by General Alexander) consisted of seven divisions in the Eighth Army, all from the British Commonwealth; twelve in the Fifth Army, five British, five American and two French; and a Polish division in reserve. Montgomery returned to England at the New Year and was succeeded by Lieut.-General Sir Oliver Leese. Montgomery was to take command in the invasion of France and it had already been decided to withdraw certain British and American divisions for this offensive.

Still, however, the Fifth Army continued its efforts. The Germans, commanded by the extremely able Kesselring, had only ten divisions in line, with three in reserve, but there were five more in northern Italy. American and French troops made progress in the mountains, and in mid-January, 1944, British troops secured a deep bridgehead beyond the Garigliano. Then, on the 22nd, the army launched a daring and promising offensive. An American corps containing a British division landed over fifty miles behind the enemy's lines at the small port of Anzio. The enemy was taken completely by surprise and a deep holding was secured. In such circumstances the first question a commander has to ask himself is, to put it in popular military slang: "Do I or do I not stick my neck out?" In this case it was decided not to, that is, it was decided to build up and consolidate before breaking out. It is clear, however, that this was an error, that it would have been prudent rather than temerarious to seize a position in the Alban Hills. Kesselring acted coolly. Concentrating some troops from the battle front and others from the north, he blocked the Allies in their Anzio bridgehead, and subsequently launched a series of strong counter-attacks which gained a considerable amount of ground and caused much anxiety before they were finally held at the end of February. The Navy lost two cruisers and two destroyers off Anzio. At the same time the Germans defeated an indifferently mounted allied attack on the strong Cassino position beginning in mid-February. Again, on March 15th, an attempt was made to reduce the position by air bombardment, the famous monastery being destroyed to no purpose, since it was not occupied by the enemy and in any case the infantry assault failed with heavy loss. Allied skill and ingenuity had fallen to a low ebb in Italy.

It could produce something better than this. The bulk of the Eighth Army was moved in secret west of the Apennines to the aid of the Fifth. The British, who were responsible for the initiation of a campaign for which the Americans were not enthusiastic and therefore had to support it, were taking a bigger part than ever. There were now, exclusive of the Anglo-American force in the Anzio bridgehead, ten divisions from the British Commonwealth (British, Canadian, New Zealand, South African and Indian), whereas only three American divisions remained with the Fifty Army outside the bridgehead. There were also two Polish divisions in the Eighth Army and three French in the Fifth. Round the Anzio bridgehead there were nine German divisions, nine in the main line, and one north of Rome. In northern Italy four were still maintained for purposes of security.

This allied offensive, which began on May 11th, was a crowning example of the principle of concentration, since some three-quarters of the available strength was massed from a short distance north of Cassino to the sea. After bitter and costly fighting —the Poles north of Cassino suffering particularly heavy losses— it resulted in the breach of the enemy's defences, an advance up the Liri valley, the break-out of the Anzio force to join the main body, and finally the precipitate retreat of the enemy. It was one of the most satisfactory battles fought by Anglo-American arms and set the seal upon the reputation of General Alexander. The British and American tactical air forces, for some time starved of targets because there had been nothing to be seen on the roads and railways behind the German front, where all movement had been carried out at night, now had their opportunities and took full advantage of them. There was, in fact, a period of a few days when the Germans were streaming north in disorder, heavily bombed from the air, and it seemed possible that they would suffer a further disaster and would to a great extent disintegrate. However, stout rearguards in the broken country saved them from this and permitted a partial recovery. Their loss in prisoners, about 27,000 in the whole period, was not exceptionally high, but they also left behind them a great deal of material.

On June 4th, two days before the landing in Normandy, the

Fifth Army entered Rome. No serious damage had been done to the city by either side. The inhabitants received the Allies as liberators. The advance continued. This offensive proved a heartening prelude to the more vital venture in preparation in the United Kingdom for the final overthrow of Germany by invasion through Western France.

CHAPTER XXI

Russia: from the Spring of 1943 to the Spring of 1944

THE early part of the summer of 1943 went by with an almost complete lull on the Russian front. The last serious fighting had been in the German-held Caucasian bridgehead beyond the Kerch Straits, and that had died down in the first days of June after strong Russian attacks had achieved only a limited measure of success. To the Soviet General Staff it appeared more and more likely, not only from such troop movements as had been observed but also from pure deduction, that the next German offensive would be directed against the Kursk salient. By dealing the Russians a heavy blow here the Germans could hope at one and the same time to postpone and hamper an offensive by the Red Army and to create for themselves a much needed strategic reserve. This was not ambitious strategy, but, as has been explained, German strategy was perforce becoming less ambitious. Yet, should the offensive develop into a sweeping success, it could be exploited by means of a northerly thrust towards Moscow.

The German armies in Russia were no longer the magnificent force which had carried out the offensives of 1941 and 1942. They had been both diluted and depleted. The divisions were occasionally as much as 60 per cent below establishment. A majority of the Panzer and Panzer-Grenadier divisions were, however, stronger, and their standards were considerably higher. These included certain new *Waffen S.S.* divisions, some of which contained a large percentage of foreigners. Their primary rôle was that of a Pretorian Guard, but, from necessity as well as with the object of giving them prestige in a nation which set a high value on military prowess, they were regularly used at the front. The combination of the conflict of opposing ideologies, Communist and Nazi, of the enlistment of mercenaries, and of a second-grade horde army, inevitably recalls the later stages of the Thirty Years' War.

On the Russian side there were also grave deficiencies, some of them inescapable in an army so vast in size. The standard first-

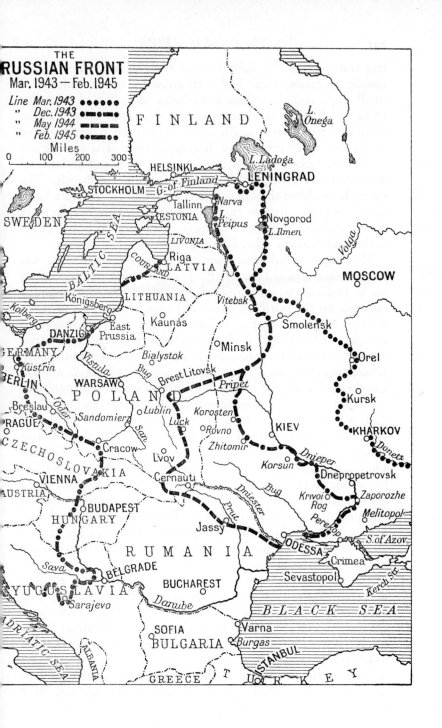

THE
RUSSIAN FRONT
Mar. 1943 — Feb. 1945

Line Mar. 1943 ●●●●●●
"   Dec. 1943 ●○●○●○
"   May 1944 ▬▬▬▬
"   Feb. 1945 ●○▬●○▬

Miles
0   100   200   300

FINLAND

L. Onega

L. Ladoga

HELSINKI

STOCKHOLM G. of Finland

LENINGRAD

SWEDEN

Tallinn
ESTONIA

Narva
L. Peipus

Novgorod
L. Ilmen

MOSCOW

LIVONIA

Riga
LATVIA

COURLAND

Volga

Vitebsk

Königsberg

LITHUANIA

Kaunas

Smolensk

Kolberg

BALTIC SEA

East
Prussia

Minsk

Orel

DANZIG

GERMANY
Küstrin

Bialystok

Vistula

Bug

Brest Litovsk

Pripet

Kursk

BERLIN

WARSAW

POLAND

KHARKOV

Breslau

Oder

Sandomierz

Lublin

Korosten

KIEV

Donetz

PRAGUE

San

Luck

Rovno

Zhitomir

Dnieper

Dnepropetrovsk

CZECHOSLOVAKIA

Cracow

Lvov

Korsun

VIENNA

Cernauti

Krivoi
Rog

Zaporozhe

AUSTRIA

Dniester

Bug

Perekop

Melitopol

BUDAPEST

HUNGARY

Prut

Jassy

ODESSA

S. of Azov

Sava

RUMANIA

Crimea

BELGRADE

BUCHAREST

Sevastopol

Kerch Str.

YUGOSLAVIA

Sarajevo

Danube

BLACK   SEA

ADRIATIC SEA

ALBANIA

SOFIA
BULGARIA

Varna
Burgas

ISTANBUL

GREECE

T U R K E Y

line transport of the infantry was horse-drawn. For highly mobile operations there had been created a certain number of small corps, including three lorry-borne brigades and some 200 tanks, but the Red Army never possessed transport enough for an adequate strength in these invaluable formations and at this time it was not so well off as it was later to become. The armour was good, but lacked the latest refinements such as wireless and armoured cars which had been developed by the British. The strength lay above all in the artillery, in which the Russians had a great superiority over the enemy. Their barrages were extremely heavy, and they employed a larger proportion of heavy pieces in the field than any other belligerent.

The Germans did what they had been expected to do. On July 5th they attacked the two flanks of the Kursk salient, making use of 30 divisions: six armoured, one motor, and seven infantry divisions on the northern flank and nine armoured and seven infantry on the southern. It was the most powerful armoured assault ever launched. Both thrusts made progress, but that on the northern side soon proved to be a failure. It did not succeed in penetrating the main defences and came to an end within a week. On the south side the enemy did better, but the maximum advance did not exceed 20 to 30 miles. The corridor, too, remained narrow, and was prevented from expanding by the arrival of Russian reinforcements on its flanks. On July 12th the Russians launched their own long-prepared offensive against the German Orel salient further north, one attack coming from the east and the second from the north. The latter began brilliantly, in fact, a good deal more rapidly than either of the German thrusts, but it was presently brought to a halt by Panzer divisions which had been withdrawn from the offensive further south. The frontal attack from the east plodded on until it reached Orel on August 5th, having covered about a mile and a half a day.

The lessons which the Soviet General Staff appears to have deduced from this operation were two: in the first place, they could now go over to the offensive with confidence, without serious concern about another major German offensive; in the second, it would pay them to avoid the Panzers in open warfare, to keep them racing about and ever hurrying to plug breaches on one part of the front after another. Meanwhile their own offensives, now here, now there, would wear the enemy out. If it came to "swopping losses" in these short advances, they could afford them better than the Germans. The Germans had not created the reserve they required, whereas fresh formations of the Red Army were still being trained and it had large resources in hardy Asiatic man-power still to draw upon. The Russians, however, looked upon this policy of attrition as only a temporary expedient. When it had gone far enough they hoped to increase the tempo.

Late in August they judged that the time had come for a more adventurous spirit to be introduced into the operations. In front of Moscow they struck hard for Smolensk, an important road and rail junction, reached its outskirts quickly, and, after a check, took it on September 25th. Further south their offensive towards Kiev was even more successful, and they reached the Dnieper on a frontage of 400 miles, though the Germans maintained bridgeheads east of the river. South of the Dnieper bend at Zaporozhe the enemy had put up strong fortifications to preserve his communications with the Crimea. There was much discussion in this country as to whether or not this deep withdrawal to the Dnieper was forced upon the Germans. It turned, in fact, upon the use of words. The withdrawal was unwelcome and made under pressure, but it was in the main deliberate. The Germans were able to carry out extensive demolitions, including the destruction of the crops which they could not carry away with them. There is no evidence that they lost great numbers of prisoners. Their policy was so far correct, and their front was slightly shortened. But if they counted on the autumn bringing Russian pressure to an end they were in error.

Early in October the Russians secured three bridgeheads over the broad river. When the Germans concentrated against them the Russians put on pressure further south, captured Zaporozhe and Melitopol, and seriously threatened the Crimea. They also squeezed the German holding in the Kuban peninsula beyond the Kerch Straits, and the enemy, making a virtue of necessity, abandoned it and withdrew the remainder of his forces into the Crimea, apparently not without appreciable loss. But there was worse to come. The Russians, merging their bridgeheads over the Dnieper, struck southwards at Krivoi Rog. Manstein threw in his armour, regained a little ground, probably saved the forces in the bend, but could not long hold up the onrush. Higher up the river Kiev was recovered by the Russians, and they then proceeded in the course of the following fortnight to carve out a deep bulge in the German front up to a distance of 70 miles west of the Dnieper at this point.

And then the Germans made another and more successful counter-attack. They had brought in an armoured division from Greece, one from Yugoslavia, one from Norway, and two from Italy. Others engaged in recent battles had been refitted, and a strong Panzer army had been consituted. The British were able to give warning to their allies of these moves, and General Martel suggested that the hostile armour would be used in strength against the "Kiev bulge", especially the southern flank, the north being protected by the Pripet Marshes. This warning, however, came only three days before the Germans began their counter-offensive.

The army group commander, Manstein, tried to repeat his exploit of the previous spring, when he had saved the German forces in the Donetz basin and recovered Kharkov. He hit hard at the southern side of the Russian salient. He recovered a fair amount of ground, including the towns of Zhitomir and Korosten. But the former German ascendancy was gone. Manstein maintained his counter-offensive for upwards of a month, but his maximum penetration does not appear to have exceeded 25 miles at any point. Measuring his achievement by the distances of Russia, he cannot be said to have accomplished more than checking the Russian advance temporarily. He did not paralyse it elsewhere, and it continued in the Dnieper bend, where it made slow but steady progress. And about Christmas Eve the Russians returned to the offensive in the Kiev salient and more than recovered the ground which they had lost to Manstein. On the Moscow front they likewise made progress in the sector of Nevel during the latter part of December.

There was no cessation that winter. The fighting had gone on all through the period of the mud, and now the Russians had hard weather in which to continue the offensive. Their prospects for 1944 were manifestly good, and after the way in which they had beaten the enemy's offensives at Kursk and Kiev they had little to fear from Germany provided they exercised common prudence and the Anglo-American offensive in the west did not break down. But was their main offensive to be launched north or south of the Pripet? If it were to be to the north, this would lead them across northern Poland to East Prussia, the cradle of German nationalism. South of the Pripet they would have the choice of advancing between the marshes and the Carpathians, which would also take them into the north German plain, or striking southward towards the valley of the Danube.

For the time being, in view of the enemy's strength and the stiffness of his defence north of the Pripet, the Russians preferred to continue to make their main effort south of the Pripet and to strain the Kiev salient to bursting-point. In January, 1944, they expanded it westward and also southward, and in the latter direction they advanced their front to the Bug. This represented a serious threat to the greater part of Manstein's army group in the Ukraine. Loth as they were to abandon a position effectively covering the Crimea, the Germans had no option but to begin a withdrawal on their extreme right. But they clung over-long to a position on the Dnieper. Suddenly the Russians closed behind this force, surrounded it, and, repeating the tactics of Stalingrad, began to force the German main body away from it. Another tremendous battle broke out round the "Korsun Pocket", which for a short time became as famous as that of Stalingrad. Manstein made strenuous efforts to relieve it, and the beleaguered force itself managed to fight its way some distance south-west towards its would-be rescuers. Some troops were withdrawn by air, and others—we shall never know precisely how many—broke out. But the Germans probably lost at least 50,000 men and enormous quantities of material.

Simultaneously the Russians had mounted an offensive in the north, which opened in mid-January and smashed the German lines of investment round Leningrad. By the beginning of February they had pushed west to the outskirts of Narva and had also advanced 40 miles west of Novgorod. Between these two advances another great sack had appeared in the German front, but this time the enemy was not caught; he cleared out at top speed from an area measuring some 50 miles by 40. The Russians continued to push him hard, and but for early thaws might have penetrated deeply into Estonia before the end of March, since early in the month they had established their front along the eastern shores of Lake Peipus.

South of the Pripet the Russian advance continued. The

Germans were obliged to abandon the position covering the Crimea and to fall back to the final hundred-mile reach of the Dnieper; but they still held the Crimea itself. In the course of February they gave up their last holding in the Dnieper bend. Due west of Kiev the Russians reached Rovno and Luck, beyond the Polish frontier of 1939, in the first week of March. Later in the month they crossed the Dniester, penetrated right up to the Carpathians north-west of Cernauti, and lined the Prut down to a point opposite Jassy.

Some of the less optimistic or more cynical observers had affected, up to the beginning of 1944, to believe that the military situation of the Germans was not nearly so serious as it appeared to the majority. Even if the enemy had abandoned ground which he would much prefer to hold, they argued, he had generally done so at his own pace and in his own time, and it might well be that the withdrawals made against the grain would prove profitable rather than otherwise in the long run by shortening the front, bettering German communications while they worsened Russian, and providing opportunities for counter-offensive action not possible when the Germans were stretched and strained. These doubts began to look foolish now. The elbow room on which the Germans had so often congratulated themselves was largely gone. The menace was approaching Germany herself, and though it was still some distance from German territory, it was very close to that of Rumania and Czecho-Slovakia and only about a hundred miles from that of Hungary. In the north Finland was virtually isolated by the success of the recent Russian offensive south of Leningrad.

The satellites were in no doubt about the serious nature of the situation from their point of view. Probably there was not one of them that would not have got off the cart now if an opportunity to do so had presented itself. Finland, never a warm ally of Germany and engaged rather in a private war of revenge against Russia with German aid, opened negotiations for an armistice, and though hitches occurred and agreement was not reached until September, contact between the two sides was maintained. Rumania, though in the hands of a Fascist government, might have been glad to take a similar step, but she was unable to do so since she was under German control and a German army group was in fact withdrawing into her territory. The Germans merely strengthened the garrison and proclaimed martial law. Hungary was not an occupied country and might make an effort to shake herself free. The Germans took no chances. On March 19th they began to rush in troops, mostly from Austria. They overthrew the Government and set up a new one favourable to themselves. In Bulgaria they reinforced the garrisons of Varna and Burgas on the Black Sea. The Germans always rode Bulgaria with a relatively light hand.

The Russians were still a long way from the Yugoslav frontier, but none of the conquered countries was causing Germany anything like as much trouble as Yugoslavia. This was due in part to the unyielding spirit of the people and in part to the mountainous and inaccessible nature of the country. The first leader who opposed the Axis was a Serbian officer, General Mihailovitch, who was appointed Minister of War by the exiled Yugoslav Government in London. He organized large guerilla bands, mainly in old Serbia, and harassed German and Italian communications. Later there appeared a rival leader, a Moscow-trained Communist who called himself "Tito" and gave himself the rank of "Marshal". The rivalry between the two was in part national, Serb against Croat and Slovene, but to a greater extent political, monarchist and Conservative against republican and Communist. The Germans brought Bulgarian troops into Yugoslav Macedonia. The wily Bulgars refused to send their sons to the slaughter in Russia, like the Rumanians and the Hungarians, but they had no objection to their employment in the occupation of Yugoslavia and Greece. Casualties were not likely to be so heavy in these countries, and besides they had territorial claims against both of them.

Periodical drives against the insurgents were fairly successful, but never succeeded in breaking up the bands, which, especially after the invasion of Italy, could be supplied from allied sources. Unfortunately, however, instead of co-operating with each other against the common enemy, the two Yugoslav forces fought each other savagely. Eventually the British came to the conclusion that Tito and his Partisans were the more whole-hearted and useful of the two. It did not occur to everyone that this was relatively easy from their point of view. The German revenge for an ambush was frequently to send troops—usually from the Croat legion formed with their approval—to the nearest village and to shoot the notables. This might well cause Mihailovitch to be cautious, but Tito, who was preparing a Communist state, did not frown upon the shooting of the mayor, the chief shopkeeper, the big local pig-dealer, or the substantial farmer. For him they were well out of the way. However, there was now ample evidence that most of the subordinates of Mihailovitch were co-operating with the Germans against Tito's Partisans, and some to the effect that this was done with his knowledge. Partly because Tito gave the better return for services rendered, partly perhaps to please Russia, allied support was withdrawn from Mihailovitch altogether. It was not generally realized how much trouble was thus being stored up for the future.

From the military point of view Yugoslavia caused a heavy strain upon Germany. At the time of the allied invasion of Italy there were actually fewer German divisions in that country than in Yugoslavia. This struck allied commentators as a very remarkable fact, but they did not in every instance realize that by no means all these troops were required to resist the Partisans. Had there been no revolt in Yugoslavia there would still have been a large German garrison in the country, as also in Greece. The German command was sensitive to the threat of invasion through these countries, especially from Salonika and up the Vardar-Morava corridor to the Danube. This was something it could never afford to neglect, even after the positive value of a footing in the eastern Mediterranean and the Ægean for the purpose of an offensive against Russia through Turkey, or against the British in the Middle East, had disappeared. The Germans still maintained a division in Crete and considerable forces in the Dodecanese. In the principal island, Rhodes, they had after the collapse of Italian power disarmed the Italian garrison, though it outnumbered their own contingent by four to one. A somewhat ill-advised British incursion into these islands, to Cos and Leros, had brought about fierce German reaction and had ended in a British disaster on November 16th, 1943. This German success had exercised an unfortunate effect upon Turkey, then considering the possibility of intervention on the side of the Allies. Scared by this exhibition of German strength and by what she considered British inanity, Turkey had once more retired into her shell.

This setback notwithstanding, it was clear to all unbiased eyes that the German cause was ruined. It was even possible that the year 1944 would see the end. There remained only two factors on which the Germans could possibly count: a breakdown in the coming allied offensive in the west and sweeping success in the use of "secret weapons", which were not yet ready.

CHAPTER XXII

Development of the War at Sea

ONE of the chief anxieties of the British Admiralty was the possibility of a German battleship getting loose upon the Atlantic trade routes. If the Germans cared to run the risk of sending out a warship of this type she might do incalculable damage. She was capable of sinking a whole convoy with its escort. The *Scharnhorst* and *Gneisenau* had sunk 22 ships before taking refuge at Brest. On May 21st, 1941, an aircraft of Coastal Command found the new battleship *Bismarck*, reputably of 35,000 tons but believed to displace something nearer 50,000, in a fjord near Bergen. That night she put to sea with the cruiser *Prinz Eugen*. Next day a British naval aircraft, in a momentary lift of the dense clouds over Bergen, discovered that the fjord was empty.

On the evening of the 23rd the *Bismarck* and her consort were sighted by British warships in the Denmark Strait, between Iceland and Greenland. At dawn on the 24th she was engaged by the British battleship *Prince of Wales* and the battle-cruiser *Hood*. She sank the *Hood*. On the 25th contact with the German ships was lost, and in the interval the *Prinz Eugen* parted company with the battleship. The *Bismarck* was again picked up on the 26th, making for a French port with speed reduced owing to damage inflicted by the *Hood*. The Home Fleet was now closing upon her from the north and the Gibraltar Squadron from the south. Even then she might have escaped, but an attack by naval torpedo-carrying aircraft jammed her rudders, so that she turned in circles. She was again hit by torpedoes, and on the 27th shelled to a flaming wreck by British battleships. But her wonderful construction kept her afloat till she was finally torpedoed and sunk by the cruiser *Dorsetshire*, some 400 miles west of Brest.

The sinking of a single battleship may not appear to be a major strategic event, but in fact it was. While she was afloat she represented a threat which involved several British battleships, because wide areas of water would have to be covered in searching for her in the Atlantic. And there was only one other ship of her class, probably the finest in the world, in the German Navy, the *Tirpitz*.

In Chapter X a brief account was given of the anti-submarine war by phases up to the middle of March, 1941. It will be convenient to continue this method of relating the struggle against the German U-boats by phases, always bearing in mind, however, that its characteristics to some extent overlapped their limits. It will be recalled that between the summer of 1940 and March, 1941, during which time the Germans extended their bases to Norway, the Channel, the Biscay ports, and the Mediterranean, the main submarine attack was in the North-west Approaches. During the remainder of 1941, the third phase of the U-boat war, there was a great extension of activity. U-boats appeared in increasing numbers in the Mediterranean and also on the West African coast. Convoys were now provided with escorts all the way across the Atlantic from the home ports to Canada and many fierce battles were fought. This could not be regarded as a satisfactory phase, but it was slightly better than its predecessor. Fifty U-boats were sunk or believed to be sunk. Losses were approximately 350 merchantmen of a total of nearly 1,700,000 tons.

The fourth phase, the first seven months of 1942, was far more deadly still, though the scene of action was altogether different. On the entry of the United States into the war the Germans neglected the North-west Approaches, the region of Gibraltar, and the West African coast route to concentrate upon American waters. The Americans were naturally less well prepared than the British and suffered terrible losses in this phase, but the British also came in for heavy blows in an area west of a line drawn from Newfoundland to Rio. There were also serious sinkings in the convoys bound for North Russia and for Malta, though in the latter case mostly from air action. A new factor was that of attacks by Japanese submarines in the Indian Ocean, as the result of which many ships, particularly tankers, were sunk. This period represented the peak of destruction, and it became problematical whether the nation was capable of sustaining it. Forty-eight submarines were sunk or probably sunk, but the losses reached the stupendous total of 670 ships of 3,500,000 tons, roughly three-and-a-third ships and 17,500 tons a day.

The fifth period, up to the third week in May, 1943, saw

heavier sinkings, but at a slightly reduced rate, the period being longer by nearly one-third. Once again its characteristics were altogether different from that of the preceding period. To compensate for the loss of skill among their submarine captains, the Germans had been organizing small fleets of U-boats which worked together and in co-operation with aircraft in what they called "wolf packs". The precautions taken by the Allies had rendered the coastal waters of North America unsafe, and the enemy now used his wolf packs mostly in the central Atlantic. The losses were enormous, and were swollen by casualties to transports returning from the landings in French North Africa. At one time in the earlier part of the period the Germans believed that victory was within their grasp. In point of fact, however, the strain of maintaining the wolf pack system was more serious than they had expected, while the British were becoming better equipped to meet the attack, especially in the matter of small escort aircraft carriers. The one bright spot in the period was the vastly increased number of submarines sunk or probably sunk. This was 159, of which 66 were accounted for by aircraft. The rise in the killing power of aircraft was significant and promising, and in fact the promise was to be borne out. The losses amounted to 786 ships of 4,500,000 tons.

The sixth phase was brief, only 120 days, up to mid-September, 1943. It was costly but triumphant. The enemy was faltering. German successes were gained almost wholly in the Mediterranean, but the Japanese in the Gulf of Aden and the Indian Ocean also hit hard. The seventh phase was somewhat similar, but with decreasing losses. And then came the eighth and final period, which represents almost exactly the last year of the war against Germany, the Japanese submarines being unable to do much harm. The Germans hoped to score great successes in this period, having brought into employment their breathing-pipe known as the "Schnorkel", which did away with the necessity for surfacing and consequently secured greater immunity from aircraft attacks. But the advantages of the Allies were far more than a sufficient counterweight to this invention. The invasion of western Europe closed port after port. Coastal Command of the R.A.F. carried out a powerful and brilliantly successful offensive on the coast of Norway. British equipment to meet the submarine menace was practically complete.

By a strange development the losses which were suffered—and they were heavy enough still—took place in waters which had been immune for four years, the waters round these islands, especially the Channel and the Irish Sea. U-boats took to skulking near wrecks to avoid detection by the "Asdic", an instrument which gave off vibrations reflected back when they encountered an obstacle in the water and indicating both its distance and direction. Submarines sunk or believed to be sunk numbered 211, the losses being 124 ships of 637,000 tons. Three thousand tons of shipping were sunk in this period for every submarine accounted for, as against 73,000 tons in the disastrous fourth phase.

It had been a close struggle for bare survival. Technical aspects apart, its main lesson is the need for unbiased thinking based upon a clear sense of proportion. For our nation the means of attack and defence and the services of sea, land, and air which wield them are all of a piece. No one form of warfare can be carried on regardless of the success or failure of another. Those who talked and wrote of "victory through air power" did not stop to think that without the aid of sea power not a drop of fuel would reach the airfields of the United Kingdom. The awakening was rude when suddenly, in the bleak central phases of the Battle of the Atlantic, it began to be a question whether the supply of oil which enabled the heavy bombers to attack Berlin could be maintained. The diversion of a reasonable proportion of aircraft production to the Navy's needs was more or less simultaneous with the effective participation of the United States in the anti-submarine war—after which American ships and aircraft sank almost as many German submarines as the British, and far more Japanese—and the two together gained the battle. But the former was carried out dangerously late, at the risk of an appalling disaster.

When we speak of the Battle of the Atlantic as the decisive struggle for survival we are saying no more than the truth, but it must not be supposed that it was in the Atlantic that the highest proportion of losses to merchant shipping were suffered. Those in the Malta convoys were higher, but these convoys were small and comparatively few. It was in the Arctic convoys that the proportionate losses were heaviest. British and American ships carrying supplies to Russia by the Arctic route lost proportionately nearly eight times as many of their number as were lost in the

Atlantic convoys; west-bound convoys returning from North
Russia lost nearly four times as many. The difference is doubtless
accounted for by the fact that the Germans relatively neglected
the home-bound convoys to concentrate against the outward-
bound. The cargoes of the latter were priceless, whereas the
former were for the most part sailing in ballast and in any case
carrying nothing more valuable than timber, since Russia had
nothing to give. The fate of one of these outward-bound convoys, that of June and July, 1942, was in itself a major disaster.
On a report that the *Tirpitz* and *Hipper* had left Trondheim, it
was ordered to scatter. The German battleships did not in fact
attack, but the convoy was hunted to death by U-boats and out
of its 35 ships only 11 reached their destination.

Mention has already been made of the arrival of the *Scharnhorst*
and *Gneisenau* in Brest harbour in March, 1941. At the end of
May they were joined there by the cruiser *Prinz Eugen*, after she
had parted company with the *Bismarck*. On February 11th, 1942,
these ships, together with an escort of destroyers, minesweepers
and other light craft, left Brest and sailed up the Channel. They
were late in being picked up by aircraft, and the attacks launched
against them by destroyers, bombers and torpedo-carrying aircraft
of the Fleet Air Arm were unavailing. They made the passage
successfully and reached a port in the Heligoland Bight.

The anger of the country over this rebuff would have been still
fiercer had it been possible to get at the truth, which was concealed
under a smoke-screen of verbiage. There was no surprise. The
ships were expected to come out; the date could be roughly
estimated; and it was known with fair certainty that they would
sail up-Channel rather than attempt to make their way home by
way of the Atlantic. The inaccuracy and ineffective results of the
repeated bombing attacks were realized. Bomber Command
seems to have been haunted by the fear that the war would be
lost if too many aircraft were taken off the task of bombing Germany. But the most important factor in the escape of the German
warships was the inadequacy of the equipment of the Fleet Air
Arm. The naval airmen who made the extremely gallant torpedo
attacks on the *Scharnhorst* and *Gneisenau*, in which the majority
came by their deaths, were sacrificed to the policy of "winning
the war by bombing", just as some of the earlier land forces had
been.

The drain of the Far East, the loss of the *Prince of Wales* and *Repulse* and other warships under Admiral Somerville's command based on Ceylon, the disaster at Alexandria caused by the Italian "limpet" bombs, and other lossess temporary or permanent in late 1941 and early 1942 had affected the Mediterranean theatre particularly. It was no longer possible to operate British cruisers from Malta, and the Italian fleet could now regularly escort considerable convoys to the forces in Libya, with little risk of interference except from submarines and aircraft. For a time Alexandria was without a capital ship. On March 22nd, 1942, Rear-Admiral P. L. Vian fought a remarkable action in protection of a Malta-bound convoy, his force consisting of five light cruisers and destroyers, whereas that of the Italians included a modern battleship and two heavy cruisers. A hit by a torpedo on the battleship was claimed, and the Italian squadron sheered off. It was a brilliant and gallant effort on the part of the British, but there might well have been a disaster had not the wind favoured Admiral Vian's smoke-screen, or had the enemy bestirred himself to get to weather of the convoy. Indeed a terrible peril had been surmounted with a very small margin to spare.

A German admiral has described the action as a turning-point in the war. The Italian fleet, he says, could not operate without the *Luftwaffe*, and the *Luftwaffe*, disgusted by the failure of the Italians to close the convoy, henceforth disregarded them and went its own way. Otherwise he thinks Malta might have been taken by a combined operation.

Yet Malta went through desperate days that summer. When Field-Marshal Lord Gort was appointed Governor and Commander-in-Chief in May, in succession to the gallant Lieut.-General Sir William Dobbie, and brought to the island the George Cross bestowed upon it by the King, he was informed that it might soon become impossible to maintain the defence owing to the crippling losses of the convoys and the difficulty in providing escorts. And the situation actually became worse after his arrival owing to the British defeat in North Africa and the retreat to El Alamein, which stripped an additional section of the Mediterranean of air cover. In June terrible losses in both naval and merchant ships were inflicted on convoys sailing simultaneously from Alexandria and Gibraltar, and the former was forced to turn back. The difficulties were increased by the fact that even when ships reached the island they were liable to be sunk in port before their supplies could be unloaded, though those which sailed back singly to Gibraltar were surprisingly successful in getting through. The Americans were now taking a hand, and their part in the defence of the island should never be forgotten. They supplied merchant shipping, including the tanker *Ohio*, which limped into harbour after being twice torpedoed in the great convoy actions of August, when Vice-Admiral E. N. Syfret, took the biggest of all the convoys from Gibraltar.

It was the arrival of the survivors of this convoy combined with the flying in of Spitfires from aircraft carriers—here again the Americans helped, using their carrier *Wasp* for the purpose—that saved Malta. After the victory of Alamein and the advance of the Eighth Army along the North African coast her ordeal virtually came to an end. Henceforward it was as an offensive outpost, for both warships and aircraft, that she was to serve. And before the year 1943 was out her dockyard was once again performing invaluable work. With the end of the land campaign in North Africa the Mediterranean was fully reopened, and the surrender of the Italian fleet made its main waters an allied lake. Henceforth the only anxiety of the naval forces and coastal air forces was an occasional raider in the air and a few submarines, no large proportion of which ever got home.

In outlining events in the Atlantic and Mediterranean the main sections have been briefly described in chapters entirely devoted to "the war at sea". With the Pacific war it does not seem desirable to proceed in this manner because to an even larger extent the naval operations were part and parcel of unified campaigns. They will therefore be described—so far as there is space for description in this narrative—in their place in the record of the general operations in the Pacific. But it is fitting to examine here the Battles of the Coral Sea and Midway because they were the heralds of a new type of naval warfare.

On May 4th, 1942, a task force of the United States Pacific Fleet, commanded by Rear-Admiral F. J. Fletcher, with two carriers, discovered by air reconnaissance that part of the Japanese transport fleet engaged in landing troops in the Solomons and its naval escort was anchored off Tulagi, Florida island. Flying over the mountainous island, the American naval aircraft caught the Japanese unready and practically annihilated them. On the

7th Fletcher caught the main transport fleet and escort in the Louisiades. The Americans first concentrated on the aircraft carrier *Shoho* and sank her. They themselves lost the aircraft carrier *Lexington*, with a great many aircraft, but the balance was heavily in their favour. The chief interest of this battle, however, is that, so far as is known, not a shot was fired by a surface ship on either side. This was something altogether new.

The second battle, that of Midway, was on a larger scale and more important, but of a similar type. Late on June 3rd, a powerful Japanese force was observed steering eastward in the direction of Midway, from which it was then about 700 miles distant. Flying Fortresses on the island, with the longest range, made the first attacks, which were followed on the 4th by assaults delivered by Army and Marine bombers, dive-bombers, and torpedo-aircraft. The Japanese in turn attacked the installations on Midway. Both sides lost heavily in aircraft, but the real battle was still to come.

Admiral Chester Nimitz, the American naval Commander-in-Chief, had had warning through a deciphered message of the Japanese move against Midway. The Pacific Fleet at full strength had gone to intercept the enemy with the only three carriers available, and its carrier-borne aircraft now entered the battle. The sole survivor of a flight of 15 torpedo-aircraft, all shot down by the enemy, saw two blazing aircraft-carriers sail past his dinghy while aircraft circled about them unable to land on their decks. The American aircraft-carrier *Yorktown* afterwards sank while in tow. Fighting continued on the 6th, and by the time touch with the flying enemy was lost the Americans claimed to have sunk four aircraft-carriers, two cruisers, and three destroyers. This estimate may have been exaggerated, but in any case the loss was crippling, and there is no doubt about the carriers, all the enemy had. And once again no shot was fired by a surface ship, and the fleets can seldom have been less than a hundred miles apart. Henceforth to the Americans the aircraft-carrier, not the battleship, was the vital unit of the fleet. The Battle of Midway was not only a turning-point of the struggle between Japan and the United States in the central Pacific; it also ushered in a new era of naval warfare. And this new era began with the Japanese grievously handicapped by the five carriers lost in the Coral Sea and off Midway.

CHAPTER XXIII

Development of the War in the Air

AT an earlier stage of this record, in Chapter XI, an indication has been given of the development of British air policy. The main feature of its offensive side was to strike at German industry by means of long-range night bombers carrying a heavy bomb-load. What were considered heavy night bombers at the beginning of the war soon became obsolete. They were replaced by several new types, but the best was the Lancaster, which gradually became the standard. By the latter part of the year 1942 the attacks had become heavy and persistent.

The Germans built up a strong system of defence. Their anti-aircraft artillery was plentiful and efficient. They also established fleets of night fighters, and against these the British bombers had relatively little defence except that of evasion. The British losses varied in accordance with the degree of skill or good fortune with which they kept the enemy in doubt about their destination, the vagaries of the weather, and other factors; but they were generally serious and sometimes heavy when distant or particularly vital targets were engaged. To take a period more or less at random, on the nights of January 1st and 2nd, 1944, 55 bombers were lost, on that of January 21st, 52, on January 28th, 45, on January 30th, 33. And these losses were due to the action of the enemy. Those brought about by crashes on landing and such-like causes were not announced, and there were times when these equalled the casualties caused by hostile action.

The latter part of 1942, in which British night attacks on Germany increased, witnessed the first serious attacks by day carried out by the Americans. The American technique, tactics, and equipment were quite different. The Flying Fortresses and Liberators carried small bomb-loads by comparison with the Lancasters, but they were much faster and more heavily armed, with about ten heavy, large-calibre machine guns. Equipped with a particularly good bomb-sight, their object was said to be "precision" bombing, and in this respect they did on some occasions remarkably accurate work. It must be added, however, that there were other occasions, according to French and later German evidence, when the night bombing of the R.A.F. Lancasters proved more accurate than the day-bombing of the U.S. Army Air Force Fortresses.

When they began their offensive the Americans had no dread of the German fighters. A single Fortress could shoot fighter after fighter out of the air with bursts of fire from the heavy machine-guns, while the enemy could not close the range sufficiently to bring his multiple medium machine guns seriously into action. It became one of the most important objects of the command to draw the maximum number of German fighters up, with the objects of inflicting on them losses which the enemy could not afford. As German tactics improved and the fighters were to a larger extent armed with cannon, the balance swung over. American losses mounted rapidly and became almost too heavy to be borne. Then there came another swing. The Americans brought into action long-range fighters which could accompany the bombers to their targets, so that once again these could perform their tasks at a reasonable cost.

The British put Berlin into a special category as a target. Not only was it the centre of government; it was also a great area of processing and finishing industries, of the highest importance to the German war effort. Disregarding the earliest attacks on the capital, which had no more than a symbolical significance, it may be said that in the first phase the R.A.F. sought out special targets. It was soon discovered, however, that the bombing was too inaccurate to produce the intended results. At the same time it was realized that, in view of the very heavy losses suffered, it would be necessary in the first place to approach Berlin by devious routes and to use every artifice to draw the night fighters off the path followed by the bombers, and in the second place to choose dark and overcast nights for the attacks, whereas clear, moonlit nights had at first appeared desirable. In these circumstances the only bombing policy could be to shovel out the greatest possible weight of bombs centrally and more or less trust to luck for the targets. And in fact it was found that far more damage was done by this means than by seeking particular targets.

But this policy was, without a shadow of doubt, that of "area" bombing pure and simple, the very method which had been reprobated by British spokesmen earlier in the war. We had accused the enemy of using such methods and stated that we did not countenance them.   Area bombing was directed against the civil populations in order to terrify them, to destroy their dwelling-houses, their supplies of heat, light, and water. Damage of this sort, it was considered, would do as much to hinder production as direct hits on factories and could be done more easily and with smaller loss.   This does not mean that attacks on special targets such as large plants and centres of communication, were abandoned: that was far from being the case.   But the policy of area bombing developed greatly, and when the Allies decided not to invade Europe from the west in 1943 but to develop a tremendous air offensive against Germany until they were ready to invade the following year, this method was accorded a high place in their programme.

There were but few who, in Parliament and in the press, ventured to criticize this form of strategy on the grounds of humanity or even on those of efficacy.   Neither editors nor writers cared to feel that they were fouling their own nest and providing propaganda for the enemy—and be sure that whenever an English-speaking German broadcaster quoted critics of the bombing policy there were not wanting kind friends at the Air Ministry ready to forward extracts and to point out that the enemy was of the same mind as the critics.   A few journalists even suffered what almost amounted to persecution.

The apologists for area bombing had a relatively easy task to prove that the policy produced valuable results.   These were, in fact, enormous.   It was much less easy for opponents to prove that they were not as valuable in proportion to the expenditure of material, man-power, and some of the best young blood in the country, as those of other methods might have been.   On the purely theoretical side there was little to be said.   The advocates of heavy area bombing to terrorize and smash the enemy to surrender had little against them because Germany was so deeply engaged against Russia and was obliged to employ so huge a proportion of her total resources in fighting Russia, that she had not enough for a retaliation in the bombing war.   This was fortunate for the United Kingdom, where population and industry were more crowded than in Germany and which could be assailed from airfields much closer to their target than those from which allied aircraft attacked Germany.

When the effects of the campaigns in Russia began to curtail the efforts of the *Luftwaffe* and to give the western allies the initiative against Germany the opportunity for alternative forms of action appeared. But by this time the advocates of strategic bombing were well entrenched. They had refused to be interrupted to any serious extent in their bombing of German towns by what they regarded as side issues. The efforts made, for example, to interfere with the building of submarine pens, which constituted one of the most deadly of all menaces to the Atlantic life-lines, were virtually nil, despite the importance of the target and its direct interest to themselves, if only they had possessed the brains to realize it. The Admiralty published successive photographs in its intelligence summary in the hope of stirring Whitehall to action, but to no effect. The pens were made impregnable while bombing of Germany went on. To some extent the same may be said of the installations for the bombardment of England by flying and rocket bombs, V.1's and V.2's. Admittedly useful work was accomplished in interrupting the building of these projectile sites and in severing communications to them and from the shelters where the projectiles were stored; but it is impossible to resist the conclusion that more could have been done.

Among those who challenged the policy of the Government was the Bishop of Chichester. Speaking in the House of Lords on February 9th, 1944, he declared that so far half Berlin was believed to have been destroyed, area by area, the residential quarters as much as the industrial. It was reported that 74,000 people had already been killed and that 3,000,000 were homeless. "The policy is obliteration, openly acknowledged." Lord Lang of Lambeth, a former Archbishop of Canterbury, speaking in the same debate, condemned the grisly note of jubilation on which these events were reported. "It is one thing to accept the destruction of military objectives and their immediate neighbourhood as a regrettable military necessity; it is quite another to exult in it."

The writer of this record, in an article in *The Illustrated London News* of March 11th, 1944, entitled "The Two Bishops"—it was a commentary on the speech of the Bishop of Chichester and a retort subsequently made by the Bishop of Fulham—put forward certain considerations in a manner as dispassionate as he could contrive to make it. He began by saying that there had been no official definition of the phrase "military objective", but that it had undoubtedly come to mean, first, factories, etc., secondly the power stations, and thirdly the dwellings of those who worked in both. He described a published diagram in which this was illustrated. "But," he went on, "it is necessarily over-simplified. There are few towns in the world such as those described, hardly any which do not contain large elements of population other than 'workers'. Logically, too, why should there not be a still more distant block of buildings on the coast, labelled 'holiday boarding-houses for workers', and another entitled 'workers' hospital, convalescent home, and nursery school'?"

All this, he wrote, was symptomatic of total war. "Once the nation begins to put all its efforts and its production to the maintenance of war, there appears a tendency to attack all the means of production, including the producers." The methods of to-day, he argued, marked a retrogression from those of the eighteenth and nineteenth centuries, and the recklessness of the age had to some extent wiped out the instinctive biological considerations which in the past had often prompted attempts to spare the lives of women. In short, he took the view that the authors of the area-bombing policy were actuated by forces and tendencies which turned them into mere instruments of fate, wielding a terrible instrument, the true significance of which their own intelligence was incapable of understanding.

Turning to the practical side, he pointed out that, according to the recent speech of the Secretary of State for War on the Army Estimates, the labour devoted to production of heavy bombers alone was believed to be equal to that allotted to the production of the whole equipment of the Army; as a result the Army had been prevented from expanding or had often had to take the second best because the best had been taken by the R.A.F. Again, he said, the losses in manpower were far more serious than mere figures revealed. "The men who are being lost over Germany would have provided the finest leadership in any service during the war, and . . . would have made very fine national leaders after the war." He hinted that results based on photographs were often exaggerated, as had been proved in our own country.

And he asked his readers to consider not only the prospects of victory through area bombing but also the kind of victory it was likely to bring and the influence of the policy on the nation at large.

Perhaps the most effective comment which can be made in

brief space upon the whole policy of bombing is that those who controlled it were not sufficiently controlled themselves. For too long they had more or less their own way, laid down their own policy, fought their own private war in a vacuum. They gave so little thought to any instrument of war other than their own that, though they depended upon the Navy for every drop of the huge quantities of fuel which they used in their operations, they begrudged any air resources transferred to the Navy. Yet in early 1942 the situation was truly desperate and supplies of oil as well as of crated aircraft were seriously interrupted. It was a policy in blinkers, for which the main responsibility must, of course, rest upon the shoulders of the Government as a whole.

One of the outstanding successes of area bombing, which may be freely admitted, was its effect upon German bomber production by the diversion to night-fighter production. By the autumn of 1944 the enemy's bomber strength had dropped to 800, whereas his night-fighter strength had risen to about the same figure; but since he was using his bombers little and losing far more night fighters, this represented a greater shift to night fighter production than the figures would imply. The sinking of the *Tirpitz* near Trömso on November 12th, 1944, was an outstanding triumph of the heavy bombers. The successful attacks on the *Admiral Scheer*, *Lutzow* and *Admiral Hipper* hardly come into the same category, because at that time the war with Germany was virtually over, but they were fine achievements.

The Germans made only one serious attempt to renew the night attacks on Britain, which they had brought to an end before launching their offensive against Russia in the summer of 1941. This was carried out in the winter of 1943–44, chiefly by fighter-bombers, and was directed mainly against London. Between 25 and 175 aircraft were commonly employed, with an average of about 70. The heaviest attacks were those of February, 1944, in which month the civilian casualty list amounted to 2,673, as compared with well over 6,000 in each of the months of September and October, 1941. It was noted that nerves did not seem to be quite as good as during the earlier and heavier attacks. On the other hand, there was now no serious dislocation such as had occurred in the winter of 1940–41, when on several occasions whole districts of London had been rendered difficult of access for several hours, even to people on foot, owing to the blocking of streets.

There is less to be said about the air war in the Pacific because its nature emerges more clearly from a narrative of the operations in general. There it scored its most spectacular triumphs. The destruction of Japan's naval forces and merchant fleet was effected mainly from the air, either by aircraft flown from carriers or by bombers from the land bases which the Americans secured with so sure a strategic eye. In Burma, in a campaign fought in front of indifferent land communications, the bold and skilful use of air transport for supply and for the movement of whole divisions made possible a victory which would have been altogether out of the question without such aid.

Great as were the distances in the European theatre, they were far greater in the Pacific. For this war the Americans evolved a more mighty and longer-range Flying Fortress, which was not required for use against Germany. The problem of area bombing did not arise in the eastern war until the Americans had closed in upon Japan and secured land bases close to her islands and the large cities of the south. Then, as will appear, the bombing of these cities was conducted as ruthlessly as that of the cities of Germany, the main difference being that the Japanese ordeal was much briefer and that almost all the attacks were carried out, according to the American practice, by day. A special significance attaches, and will do so as long as humanity endures, to the war against Japan owing to the fact that this war witnessed the first employment of the most deadly weapon ever conceived, the atomic bomb.

The outstanding feature of the final stages of the war in the air was the plenitude of the allied resources. Production became so great that there was enough for all purposes. The old controversies about the allotment of air power to the armies and navies ceased because the allied production was so vastly superior to that of the enemy that it was possible to find aircraft for every sort of task. The armies had their great tactical air forces; the artillery was permitted its own miniature air force—that of the British being known as the Air Observation Post—for fire control; fleets of gliders were available for airborne forces; fleets of transport aircraft were provided for the movement of troops and supplies; regular passenger services were created on a lavish scale; the naval forces no longer lacked modern dive-bombers or torpedo-carriers. It would be a grave error, however, to allow a complacent picture of this state of affairs to blot out that of earlier days when the British Army was constantly defeated and the Navy came near to losing its vital battle with the U-boat by reason of their starvation from the point of view of air support. The lessons of the earlier period of the war are not less important, perhaps even more important, than those of the triumphant conclusion. They inculcate above all the need for the combination of all weapons, a combination which can be achieved only by combined thought.

The German attack on Great Britain with long-range weapons can most conveniently be recorded under the category of air warfare because the means of defence against them were the air arm and anti-aircraft ground weapons until the best and only decisive measure of defence, the capture of their sites, was achieved by the allied armies of invasion. About a year before their exploitation in the summer of 1944 information had reached the British Government from neutral sources that the enemy was preparing weapons of long-range bombardment. The first discovered and the first used was a jet-propelled "pilotless plane" or "flying bomb". The second was a gigantic rocket-bomb. The former came to be known as the V.1, the latter as the V.2.

Both sides had for long been experimenting in jet propulsion. The Germans were slightly ahead in the race and their first jet-propelled aircraft came into action a little earlier than those of the British, but their productive capacity was not now great enough to render the menace serious. By far the greatest danger in the realm of jet-propulsion came from the V.1, which had a bursting charge of over 2,000 pounds.

On August 17th, 1943, a powerful air attack on Peenemünde, the experimental centre for the V.1, is believed to have accounted for a number of scientific experts and checked the development of the weapon. Attacks on installations on the French coast by bombers began in December, 1943. It has been suggested that they might have been heavier, but they delayed the preparations for the attack, which began on June 13th, 1944, almost simultaneously with the allied invasion. It was maintained until the launching sites were over-run in September. London was the chief target, and perhaps owing to a slight tendency of the bombs to fall short, its southern suburbs suffered particularly. The destruction of housing was immense. Considerable depression became noticeable; there was absenteeism in factories and a sharp drop in output.

At the beginning the artillery of Anti-Aircraft Command was widely dispersed, covering ports from which the invasion was to be launched. General Sir Frederick Pile, the Commander-in-Chief, reorganized it with promptitude and skill. The bulk of that stationed in and immediately round London and the anti-aircraft balloons were moved outwards, since there was no object in bringing down bombs on London. Special zones were allotted to artillery and to fighter aircraft, of which one new type, the Tempest, proved highly successful in shooting down the V.1s. Pilots showed great courage in dealing at close quarters with these deadly missiles. The percentage of bombs shot down to those launched increased rapidly as airmen and gunners gained experience.

The bombardment by the V.2 started later but continued longer. Owing to the superior range of this weapon it could be fired not only from France but also from sites in Holland which were not reached by allied land forces until the final surrender of the enemy. England, however, did not have to wait quite so long to be rid of the pest, since for technical reasons it could no longer be employed after its communications with the Ruhr had been cut in March, 1944.

The damage done was serious in its immediate repercussions and great enough to exercise an important adverse effect upon the whole problem of post-war rehabilitation in south-east England. Yet it was small by comparison with what had been escaped. The Germans had intended to make the bombardment from both these weapons several times as heavy as it ever in fact became. They were preparing others, and they were also at work upon the method of nuclear fission which produced the atomic bomb used by the United States against Japan. There is cause to suppose that, with only a little more time at their disposal, they could at the least have rendered London uninhabitable; they might also, even without stopping the invasion, have put its communications and supplies into the gravest peril. So, just when they were obviously on the eve of complete victory with the aid of established weapons, the Western Allies, and Britain in particular, narrowly contrived to escape a hideous danger from artifices of a new kind.

CHAPTER XXIV

Invasion from the West

THE title given to the plan for the invasion of the European Continent from the west, Operation Overlord, possessed a special significance. It was the over-riding operation. Whereas the planning of successive operations in Tunisia, Sicily and Italy had been conducted by the same staffs—though there were also special planning sections—and these staffs were engaged in preparing for the next phase while conducting the fighting in its predecessor, commanders and staffs concerned with Overlord were withdrawn from the battle and given nearly half a year for preparation. General Eisenhower left the Mediterranean at the beginning of 1944 to become Supreme Commander, with the British Air Chief Marshal Tedder as Deputy. General Montgomery returned to command the British 21st Army Group. General Sir H. M. Wilson, until then Commander-in-Chief in the Middle East, succeeded General Eisenhower in the Mediterranean command. A conference held at Teheran and attended by Mr. Churchill, President Roosevelt, and Marshal Stalin, discussed the plans and announced, slightly optimistically as it was to prove, that it had "reached complete agreement as to the scope and timing of the operations which will be undertaken from the east, west, and south". Certain troops, among them the famous British 7th Armoured Division, were brought home from Italy to train for the invasion.

The preparations were the most elaborate in the history of warfare. They involved the whole economic life of Britain, since a great proportion of her shipping had to be withdrawn from commercial use and stocks had consequently to be accumulated to cover the deficiency thus created. Numbers of camps were established, the British in the maritime counties from Norfolk to Hampshire, the Americans thence to Cornwall and South Wales. Special arrangements were made for "sealing" these camps from the outside world. Under General Eisenhower two British naval and air commanders-in-chief were appointed, Admiral Sir

Bertram Ramsay for the Allied Naval Expeditionary Force and Air Chief Marshal Sir Trafford Leigh-Mallory for the Allied Expeditionary Air Force. There was no parallel appointment of commander-in-chief of the land forces, but General Montgomery was appointed to act in that capacity for the assault period, it being General Eisenhower's intention to take over command of the land forces himself when open warfare developed and that at the same time the American army group commander, General Omar Bradley, should become independent of Montgomery.

The Germans also had a supreme commander, Field-Marshal von Rundstedt, whose title was that of "Commander-in-Chief West". Under him were all the land, naval, and air forces in France and the Low Countries. The northern and larger army group was commanded by Field-Marshal Rommel, Montgomery's old opponent. At the date of invasion the divisions in Rundstedt's command numbered 60, approximately one quarter of the German field divisions. The coast defences were strong, and particular attention had been given to the defence of ports, on the theory that, should an invader fail to secure a port at an early stage, he could neither land his heaviest equipment nor organize his services of supply. This form of defence was countered by the provision by the Allies of material for two artificial harbours, to which were given the code-word "Mulberry", a brilliant conception which upset German calculations. In the preliminary stages the Allies possessed 37 divisions, including airborne, and a number of brigades which amounted in effect to several more. They could eventually count upon being reinforced by another army group which was to land in the South of France in August— it would have landed earlier if landing craft had been available. Many more American divisions would across the Atlantic, and the British were to scrape together a few more.

The fact remained, however, that the original landings were to be carried out on a total frontage of only five divisions, plus three airborne, and that the "build-up" was strictly limited in speed. (Had it not been for Montgomery and the support he obtained from Eisenhower, the frontage of assault would have been one of three divisions only and the whole venture would probably have failed. Everything therefore depended upon a correct appreciation of the speed at which the enemy could concentrate and upon the efficiency of the measures taken to delay his concentration.

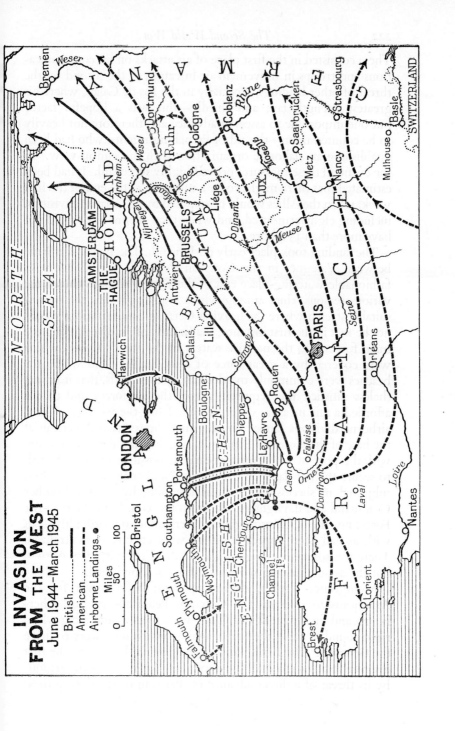

INVASION
FROM THE WEST
June 1944-March 1945

British
American
Airborne Landings.●

Miles
0   50   100

N O R T H   S E A

ENGLAND

LONDON
Bristol
Southampton
Portsmouth
Weymouth
Plymouth
Falmouth

E-N-G-L-I-S-H   C-H-A-N-N-E-L

Harwich
Calais
Boulogne
Dieppe
Le Havre
Rouen
Caen
Falaise
Orne
Domfront
Cherbourg
Channel Is.
Brest
Lorient
Laval
Nantes
Orléans
Loire

F R A N C E

PARIS
Seine

Lille
Somme

BELGIUM
Antwerp
BRUSSELS
Dinant
Liège
Meuse
LUX

HOLLAND
AMSTERDAM
THE HAGUE
Nijmegen
Arnhem
Maas
Roer
Wesel
Ruhr
Dortmund
Cologne
Coblenz
Rhine
Saarbrücken
Moselle
Metz
Nancy
Strasbourg
Mulhouse
Basle
SWITZERLAND

G E R M A N Y

Bremen
Weser

These consisted in the first place of air attacks on his communications and troops in movement or in camp; in the second on the threat of other landings, especially in the Pas de Calais, where his greatest strength lay; and thirdly—this was a hopeful factor but one impossible to assess in advance and therefore not heavily to be counted upon—the aid of French insurgents, who had been establishing an elaborate organization with this end in view. In the event all these measures proved highly successful. It had been estimated that there might come a moment, at the end of the first week, when the Allies would be opposed by 20 German divisions, including eight armoured, and when they themselves would not have more than 15 ashore.

The landing took place early on June 6th. The Bay of the Seine between Valognes in the Cotentin Peninsula and Cabourg, a fashionable watering-place east of the Orne, had been chosen for various reasons, chief among which was that it was the nearest suitable stretch where the heaviest German concentrations would not be met in the first instance, that it did not involve sending the main forces into the narrow waters of the Pas de Calais, which were covered by a great force of coast artillery and where the beaches were commonly overlooked by high cliffs, that it nevertheless satisfied the requirements of the air forces, and that it afforded a fair measure of protection from the weather. Three airborne divisions landed in the small hours, two American at the base of the Cotentin Peninsula, which it was desired to secure with the port of Cherbourg as early as possible, and one British to secure the left flank on the Orne. Neither the coast batteries, subjected in succession to night bombing by British Bomber Command and daylight attacks from the U.S. Eighth Army Air Force, nor the defences in general were quite so thoroughly dealt with as had been hoped, but they were effectively neutralized. There was some heavy fighting and a disquieting incident or two, but the assault landing was successfully accomplished.

Montgomery's plan, drawn up long before, was for the Americans to overrun the Cotentin Peninsula, capture Cherbourg, and finally break out. They were to carry out a big wheel right round towards the Seine, against which they were to drive the Germans. The British army group on the left was in the first instance to attract to itself the maximum weight in hostile armour by its threat of a direct advance on Paris, in order to keep these forces from interfering with the American operation. It was then itself to wheel round on the hinge of the Orne and advance on the Seine in co-operation with the Americans.

In the course of the first week the allied holdings were linked into a single one 50 miles long with a maximum depth of 12 miles. The accumulation of supplies and material was, however, getting behind schedule as the result of stormy weather, which delayed landings. For a brief period only a limited offensive could be attempted, the primary objectives of which were Cherbourg and Caen. The Americans cut across the Cotentin Peninsula, reaching the west coast on June 18th. The British, outflanking Caen, thrust out to Villers Bocage, but were compelled to withdraw from it. On June 25th the Americans entered Cherbourg, but the port had been blocked and demolished with exceptional thoroughness, and it was about two months before it could take heavy lifts alongside berths. Meanwhile the British carried out a deep thrust southward some six miles west of Caen and secured a bridgehead over the Odon. By the 30th they were engaging no less than seven Panzer divisions, two-thirds of the German armoured strength in the theatre, and since these had been committed to the defensive the prospect of driving the Allies out of France, which could be effected only by a major armoured counter-offensive, were rapidly receding, if not already gone.

Still, Montgomery had some troubles also. He had originally hoped to make his break-out by July 3rd. The American commander, Bradley, had to obtain a good starting line before he could strike, and this meant that he had to push well south of the flooded, marshy country at the base of the Cotentin Peninsula. He was not ready until the 25th. In the interval the British kept up the pressure. After beating off a succession of extremely fierce though not simultaneous assaults by S.S. divisions, which were largely smashed by artillery concentrations, they captured Caen on July 9th and in the following days somewhat extended their bridgehead over the Odon. East of Caen a great attack was launched on July 18th after one of the heaviest air bombardments ever attempted, carried out by 1,100 bombers of Bomber Command—the night-bombers of old days now able to operate in daylight owing to German inferiority in the air—600 heavy and 400 medium American bombers. The main attack was carried out by three armoured divisions. They made very good progress at first, but were held up with heavy losses after an advance of between five and six miles. This was disappointing, but useful ground had been secured for the break-out.

It is fitting to mention at this stage an astounding event which occurred on July 20th, an attempt to kill Hitler by a bomb at his headquarters. It came near to success, and there is evidence that he was never quite the same man afterwards. It was followed by a drastic purge, though it is certain that the authorities never discovered all the ramifications of the plot. It was significant of the growing belief among the German militarists that the country was being led to perdition by a madman. Yet it does not seem to have exerted any serious effect upon the fighting in France or upon the quality of German resistance in general.

The American break-out began on June 25th. Five days later Avranches, the gateway to Brittany, was attained. General Patton, the Third Army commander, then according to plan ordered one of his corps to drive into Brittany. Here the German garrison was cut to pieces, and the Americans pushed rapidly westward towards Brest. The wheeling wing of the Third Army reached Laval and the First Army Domfront. On August 7th the Canadian First Army launched a strong attack southward towards Falaise.

Then for the first time, when there were already some 35 allied divisions in France, the enemy launched a major counter-offensive, as opposed to the countless local counter-attacks carried out all through. With the better part of five armoured divisions he struck west with the objects of reaching the sea and cutting off all American forces south of Avranches. He gained some early success, but the Americans, well supported by the tactical air forces, stood their ground. The allied command acted quickly, the first decision being apparently taken by Montgomery. He had always been hoping to catch the enemy in a pocket on the Seine; now, however, he saw a heaven-sent opportunity of catching him in a pocket west of Falaise-Argentan. He ordered the Americans to swing north towards Falaise. Very fierce fighting took place before the pocket was closed, and a proportion of the Germans got out. But the losses from bombing and artillery fire were enormous.

While this battle was being fought out the Americans did not cease to press on towards the Seine, which they reached near

Mantes on August 19th. British and American troops destroyed or captured all the German forces remaining in the "Falaise pocket". Then the British also raced towards the Seine. About 40 of the German divisions had been cut up, including some virtually destroyed. Some 10,000 vehicles, including 1,500 tanks had been left on the battlefield. The enemy must have suffered not far short of half a million casualties. And yet 30,000 vehicles got away across the river. Had a complete block been established by the air forces on the Seine, the war would have been nearly over.

To many observers it appeared that the end was near when the Allies swept over the Seine in a flood. On the right the Americans reached the Moselle by September 7th. Liége was captured on the 8th. The British armour dashed over the Somme, reaching Brussels on the 3rd and Antwerp on the 4th. The great port was intact, but of no value while the Germans held the approaches from the sea. On August 15th a new expeditionary force from Italy, of a total strength of three American and seven French divisions, supported by ten groups of fighter and fighter-bombers and naval aircraft from nine aircraft carriers, began landing west of Cannes. Resistance, after a very heavy naval bombardment, in which six allied battleships or monitors took part, was light by comparison with that encountered in the north, so that the "build-up" was rapid and a whole Franco-American army group was soon ashore. The Germans retreated at top speed up the Rhône valley. They lost heavily in prisoners, but their main body escaped to join the armies retreating towards the frontier farther north. The Germans in the south-west also fled, harried by the French resistance forces and in many cases intercepted by the Americans. By early September the enemy had lost nearly a quarter of a million prisoners.

On September 1st Montgomery ceased to act as Eisenhower's land commander and Eisenhower assumed direct command of all the land forces, to which were shortly afterwards added the army group from the south. From now onwards operations were conducted in accordance with American doctrine, an advance on a broad front, probing for weakness, rather than the concentration on a narrow front for a thrust of overwhelming strength favoured by Montgomery. It must always remain a matter of speculation whether or not the results would have been more favourable had the advance been conducted on Montgomery's lines. He himself was promoted to the rank of field-marshal.

By the time the heads of the allied armies reached the Moselle and the Maas the administrative machine, despite all efforts, was beginning to run down. Probably in such circumstances it would have been the soundest course to open the deep-water port of Antwerp as the next step. It was, however, decided to make one more effort to leap the barriers of the rivers, the Maas, Waal and Lower Rhine, with the aid of two American airborne divisions and one British. Bad weather and the speed of the enemy's concentration prevented a full success. The crossings of the Maas and Waal were secured, but that of the Lower Rhine at Arnhem had to be abandoned after a heroic fight.

The next step was then inevitably the opening of Antwerp. Meanwhile the majority of the ports in which the Germans had dropped garrisons had been captured. On the capture of Boulogne a petrol pipe-line was laid to it. The clearance of the West Scheldt estuary by troops under the orders of the Canadian First Army, which involved the capture of the island of Walcheren and a whole series of complicated and often bloody combined operations, was not completed until the first week of November.

Even the opening of this port and the restoration of the main railways, involving the erection of hundreds of bridges, did not compensate for the coming of winter and the opportunity for recovery which had been afforded the enemy. The Americans found the German frontier defences, the Siegfried Line, formidable, but the mud almost more so, and their losses were heavy. By early December, however, the Rhine had been reached by the French at Mulhouse. The Americans were on it at Strasbourg, were pressing into the Saar, and stood beyond the Our. The British were in general lining the Maas. General Eisenhower was looking forward to forcing the passage of the Rhine as soon as there was an improvement in the weather.

The Allies were to endure some evil moments before this took place. The dispersion of the attacks, which relieved the enemy of anxiety about a dense concentration, a certain lack of balance in the dispositions, and the muddy state of the ground, which enabled defence to be carried out with a relatively small number of troops, afforded Rundstedt, the German commander-in-chief, an opportunity which he was not the man to neglect. He had drawn a proportion of his troops into reserve, refitted eight armoured divisions, and received some accretions from the eastern front. He had assembled two Panzer armies, largely equipped with Panther and Tiger tanks straight from the factories. He had even concentrated the first powerful air striking force which the Germans had been able to muster for months, and this was launched in the early hours of December 16th in heavy and effective attacks on allied airfields. The Germans had not the resources to maintain an air offensive; in fact, they counted on thick weather to limit air operations to a minimum, and in this respect their hopes were fulfilled in the early stages.

The blow struck that morning was delivered against the thinnest sector of the American front, between Echternach and Monschau. The enemy's object in the realm of higher strategy was to strike the Allies with such force that they would not readily recover, so that he himself could take advantage of the respite to move troops across to the eastern front. The direct object was to cross the Meuse above Liége and perhaps as far up as Givet, capture and destroy the allied stores accumulated for the offensive, especially in the Liége area, and exploit in the direction of Brussels, even to Antwerp if possible. Complete success would have brought about a very damaging situation for the Allies, since their forces north of the zone of the enemy's thrust would have been cut off from the rest, with their supply routes severed; but to risk the last good army which the Germans could ever hope to raise in the west in an all-out offensive without air superiority was a terrible gamble. It can only be supposed that it was on the one hand the refusal of Hitler to recognize facts and on the other the desire to gain time for the exploitation of further secret weapons which led to its being undertaken.

The enemy advanced deep into the Ardennes in the general direction of Dinant, though not at the speed of his earlier offensives, perhaps in part because the tanks on which he chiefly relied were slower than those previously employed. The maximum advance was over 50 miles, but he was defeated by the speed with which allied reinforcements moved on to the flanks of his array, by fine weather after Christmas which gave their air forces full opportunity to pound his transport and troops against the background of snow, and by the stout resistance of the American troops, especially perhaps round the road junction of

Bastogne. When the Allies struck back he began to pull out of the salient. He did this cleverly, covering the retreat by stout rear guards, and though he lost a large number of men and much material, did not at any time stand in danger of being cut off. The withdrawal being over, Rundstedt at once sent his Sixth Panzer S.S. Army to the east, and it next appeared in Hungary.

It is estimated that the delay imposed upon the Allies by the Ardennes offensive was one of six weeks. On the other hand, it is not to be doubted that the Germans had weakened their own strength proportionately more than that of the Americans and British. Had there ever been the smallest doubt about the ultimate issue, that had now been settled.

CHAPTER XXV

Invasion from the East

SUMMER was of course the main campaigning season in Russia, but winter also witnessed large-scale and swift-moving fighting, while the rains and early snows of autumn did not create insuperable obstacles to mobility. But the fourth season was barren. The spring thaw made major offensives impossible, and in this respect the spring of 1944 followed the precedent of those of 1942 and 1943 by bringing with it a lull while snows melted, rivers became swollen and in many cases overflowed their banks, and roads turned to quagmires. But in April, 1944, there was one sector outside the main continental conditions where operations were still possible. The Russians could recover the Crimea, in which they had for some time possessed a footing at Kerch. On April 11th they broke in through the Perekop Isthmus, and a few days later their armies from Kerch and Perekop joined hands. They announced the capture of 30,000 prisoners in this lightning campaign. Sevastopol held out until May 9th.

On June 10th, just after the invasion of Normandy, the northern armies turned on the Finns. The improvement in their tactics and armament since the early days of the Second World War was made manifest when they broke the Mannerheim Line by a single blow. This offensive was acclaimed with some irony in the west, where something bigger and more significant had been hoped for. The Russians confided in no one, but they were in fact preparing a more important venture about which there could be no crtiicism, and it may well be that they opened it at the earliest possible moment having regard to the vast amount of work they must have been putting into their communications. This was carried out in White Russia. Vitebsk surrendered on June 17th, and there followed a swift advance on Minsk from north-west and south-east. The Germans retreated hastily, but not always fast enough, and a considerable number of prisoners were captured here, some of them being trapped well east of the town when the Russians closed upon it on July 6th.

In Poland Lublin, Bialystok, Lvov and Brest Litovsk were captured, and the advance on Warsaw continued. It was hoped that the Russians would continue their drive across the Vistula and take the Polish capital in their stride in early August. On this occasion, however, there was to be a check, followed by a ghastly tragedy which created international bitterness. As the Russians under Marshal Rokossovsky approached Warsaw the organized Polish "Underground Movement" rose in revolt against the Germans. With the aid of surprise they gained possession of the greater part of the city. The Germans struck at Rokossovsky and drove him back from the immediate neighbourhood of the place, though only a few miles.

Finding that the Russians had halted, the Germans turned upon the Polish forces in the city. Weeks of fierce fighting in the streets followed. The Poles were short of arms. Polish airmen of the R.A.F. attempted to supply them. It would have been a difficult but by no means impracticable task had the Russians afforded them landing grounds where they could refuel between their outward and homeward flights, but this boon was refused. Ammunition was particularly short and the lack of food soon became equally serious. In these circumstances there could be but one end to the struggle, and the Polish patriots finally surrendered.

The tragedy was complicated by its political background. Russia had broken off relations with the exiled Polish Government in London, which refused to acknowledge Soviet claims to the territory seized by the Red Army in 1939 in collaboration with Germany. The Polish Underground Movement professed allegiance to this government, with which it was in close touch. Poles in the United Kingdom, and many of their British friends also, either hinted or announced publicly their belief that the Red Army had stood by and watched with satisfaction the slaughter and capture of elements which might have proved troublesome to it when it set about organizing as Soviet territory the belt of Poland which it had recovered or was in process of recovering. It seems most improbable that this was in fact the case or that Rokossovsky, himself of Polish blood, deliberately halted in order to let the Germans wreak their fury upon the Poles. It is, in fact, known that the enemy had concentrated considerable armoured strength on the Vistula in the region of Warsaw, as had been his practice on several previous occasions when the pace of his retreat was becoming disastrous and he felt that he must call at least a temporary halt.

Yet the Russians had certainly made no sacrifices in aid of the Poles, and they had only themselves to thank for the sinister interpretation which these observers put upon their conduct. Apart from their refusal to assist the R.A.F. in supplying the Poles or to do so themselves—though they did send in some arms towards the end when it was too late—their public comment upon the affair was callous, while their *protegés*, a committee of Poles favourable to themselves which they had set up in Lublin and accorded some of the functions of a provisional government, did not hesitate to accuse the Polish insurgents of treachery. The whole episode was deplorable and put an end to any faint hopes there may have remained of an accommodation between the U.S.S.R. and the Polish Government.

Meanwhile the Russians had made further progress in the north, especially in Latvia. Here they advanced to the Gulf of Riga, cutting off the German troops remaining in the province of Livonia and in Estonia. But here also they suffered a check. About August 20th the Germans launched a heavy attack and re-opened a corridor between Courland and Livonia.

From this time forward Russian progress on the northern and central fronts virtually came to an end until the autumn. It has already been stated (in Chapter XXI) that the southern Russian armies had in the spring reached the Carpathians and established themselves on the Prut. Subsequent Russian action was governed by a nice combination of military and political motives and measures. The vital front, that on which Germany could be most swiftly defeated, clearly lay between the Carpathians and the Baltic. But it was this front which was mostly likely to be strongly defended, and the Russians had carried out upon it a deep advance, which had strained their communications. They now decided to leave it alone for a time, while they improved communications, built up supply depots, and improved the mobility of their forces by increasing their mechanization.

Yet they must go on fighting the Germans and keeping them on the stretch, and for this purpose the southern front, though, as has been said, the less vital strategically, offered considerable attractions. The outermost of the satellites, Rumania and Bulgaria, were obviously intent on surrendering as soon as they could, that is to say as soon as the German grip upon them should have been sufficiently loosened. That would be in itself an enormous advantage. It would probably permit the Red Army to leap the barrier of the Carpathians and penetrate without serious fighting into the great Hungarian plain, where its armour would find full scope. Rumania might be induced to fight against her former ally, and the prospect that Bulgaria would be prepared to do so was even better since there was a long sentimental attachment between the two countries, though they had been foes in the First World War. Great political advantages were also in the offing. The U.S.S.R. was already prudently looking forward to post-war conditions. It hoped to set up in Rumania and Bulgaria, and if all went well later on in Hungary and Czechoslovakia, possibly even Catholic Austria, *régimes* favourable to itself and of its own Communist complexion. This would be a good start if it subsequently desired to exercise pressure upon Turkey in order to obtain a base upon the Dardanelles. If the Red Army broke through to Yugoslavia it could also ensure that Marshal Tito was placed at the head of a Communist government in that country and that his rivals were liquidated. This would carry Russian influence to the Adriatic.

All went well with these plans. The offensive launched in August against Rumania caused the Rumanians at once to break loose from Germany, for whom their troops had made such heavy and useless sacrifices. The Russians entered Bucharest on the 31st, and immediately marched up the Danube in consort with their new allies, to reach Yugoslav territory within a week. On September 8th they entered Bulgaria. Here the process was repeated. A new government was set up; the army came over; and it also was sent into Yugoslavia by Marshal Tolbukhin to attack the flank of the German forces which were now beginning to move slowly northward out of the Balkans. Belgrade, the capital of Yugoslavia, was set free on October 20th, and thenceforward the Russians virtually handed over the campaign in that country to Tito and the Bulgarian Army.

With Hungary the Russians again combined political warfare with military action. Sections of the Hungarian Army in Transylvania came over to them, so that they were enabled to make their way across the mountains and reach the Hungarian plain. In December they reached and surrounded Budapest, but the city was stubbornly defended and the Germans also put up a strong resistance farther south, on either side of Lake Balaton. They even threw in a counter-offensive which enjoyed some temporary success. Simultaneously the Red Army cleared the greater part of the Baltic States which still remained in German hands. On October 19th they crossed the East Prussian frontier and stood on German soil, but though they made early progress upon it they were shortly afterwards brought to a halt and even compelled to yield some ground. Germany was in a state of dislocation. Refugees were pouring out from East Prussia and those parts of Poland which the enemy had colonized, and the confusion was made worse by the allied bombing.

The winter had been exceptionally mild, so that the Polish plains had not hardened until unusually late in the season. It was doubtless for this reason, as well as for those political reasons of which mention has been made, that there had been a delay in launching a major offensive in Poland, the vital front on which the Russians were facing the crucial objectives in Germany: Upper Silesia—to which the enemy had transferred much of his production in order to avoid bombing from the west—Brandenburg, Pomerania, East Prussia and Berlin. There had been some irritated criticism, particularly in the American press, but the weight and success of the next offensive was hailed with delight.

It was launched by Marshal Koniev from a bridgehead which the Russians had long held beyond the Vistula at Sandomierz, near the point where the San enters the greater river. In the first two days something like 25 miles were covered, in the general direction of Cracow and the Silesian frontier. The Russians were now employing a very heavy infantry tank, known as the Stalin, powerfully armoured and gunned, which was used to smash resistance in the forward zone before the cruiser tanks passed through to exploit the victory and keep the warfare mobile. Three days later Zhukov, on Koniev's right, advanced from the Vistula. Next day came the announcement that Rokossovsky was on the move still farther north. His advance, also extremely successful, outflanked East Prussia, which had already been entered from the east by Cherniakovsky.

The plan was now for Rokossovsky to wheel right-handed into East Prussia while Cherniakovsky continued his westward advance, for Zhukov to drive straight into Brandenburg with his centre approximately on Berlin, for Koniev to overrun Silesia, the great industrial area lying partly in Germany and partly in Poland which yielded something like 20 per cent of the total German output of coal, and was also the centre of a great industrial production, now largely devoted to the needs of war. The country was in general open, which favoured the Russian numerical superiority and strength in armour. The Germans were none too strong in armour on this front. Their Sixth Panzer S.S. Army was still engaged in the west; they were employing armoured forces south of the Danube; and when they despatched the Sixth Panzer S.S. Army eastward after its withdrawal from the Ardennes it also went, somewhat to the general surprise, to Hungary rather than to the northern front.

The whole Russian offensive was a brilliant success. The defence of East Prussia was desperate, and Cherniakovsky made only slow progress, but Rokossovsky gradually fought his way up to the coast, thus cutting off all German forces still remaining in the province. Zhukov made one of the deepest and most rapid advances witnessed in the course of the war, proving beyond a doubt the greatly increased mechanization of his forces. He reached the Oder near Küstrin. The main body then closed up on the river and at the end of the first week in February the Germans reported that the Russians were in possession of four bridgeheads beyond the Oder. Koniev made for the upper Oder, likewise established bridgeheads, and pushed on into the heart of the industrial area. Some of the towns which he captured were scarcely damaged, since the Russians had never gone in for strategic bombing on a large scale.

The great question was now whether Zhukov would push straight on for Berlin, leaving considerable hostile forces on his right flank. With increasing success the Russians were becoming more rather than less cautious in such circumstances and were more inclined than formerly to clear their flanks after a deep thrust into the enemy's array. Now, without seriously attempting to enlarge his bridgeheads over the Oder, Zhukov began to extend his front to the northward in the direction of Stettin. It is not at present clear whether he would have quickly renewed his drive in the direction of Berlin had the weather been more favourable. The sudden thaw in February put this out of the question for the time being.

The remainder of the front had not been inactive. On Koniev's left Petrov had made a considerable advance in the Carpathians. In Hungary the German counter-attacks were fought down and the Russians regained the initiative. In Budapest the Germans fought fiercely, and one of the city battles, typical of the Second World War while unknown in the first, raged on for week after week, destroying large sections of the capital, which had hitherto suffered little from the ravages of war. The Russians gradually compressed the garrison into smaller space till all of it that remained was enclosed in a corner of Buda. Here the end came on February 12th. By the end of February the front was well west of Budapest and further south had flowed some 75 miles west of the Danube.

It must be evident from the combined pace and depth of the recent advances that the Russians had created a more elaborate and skilful organization of transport than in their former offensives, and that they were in possession of greater resources in this respect. Their vast numerical superiority, about two-and-a-half to one at this period, perhaps more if the defection of Germany's allies be taken into account, had been an important factor. So too had been the allied offensive in the west. Its influence may be concealed by the fact that the proportion of divisions on either front did not greatly change unless the system on which Germany was now using her drafts be understood. In this time of failing man-power she had maintained the number of her divisions, but had allowed their strength to drop. Many, for example, possessed only two infantry regiments, and these far below establishment. It was the custom, however, to direct the flow of trained reinforcements and largely also of material to divisions forming part of armies or army groups most heavily engaged. This was a makeshift system, and the fact that it worked at all afforded evidence of the remarkable quality maintained in German training establishments and of the still high standard of junior leadership. It is true that this had deteriorated; the Western Allies had discovered in the Ardennes that even in the best armoured divisions the tactical standard was not quite what it had been. Yet it was astonishing that it should have remained as good as it was when divisions had been allowed to run down to little more than cadres and then filled up with drafts.

The invasion from the west had brought such a flood of reinforcements and material to the formations on that front, though the former included men of almost every race, even Russians. The virtual cessation of the Russian offensive on the northern front in the east meant that the German casualty list dropped, and at the same time the normal wastage of a quiet front was not replaced. For a time, therefore, though the Americans and British were facing only about 90 divisions in the west and in Italy, while the Russians were facing 200, the disproportion was not so great as the bare figures would imply. Later on the Russian northern offensive drained German resources heavily once more, and the fact remains that from the time when the U.S.S.R. was attacked by Germany in 1941 the Red Army bore the brunt of the war with the German Army.

Other causes underlying the Russian victories and prodigious advances were the physical hardihood and endurance of the troops, particularly in winter warfare; the discovery of young commanders, such as Rokossovsky, who had drawn most of their experience from the present war; the greatly improved staff work, acknowledged recently by Marshal Stalin in his habit of addressing congratulatory Orders of the Day not only to army group commanders but also to their chiefs of staff; the strength of the artillery, an arm which, in Stalin's view, the Germans had neglected to their cost; and the generally high standard of armament and equipment. No mass army numbered by hundreds of divisions could be equipped and mechanized on the American or British standard, but the great feat of the Russians was that they had put into the field a mass army of many millions with so relatively high a standard. They had combined so far as was humanly possible mass, which commonly stands for a low scale of efficiency, with the most modern type of equipment, and had made a remarkable success of the venture. One form of attack they had never had to face in full force: the devastating fighter-bomber assault with which the Americans and British preceded and accompanied their land offensives. Doubtless, if they had, their military economy would have been altered by now and they would have been producing more aircraft and maintaining fewer divisions.

Mention has been made of the movement of Bulgarian troops under Russian direction into Yugoslavia to attack the German forces, which were described as moving slowly northward out of the Balkans. At last the eastern Mediterranean holding was being abandoned. The Germans could not take away their garrisons from Crete and the Ægean, and these were left to their doom, but they withdrew from Greece. On October 4th, 1944, the first British troops landed at Patras, where an airfield was quickly secured.

The liberation of Greece was swift and accompanied by little fighting. The British did not possess the strength to do more than harass the retreating enemy. The Greek partisan forces did relatively little to help. The Germans extricated themselves without serious loss. In Yugoslavia they had harder fighting, particularly against the Bulgarians, who advanced in three columns, the northernmost on Nish. The Germans, however, proceeded along the valley of the Jbar, losing some men and more material but taking no great hurt and inflicting sharp losses upon the Bulgarians. In the end they reached their allotted station in northern Yugoslavia, while some passed into Hungary. They had avoided the risk of being cut off. It was a notable proof of what good troops could accomplish in mountain country and of how good these Germans still were.

In Greece they left behind them a sorry legacy. The old political bitterness from which that country has seldom been free had burst into flame in Egypt, where there had been a mutiny among naval and land forces inspired by anti-royalist and Communist sentiment. After much political excitement and civil disturbance a rebellion against the Government—from which the left-wing ministers had just withdrawn as a protest against the method of demobilizing the irregular bands—broke out on December 3rd. According to a majority of observers, the Athens police were responsible for the uprising when they fired on a prohibited but unarmed procession. The suppression of the insurrection fell mainly on British troops, who had to carry out unpleasant and difficult street operations.

The affair was fiercely debated, mainly on party lines, in the United Kingdom, and the Government came in for much criticism. The criticism with which it should have been faced was, however, seldom or never heard. The policy of arming civilians, including every kind of bandit and criminal, had brought about its just retribution here as in several other countries. Chickens of this sort invariably come home to roost. The solution of the Greek problem does not belong to war history, since it was not reached during the course of the war. Its chief influence upon hostilities was that it occupied troops who would have been more profitably employed in Italy.

After the surrender of Finland the situation of that unhappy country was complicated by the strength of the German forces, some ten divisions, in the northern part of the country. Had they been prepared to withdraw of their own accord the Finns would probably have let them do so, but as they hung on the Finnish Government at Russian dictation agreed to co-operate in expelling them. It was a slow process. In October, 1944, however, the Germans withdrew into Norway, again, as in their retreat from the Balkans, without serious loss. The Russians crossed the Norwegian frontier, but their advance could not be called a pursuit. They lost contact with the enemy and did not seek to regain it. Having this extra force of high quality in Norway, the Germans spared a few divisions from it to reinforce the main European fronts and might have sent more had their communications been better. They laid waste the Finmark, the northern province, to hold off the Russians, but there was no fighting except for skirmishing with a small Norwegian force landed in the north.

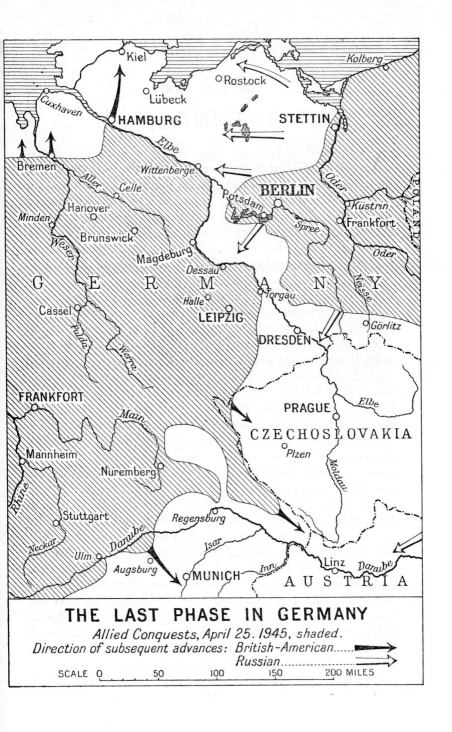

THE LAST PHASE IN GERMANY
Allied Conquests, April 25. 1945, shaded.
Direction of subsequent advances: British-American ....➔
Russian ----------➔

SCALE 0   50   100   150   200 MILES

CHAPTER XXVI

The End in Europe

AT the end of February, 1945, the Red Army was every-where established on the shores of the Baltic from the Gulf of Finland to the Gulf of Danzig, except that the Germans held the triangular Courland peninsula in Latvia, which they mantained largely through the port of Libau. Then the front ran westward, keeping fifty or sixty miles from the sea, to the Oder, and then southward along that river, and on to the mountains which formed the frontier of Czechoslavakia. It followed these south-eastward, crossed the frontier south of Cracow, and then bent south-westward to form another great salient in Hungary, of which only a small part, on the Austrian frontier, remained un-conquered. The front facing Berlín was 1,100 miles due west of Voronezh, where it had stood at the end of 1942, and about 1,700 miles from the war industries in the Urals, which were linked with the Moscow network by only two or three main railways. When there is taken into account also the amount of destruction between Moscow and the front some faint indication will appear of the magnitude of the task of transportation and supply.

Early in March the Russians thrust due northward and reached the Baltic at Kolberg in Pomerania, thus creating an almost straight north-to-south front from the sea to Silesia, but leaving another German pocket of considerable strength between Danzig and Kolberg. About the 22nd of the month they began to push forward again in Silesia, over-running more industrial territory the loss of which was serious to the enemy. Some three days later they launched a powerful new offensive in Hungary, west of Budapest, and before the end of the month had crossed the Austrian frontier. On April 4th came news that their armoured advanced guard was within 12 miles of Vienna, and next day they were in the suburbs. Another long and savage city battle, only a degree less destructive than that of Budapest, followed, but, as in the former instance, the Red Army did not allow its progress to be stopped by the fighting in the city.

On April 16th the final and decisive offensive, for which

Zhukov had long been preparing, was launched from the bridge-heads established beyond the Oder in the direction of Berlin. The Germans had put up a most stubborn defence on the river, aided by wet weather, and this sector of the front had not seriously altered since the first week in February, but now the enemy was pushed swiftly back towards the capital. By April 22nd the Russians had actually driven past Berlin on the southern side. At this date the Western Allies were lining the Elbe over a great part of its length. The end could not now be long delayed.

Some of the most determined Nazis had broken away and were trying to make their peace. Goering had deserted and was to make some vague but unsuccessful attempts to open negotiations. Himmler, who claimed that he spoke for Germany since the Führer in Berlin was no longer in a position to do so, approached the Swedish Government with an offer to surrender all the forces facing the Western Allies. The Germans were striving to make a separate peace with them, not merely in hopes —which must have in any case faded by now—of dividing them from the Russians, but still more in their terror of the latter and of the treatment to be expected from them. For this reason also thousands of troops originally aligned against the Russians were pouring westward so that they might find themselves in British or American hands when the curtain fell upon the last scene. When it was made known that only unconditional surrender on both fronts would be accepted Himmler disappeared into hiding, to be apprehended and to end his life by suicide after the capitulation. The head of the German Navy, Grand Admiral Doenitz, was afterwards to assume the mantle of Führer on the assumed death of Hitler, and it was on his behalf that representatives approached Field-Marshal Montgomery and surrendered the forces immediately in front of the 21st Army Group.

In Berlin, however, Hitler had gathered about him a small group, including Dr. Goebbels, his most faithful henchman, who had no thought of surrender. They were prepared to defend the city to the last house and had assembled a force, largely of fanatical S.S. troops, who would do their bidding. Hitler himself directed the final defence, so far as in his hysterical frame of mind he was capable of understanding the position, from a nest of underground chambers, impervious to any form of bombardment, in the grounds of the Chancellery. Ferocious street battles were fought, the defence making considerable use of the underground railway system, with exits into the streets covered by steel cupolas or the turrets of tanks. The Germans made many counter-attacks and some points are believed to have changed hands half a dozen times. By April 25th Berlin was completely surrounded by a ring of steel. And on this date the first contact between American and Russian forces was made at Torgau, on the Elbe. On the 30th another link was established further north near Dessau.

Even this did not immediately bring the battle in Berlin to an end, but on May 2nd all resistance ceased, and the dirty, ragged, bearded defenders came forth from their lairs to stack their arms and pass into captivity. It was the seventeenth day since the advance from the Oder.

Some mysterious features surrounded the end of Hitler, and there were conflicting versions from German sources. The bulk of the evidence was in favour of his having committed suicide at the last moment with his mistress Eva Braun, to whom he had recently been married. Goebbels and his entire family un-doubtedly took poison, and the probability that Hitler did like-wise is very strong. The accounts given of the burning of his corpse with petrol were not particularly convincing, but it seems likely that this was done. At all events his body was not found. He had always vowed that he would fight to the last and never surrender, and now he had fulfilled his promise. Such was the end of the Third Reich and its founder. The part played in the last scene by the Western Allies has now to be described.

The delay imposed upon them by the Battle of the Ardennes had been compensated for by the enemy's loss of some 220,000 men, including 110,000 prisoners, the depletion of his strategic reserve, and the disillusionment caused by the failure of an offen-sive on which such high hopes had been based. The Germans also attacked in the Bavarian Palatinate, and the American Seventh Army had to withdraw to the old defences of the Maginot Line in order to provide reinforcements for the struggle in the Ar-dennes, but this was not regarded as a serious matter.

Before the main battle of the Rhineland could be begun, there was still work to do. In the latter half of January, 1945, the British cleared the enemy from a small triangle south of Roermond between the Maas and the Roer, a difficult infantry operation on waterlogged ground. Simultaneously the French and Americans carried out an attack in Alsace which drove the enemy with heavy loss from his last holdings west of the Rhine from the Swiss frontier to Strasbourg. Further north the Americans continued to press him back from the Siegfried Line and on February 10th the First Army obtained control of the Roer dams. The enemy flooded the Roer valley, but was forced to release the waters at a moment not unfavourable to the Allies. He would certainly have held them up longer had he been permitted to do so.

General Eisenhower's plan was now to destroy the maximum strength of the enemy west of the Rhine north of Cologne, seize bridgeheads over the river, and afterwards isolate the Ruhr. The American Ninth Army was placed under Montgomery's command. What proved to be the last major battle that the western Allies had to fight began on February 8th with an attack by the Canadian First Army from the Nijmegen bridgehead in a general south-easterly direction through the Siegfried Line and the Reichswald, followed on the 17th by the Ninth Army, which was delayed by the flooding, towards the north-east. Heavy and bitter fighting lasted until on March 3rd contact was obtained between the two armies in Geldern. The enemy had fought his main battle west of the Rhine as the allied commanders desired, but he did not persist to the end and contrived to withdraw a fair proportion of his strength across the river. Simultaneously Patton's Third Army had fought its way through the tangled country of the Eifel. He reached the Rhine at Coblentz on March 9th and two days later the west bank was clear from thence to the north. On the 7th, by a combination of good fortune and initiative the American First Army had seized intact the Ludendorff Bridge at Remagen. On the 14th Patton bridged the Moselle south-west of Coblentz and struck at the Saar pocket. While this was being cleared his Third Army secured a second bridgehead over the Rhine at Oppenheim, which it expanded rapidly.

Eisenhower was now ready for the main assault. American strength now amounted to 60 divisions, including an airborne division ready to fly in. Montgomery had been compelled to disband a couple of divisions for want of men to fill their ranks, but had been promised a strong reinforcement from the Mediterranean, the headquarters of the 1 Canadian Corps, with two

9

Canadian and three British divisions, which would bring up his strength to 21 though two of these were not destined to arrive, one being retained in Italy and one sent to the Eastern Mediterranean. There were seven French divisions. Facing this formidable array—small, however, measured by divisions by comparison with that of 1918, when the final campaign was fought in the west—the Germans possessed a maximum of 56 divisions in being, most of them seriously under strength, the skeletons of certain others, and a large but unimportant body of hastily enrolled militia known as the *Volksgrenadiere*. The allied superiority in armament was even greater. In the air the allied advantage was overwhelming. The last great effort of the *Luftwaffe* had been made in the Ardennes, and little more was to be seen of it. Before the final offensive west of the Rhine nearly 10,000 sorties had been made on a single day, February 22nd, against the German railway system.

The passage of the Rhine proved a relatively easy matter. After a great air and artillery bombardment, it began on the evening of March 23rd. On the following morning two airborne divisions, one American and one British, landed beyond the Rhine north and north-east of Wesel. These divisions were landed within range of supporting fire from the west bank and after the heads of the land columns had crossed the river. There was no need on this occasion to subject them to heavy risks.

Fine equipment and excellent work by the engineers enabled large striking forces to reach the east bank rapidly. Then the American First and Ninth Armies, the latter under Montgomery's command, enveloped the area of the Ruhr, in which they trapped elements of 18 German divisions. The rest can be told briefly because except at isolated points, especially where the personnel of training establishments were encountered, as at Paderborn, there was no more serious resistance. In the words of General Marshall, "the magnitude of the offensive smothered resistance all along the Western Front". The disruption of the German transport system prevented co-ordination of resistance, and the dispersal of production, in itself a sound and logical reply to bombing, now told heavily against the enemy because he was unable to assemble his material, so that some sectors were starved of it although the total stock was plentiful.

During the last week of March both armies of the Southern

Group under Devers, the French First and the American Seventh, crossed the Middle Rhine, the former at Gemersheim, the latter below Mannheim. The French then pushed southward through the Black Forest and Stuttgart towards the Swiss frontier and Lake Constance. The Seventh captured München and thrust rapidly forward to the Inn and the Brenner Pass, through which it finally made contact with the troops of the 15th Army Group in Italy, whose great success will shortly be described. How astounding an outcome, how completely unpredictable, that this army, which had left Italy to invade France, should have been the first to pass through the Brenner, and from the north! The outstanding feats were those of Patton's Third Army, the strongest in the allied array, containing 18 divisions, six of them airborne, and commanded by a man of extraordinary energy and boldness. Patton crossed the Main and wheeled round to the Danube near Regensburg. Another detachment of his army penetrated into Czechoslovakia, and he could doubtless have over-run all Bohemia if it had not been considered more prudent politically to leave the major part of this task to the Russians. Indeed, since the Germans were opposing the Russians more strongly than they were the western Allies, it is possible that the latter could also have been the first into Berlin. The American First Army, besides playing its part in the envelopment of the Ruhr, thrust through the Harz to Leipsic and the Elbe. The Ninth passed through Brunswick to the Elbe at Magdeburg.

The British Second Army crossed the Weser and its tributary the Aller on the front Celle—Rethem—Bremen, then pressed on to the Elbe between Wittenberge and Cuxhaven at the mouth of the river. Finally, two of its corps, with an attached American corps, crossed the river above Hamburg and thrust towards Wismar, Lubeck and the Danish frontier with Schleswig-Holstein. On its left the right wing of the Canadian First Army advanced on a very wide front between the lower reach of the Weser and the Zuyder Zee. The left wing swung due westward into "Fortress Holland", the part of the country covered by water barriers and inundations. Its advance was, however, soon halted by Montgomery's orders. The enemy in western Holland was completely cut off, but his position behind the floods was impregnable except to an effort for which there were no resources —and no necessity—at this stage. The German Civil Commis-

sioner, Dr. Seyss-Inquart, offered a truce which would permit
the introduction of food to the starving population. This was
readily accepted and observed until the final German surrender.

The Italian theatre of war had been relegated to a secondary
level; the allied command constantly saw its projects over-ruled
and its efforts handicapped by the successive calls made upon it
for forces for the western invasion of France, for the southern
invasion, for reinforcements to the 21st Army Group, and, as
recorded in the last chapter, for Greece. This is not to suggest
that the policy was incorrect, but it proved trying to commanders
and troops alike.

The advance of the summer had brought the British Eighth
and American Fifth Armies up against the "Gothic Line", a
strong system of defence which the enemy had prepared early in
the year when in doubt as to whether he would be able to hold
out south of Rome as long as he actually contrived to do. Despite
the diversion of forces to other theatres, another general offensive
was launched on September 10th with the object of breaking
through into the plain of the Po. On the whole, this was a disappointing venture. The works were carried, but the mountains
themselves barred the way till the weather broke. The deepest
advances were made on the Adriatic coast, through Rimini
towards Ravenna, and in the centre, from north of Florence towards Bologna. In December there were high hopes of a drive
on Bologna, but some pressure on the left flank of the Fifth
Army, where a Negro division gave way before a German counter-offensive, and the diversion of troops from the Eighth Army
to Greece stood in the way. Meanwhile the able German commander, Kesselring, had reorganized his defence. Mussolini, who
had been in allied hands but had been rescued by the Germans,
had set up a Fascist republican system in the north, and now some
four new Italian divisions were available in aid of the German
defence. In December General Sir H. Maitland Wilson, Supreme
Commander in the Mediterranean, succeeded Field-Marshal Dill,
who had died in the United States, as senior representative in
Washington of the British Chiefs of Staff. Wilson, who was
promoted field-marshal, was succeeded by Alexander, also promoted to that rank, and the command of the allied armies in Italy
was taken over by the American, General Mark Clark. General
Sir Oliver Leese, Montgomery's successor in command of the

Eighth Army, had gone in October to the Far East, to be succeeded by Lieut.-General Sir R. L. McCreery.

The winter operations made heavy calls upon the troops, but the results were too small for detailed examination here, though some of the gains embodied value for the future. On April 9th, 1945, the 15th Army Group launched yet another major offensive. Counting by divisions—it now included one Brazilian—it was inferior in strength to the enemy; its superiority lay above all in air power and to a lesser degree in artillery. At last complete and undiluted triumph was won. The Eighth Army led the offensive with an attack across the Senio, west of Ravenna. Despite an extremely heavy air and artillery preparation, resistance was still determined. The enemy was given five days in which to alter his dispositions for the purpose of holding this attack, and then the Fifth Army struck in its turn, from the mountains south and south-west of Bologna. After a week's hard fighting the enemy's front broke. Americans of the Fifth Army and Poles of the Eighth entered Bologna almost simultaneously, the former from the south-west, the latter from the east. Between the 23rd and 25th both armies crossed the Po in strength, and on the 25th the Americans took the naval base of Spezia, on the west coast. The very stubbornness of the German resistance was now the enemy's undoing. As so often happens to an army defeated with a mighty river at its back, the Germans lost a great proportion of their stores and equipment, which they were unable to withdraw across the Po.

Resistance had now completely collapsed. On the right the Eighth Army raced up the plain, captured Padua, Venice and Treviso, and heading for Trieste, established contact with the Yugoslav forces of Marshal Tito at Montfalcone. In the centre the Fifth Army made for Verona and the Brenner, and, as has already been stated, established contact with the American Seventh Army from Bavaria. On the left it reached Turin, where, by a curious irony, the first troops to arrive belonged to an American regiment of men of Japanese blood, born in United States territory. From Genoa it made yet another contact with forces from another theatre, meeting French troops which had moved along the Riviera to Savona.

Before the last of these events, however, the struggle was really over. German emissaries had come to the headquarters of Field-

Marshal Alexander with proposals for a surrender from General von Vietinghoff, and after brief negotiations the whole German army group, which covered certain Austrian districts in addition to the Italian theatre, laid down its arms in unconditional surrender on May 2nd. The armies of Italy, which had been fighting in that theatre for nine months before the landing in Western France, thus secured the first great wholesale surrender. Mussolini was killed and his corpse was mutilated by Italian partisans.

So complete was the success in Italy that it must be a matter for speculation how much the allied armies could have achieved if they had retained the ten divisions employed in the invasion of Southern France in August, 1944. Maitland Wilson, the Supreme Allied Commander in the Mediterranean at the time, had proposed as an alternative to this operation an immediate advance into the plain of the Po, followed by exploitation through the Ljubljana gap into the plains of Hungary. He could have done it —he had at his disposal at that time some 5,000 allied aircraft against a couple of hundred German. The decisive reason why his project was turned down was General Eisenhower's need of the port of Marseilles. It would doubtless also have been difficult to persuade General de Gaulle to use the French divisions for any purpose but the liberation of France. But it must be said that, apart from taking Marseilles and providing reinforcements for General Eisenhower, the landing in the south of France proved almost superfluous.

It was only by two days that this surrender in Italy preceded that of the German forces facing the 21st Army Group in northwest Germany, Denmark and Holland. This took place at Field-Marshal Montgomery's tactical headquarters on Luneburg Heath on May 4th. On the 5th the German Army Group G in Austria agreed to surrender to the American 6th Army Group. Next day the military emissaries of the German Government surrendered to General Eisenhower at Rheims. Eisenhower had certainly not bottled up an unnecessary reserve for emergencies, a common fault of commanders. On the day of the surrender he had under his orders 90 divisions—61 American, 18 British and Canadian, 10 French and 1 Polish. One airborne and two infantry divisions were in France; all the rest were in Germany, Austria, Czechoslovakia or Holland.

The German force in Norway, the only undefeated German army, surrendered to British staff officers sent in two flying-boats to Oslo Fjord by General Sir Andrew Thorne, the Commander-in-Chief in Scotland.

CHAPTER XXVII

Allied Offensive in the Far East—Burma

THE Burmese theatre of war may be regarded from various
points of view. To the British it represented first of all the
area in which the Japanese threat to India must be faced and
defeated. That accomplished, it would be the field in which the
principal Japanese force on the Asiatic continent outside China
and Manchuria should be overthrown and a stepping-stone to
the recovery of Malaya and the Netherlands East Indies, from
which bases, apart from their enormous economic significance,
the forces of Britain and of the British Commonwealth might
hope to take a more extended part in the reconquest of Pacific
territories snatched by Japan and in the final destruction of
Japanese power.

In inter-allied councils, however, Burma appeared under another aspect, that of its connection with China, and this was particularly prominent in American eyes. American sentiment for
China was strong, so strong that Chinese shortcomings from time
to time produced in the United States rude shocks of disappointment not experienced in this country because here less was expected. But behind this sentiment was a strategic consideration,
which may be expressed in the words of General Marshall: "If
the armies and government of Generalissimo Chiang Kai-shek
had been finally defeated, Japan would have been left free to
exploit the tremendous resources of China without harassment.
It might have made it possible when the United States and Britain
had finished the job in Europe, and assaulted the Japanese home
islands, for the government to flee to China, and continue the war
on a great and rich land mass." The American authorities regarded
Burma largely in the light of its aid to China, and it is probably
fair to say that this was one of the reasons which induced the
United States to put such large resources into the Burma campaign. The extent of those resources has not even yet been fully
recognized in Britain, perhaps because the number of fighting
men employed was relatively small. The aid afforded was vital

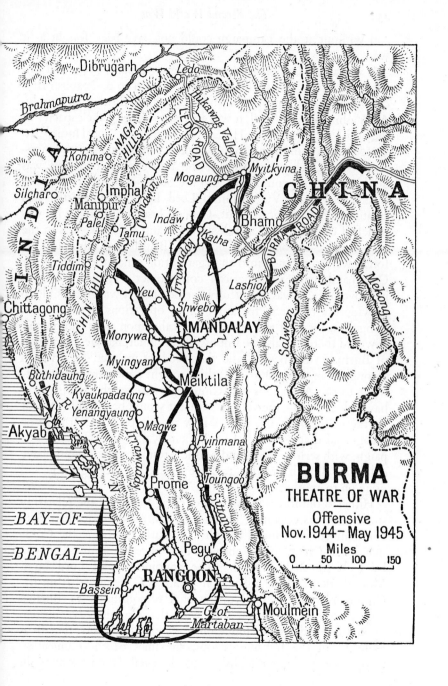

BURMA
THEATRE OF WAR
—
Offensive
Nov. 1944 – May 1945

Miles
0   50   100   150

and without it the campaign could not have been fought as it was.

It was at the Casablanca Conference in January, 1943, that this subject was first discussed and it was decided to re-establish land communications with China and increase the flow of air supply. At Washington, in April, it was agreed to increase the capacity of the aerial route over the Himalayas, known as "the Hump", to 10,000 tons a month and to undertake a campaign after the monsoon. At Quebec, in August, the figure of 10,000 tons was doubled. At this conference also the South-east Asia Command (S.E.A.C.) under Vice-Admiral Lord Louis Mountbatten was created. The American Lieut.-General Joseph Stilwell, who was Chief of the Staff to Generalissimo Chiang Kai-shek, was in the first instance appointed his deputy. British and American air forces were combined into an organization called the Eastern Air Command, with an American commander. Finally at Cairo, in November, it was regretfully decided that it was impossible to provide the resources for amphibious operations in the Bay of Bengal, in view of the other heavy calls upon such equipment. It would therefore also be impossible to undertake the reconquest of Burma in the natural and the speediest manner, by invasion through Rangoon. But—and this brought a measure of contentment to the Americans and Chinese, whatever the British may have felt about it—the view was that it would be possible to clear northern Burma and to drive a new road into China. It must be recognized that the lack of equipment was to prolong the campaign, with serious moral and political results, since it would have enhanced British prestige to have finished it more quickly and gone on to another.

Hitherto the forces in Assam covering India and the relatively small numbers operating beyond the Burmese border had been commanded from India, the ultimate authority being the Commander-in-Chief, an appointment held since the summer of 1942 by Field-Marshall Wavell. The appointment of Lord Louis Mountbatten and the formation of S.E.A.C. removed from the Commander-in-Chief all operational responsibility in Burma, but at the same time left him with the administrative burden upon his hands, since India must inevitably supply the great majority of the fighting troops, the lines of communication troops, the training establishments, hospitals, food (coming in through Indian ports when not produced in India), and many supplies and stores, and must provide the main base for the campaign.

S.E.A.C. was a conception which attracted the attention of the world—and to start off with a good press has become an important consideration even in a military campaign. It must, however, be realized that it never fulfilled its full function and would not have been set up on such a scale had it been known from the first that its activities would be confined to Burma and that the war with Japan would be brought to an end before it could break forth to fight larger-scale campaigns with added resources released by the defeat of Germany. Indeed the whole superstructure of the forces operating in the Burma theatre was excessively heavy. At the top was S.E.A.C., with a vast staff but no real administrative responsibility. It was the co-ordinator, but had not a great deal to co-ordinate. Below it was established an army group headquarters—the commanders being successively Lieut.-General Sir George Giffard and Lieut.-General Sir Oliver Leese—but without a group of armies under it.

The Supreme Commander was a young naval officer not long past forty, of great ability and personal charm and a kinsman of H.M. the King. He had had some valuable experience as Chief of Combined Operations, though here unfortunately combined operations by naval and military forces could not be carried out for a long time and then only on a limited scale, while the Admiralty clung to its fleet based on Ceylon and refused to let him exercise a control of it to which his appointment appeared to have entitled him. The Army on its side provided a highly experienced and capable staff officer, Lieut.-General Sir Henry Pownall, considerably older than his chief. So something of the atmosphere of commands in certain old wars was created: the attractive, clever, young prince, with the veteran mentor and coadjutor, hiding himself behind his chief, intensely loyal to him and scrupulously careful of his reputation. All this has, of course, to be translated into modern terms, but the parallel can hardly be avoided. S.E.A.C. was a well-run institution which accomplished its task with credit, but an unkindly satirist with a lively pen could create an amusing picture of it without more than legitimate distortion.

So much for the higher strategy and its instrument, discussion of which has carried us some way beyond where the forces in Burma were left after they had made their way back, weary, disease-ridden, and defeated, to the safety of Assam during the monsoon of 1942. Not that the early events of the following fine-weather season were of high importance, since they were confined to an abortive British advance mainly carried out by a single Indian division into the Arakan, the coast territory on the Bay of Bengal. The Japanese gave ground till they reached previously prepared defences near the end of the Mayu peninsula north of the little port of Akyab in early January, 1943. There they withstood all attacks, and in April forced a withdrawal to the region of Buthidaung, some 35 miles from the southernmost point reached. It had been a disappointing offensive, which proved that in jungle fighting Indian divisions had still much to learn from the enemy, though this was being remedied already.

Simultaneously another adventure was carried out which aroused much interest. A specially trained force under a remarkable young commander, Brigadier Orde C. Wingate, crossed the Chindwin deep into Japanese-controlled territory in February. It had no lines of communication and depended on supply from the air. In March it cut in 75 places the railway from Mandalay to Myitkyina. The force, or its survivors, returned in May. It had carried out a remarkable experient, which, however, gave birth to a great deal of absurd comment in which Wingate was contrasted with the typical "brass hat", naturally to the latter's disadvantage. In point of fact it had in some respects a bad moral effect, since sick and wounded in considerable numbers had to be left to the mercy of the Japanese. Yet it was to bear fruit.

During the monsoon careful training was undertaken both in India and in Burma and a large number of patrol actions were carried out. These were well prepared and in the vast majority of cases successful. By these measures self-confidence was implanted in the Fourteenth Army, which was ready by the end of the wet weather to begin operations, in concert with another force in the north, to clear Burma down to Myitkyina. The northern force, under General Stilwell, consisted in the first instance of two Chinese divisions which entered the Hukawng Valley from the Ledo area, where they had covered the new road, at the end of October and were joined early in 1944 by an American "jungle team", a brigade of all arms, under Brigadier-

General F. D. Merrill. Later in the year two more Chinese divisions were flown to Assam and eventually moved into the Hukawng Valley.

This force was confronted by only a single Japanese division based on Myitkyina. The Indian divisions did not require comparable odds to defeat the Japanese, but it is noteworthy that the enemy was always inferior in numbers, besides being at a heavy disadvantage owing to allied air ascendancy. There has been a disposition to under-rate the military qualities of the Japanese Army, though never the desperate, fanatical bravery of the individual Japanese soldier; but even as an instrument the Army was exceedingly formidable. In both the offensives which it carried out against the Fourteenth Army its strength was inferior to that of the defence, yet its performance, especially in Assam, was astonishing and came within measurable reach of success.

No more difficult campaign from the point of view of communications can have been undertaken in modern times. There were no roads from Assam across the mighty jungle-clad ridges barring the way to the valleys of the Chindwin and Irrawaddy. India itself possessed certain shortcomings as a base, and since the Burmese theatre was perforce on a low priority a great deal of material which would normally have been considered indispensable for a campaign in such a country could not be provided. The British performed prodigies of administrative improvisation. The Americans brought their remarkable engineering capacity, power of organizing, and modern material to their aid. Their port battalions performed excellent work in Calcutta, and their railway battalions more than doubled the capacity of the Bengal-Assam Railway. Their road engineers pushed forward the Ledo Road at an astonishing speed until in January, 1945, the first truck convoy was able to cross the frontier from Burma into China.

The greatest American contribution was, however, in air transport. This was given at a time when the R.A.F. was incapable of supplying the army's needs in this respect, but as the campaign progressed the British took over an increasing proportion of the work and the American squadrons were gradually withdrawn. In Burma the revolutionary use of transport aircraft transformed the campaign. A division cut off by hostile envelopment or advancing rapidly through country in which it could not maintain lines of communication was supplied from the air, not as a matter of emergency but almost as a matter of routine. A division could be picked up and transferred from one sector to another. Reinforcements could be flown in to a hard-pressed garrison and administrative troops who in the circumstances were only an embarrassment to the defence flown out; in fact, these things were done on a large scale during the Japanese offensive in Assam.

During the monsoon the Japanese had doubled their forces and clearly meant to pass to the offensive both in the Arakan and Assam. In the Arakan they might employ two divisions and a brigade of renegade Indian troops against the two Indian divisions on that front. On February 3rd, 1944, they struck, carrying out a typically bold and simple Japanese tactic of envelopment which place a strong force astride the communications of one of the Indian divisions. They expected that it would withdraw in confusion through a dangerous pass and would be destroyed. Having dealt with the second Indian division they would then push on to Chittagong and with the aid of their "Indian National Army" raise a revolt. Then, when British reserves had been drawn in, they would strike in Assam.

But the Fourteenth Army was ready. Lieut.-General Slim put the two divisions on to air supply at once. General Giffard sent in two more divisions; the enveloping Japanese force was enveloped in its turn; and after some hard fighting it was broken up into fragments fleeing through the jungle, with 5,000 men left dead upon the field. The British had won their first victory over the Japanese.

Meanwhile Wingate had launched another expedition. This time two of his brigades were flown in by glider to landing-places astride the Irrawaddy and the railway in the area of Indaw and Katha in early March; the third marched south from Ledo. It should be noted that the force, described for purposes of deception as the "3rd Indian Division", was in fact British. It was, as before, entirely maintained from the air. This force cut the railway and road from Mandalay to Myitkyina and the road from Bhama to Myitkyina, and on this occasion kept them cut for a long time. The Japanese had, it must be confessed, not taken the first Wingate expedition seriously. They now did not realize that this was much stronger, and did not employ a major force to clear their communications. Their efforts to do so were unsuccessful and very costly. On the other hand, the Wingate venture failed to fulfil one of its main objects, which was to compel the Japanese division facing Stilwell to withdraw.

On March 15th the Japanese launched their main offensive in Assam. It was a sufficiently bold venture, since they were prepared to put into it only three divisions and another Indian renegade formation of the strength of a division but inconsiderable fighting value, together with smaller formations. In the area Kohima-Imphal-Tiddim there were three Indian divisions. This time the Japanese sought to penetrate to the Brahmaputra valley, thus cutting General Stilwell's communications and over-running the airfields on which supply to China depended. The tactics were as daring as the strategy. The enemy thrust two divisions in between Kohima and Imphal, while a third attacked northward along the Tiddim-Imphal road with the aid of a smaller force operating from Tamu.

Once again Slim had foreseen what would happen and prepared to meet the threat with the aid of air transport. A division from the Arakan was flown in to the Imphal area. Many thousand useless mouths, administrative troops, were flown out. A British division was brought down from the Manipur Road railhead, and one of its brigades also flew to the defence of Kohima. Finally yet another division was flown in from the Arakan to the northern flank. All beleaguered forces were put on to air supply.

This was one of the longest battles of the war, lasting three months. The fighting was very bitter both during the Japanese offensive and after the Fourteenth Army had regained the initiative. By the first week of June the opposing forces formed an extraordinary double sandwich. To the north, round Kohima, were two British divisions; between Kohima and Imphal were two Japanese divisions; then in the area Imphal-Palel came four more British divisions; and finally, on the southern flank, a Japanese division and a brigade. The enemy could not stand the strain of attack at odds of two to one. After a last desperate assault on Imphal he broke and fled across the Chindwin in rout, abandoning a great part of his equipment. His permanent losses in the Arakan and Assam were estimated by British intelligence to number 75,000.

While the struggle in Assam was at its height, Stilwell had

thrust through terrible country down to Myitkyina. Wingate's force advanced northward to take Mogaung and join hands with the northern forces. The Japanese division in this area was largely destroyed, though remnants held out in Myitkyina itself for a considerable time.

Despite the breaking of the monsoon, the Fourteenth Army pursued the flying enemy, though it might have been able to do so more effectively but for the exhaustion of the splendid air transport squadrons who may well be described as the chief heroes of the victory of Imphal. By early December the Fourteenth Army held three bridgeheads over the Chindwin.

Slim's orders were now to occupy central Burma as far south as Mandalay and if possible exploit to the south. The enemy's total strength in Burma was now ten Japanese and two "Indian National Army" divisions, a large force of lines of communication troops, and seven battalions of Burmans. Only five of these Japanese divisions were, however, likely to oppose the Fourteenth Army, owing to the demands of the northern front (where the American Lieut.-General D. J. Sultan had succeeded General Stilwell and had a British division under his orders), the Arakan (where there was a British corps not now under the Fourteenth Army), and the south, which the enemy could not strip clean. Some five divisions with outside strength might oppose the Fourteenth Army, which had six, also with outside strength, but could not maintain them all beyond the Chindwin.

The first plan was to bring the Japanese to action and defeat them in the Schwebo plain north of the Irrawaddy. But the Japanese had grown more wary. When the British crossed the Chindwin in December, the enemy drew back behind the Irrawaddy. Slim now recast his plan and aimed at getting a striking force behind the Japanese along the river about Mandalay while he also attacked from the north. By a remarkable strategic "scissors" movement he brought his left-hand corps across to his right flank, to the bewilderment of the Japanese, and after extraordinary marches through the most difficult country it seized a crossing over the Irrawaddy below Mandalay. The enemy concentrated in strength as soon as he realized the menace, but could not interrupt the development of the operation. Mandalay and Meiktila were captured, while in the north the Chinese secured Lashio. The Japanese fell back, still determined to defend the routes south along the Irrawaddy and the Sittang, but having suffered very heavy loss and being greatly hampered by hunger, disease and fatigue among the remnants of their forces. The British, fortified by a new drug far more effective than quinine in warding off malaria, were able to pursue them through the most malarious areas without hesitation or any special extra precautions.

The rest of the campaign was brilliantly handled, strategically and tactically. Air transport was used once again with great effect both for supplies and troop movements. An advance in the Arakan opened up new airfields and growing command of the sea enabled supplies to be carried by sea to points upon the newly-won Arakan coast-line from which they could be flown to the front, thus securing a vast saving in the capacity of the transport squadrons as compared with the time when they had had to fly all the way from India. Rangoon was recovered on May 3rd, 1945, though hard fighting was still called for to rope in the thousands of Japanese striving to make their way eastward across the Sittang. All preparations were now set on foot for a landing in Malaya in overwhelming strength, but this never took place because the general Japanese surrender occurred just before it was ready.

It had taken a long time to destroy the Japanese forces in Burma and reoccupy the country, but this was largely on account of the woeful lack of material resources. With what they had to use the commanders had made a remarkably fine job of it, and the British, Indian, East and West African, and Chinese forces, with their American contingent, their American, R.A.F., and Indian air support, their effective aid from the Navy in the later stages, shared with American forces in the Philippines the distinction of being the only ones ever to engage and utterly defeat a major Japanese army in the open field.

CHAPTER XXVIII

Allied Offensive in the Far East—The Pacific

THE American campaigns in the Pacific provide the supreme example of combined operations that the world has witnessed. The old and useful term "amphibious" has become out-of-date to describe them and all operations of a similar type, since these are no longer merely "connected with both land and water" but conducted in the three elements of land, water and air. If we reject the appalling term "triphibious", invented in jocular mood by Mr. Churchill, "triune" remans the most satisfactory epithet. Efforts have been made to present to the public a picture in which air power appears as the victor in these campaigns. It is false; victory was won by a partnership between the three powers. Air power may be considered the senior partner, yet no phase could have been undertaken without the participation of all three. Some of the land fighting was among the fiercest and most bloody of the war, that in Okinawa for example. The most important naval battles of the war took place in Pacific waters, the only others being those fought in the Mediterranean. The only great naval battle, to be ranked in history with Lepanto and Trafalgar, belongs to the Pacific. Yet, owing to the nature of the area and the development of the power of aircraft flown from carriers, two striking characteristics of these campaigns appear: first, the increasing rôle of the air arm in naval warfare, and, secondly, the relatively small number of land forces which were required or could be employed in proportion to the strength of the land forces of Japan—though it must not be forgotten that the Allies were preparing to bring into action far greater land strength when the end came.

Omitting the Burmese theatre and China, at the end of hostilities the Americans had in the Pacific 21 Army divisions (the great majority in the Philippines) as against 67 in the European theatre. In addition to these are were the Marine divisions and the Australian and New Zealand forces under General MacArthur's command. Yet even this represented a considerable expansion. In July, 1943, two years earlier, General MacArthur's strength in land forces was four American and six Australian divisions, while in the Central Pacific there were at the disposal of Admiral Nimitz nine Army and Marine divisions. The key to this riddle is, of course, the power of these commanders, by reason of their naval and air strength, to land their soldiers and marines in superior local strength and to provide them with immensely powerful support.

For the same reason the technique of landing from the sea became different in the Pacific to that practised against the Germans on the European Continent. In most cases tactical surprise was less essential since the Japanese could not concentrate to meet the attack as the Germans could. On the other hand, the Japanese were more fanatical defenders, who fought to the last and might inflict dreadful losses upon the assailants even though the issue was a foregone conclusion. The Americans therefore carried out more prolonged and thorough bombardments of the beaches from air and sea before they put their troops ashore on an island objective than they could have afforded in Europe, where no time could be wasted if it was hoped to anticipate a concentration of hostile strength. The Japanese, for their part, soon learnt that no life could exist on the beaches under such bombardment and took to withdrawing a short distance inland, hoping to break the attack on their retired position and then clear the beaches by counter-attack.

The control of operations in the Pacific was retained by the United States Chiefs of Staff, whereas that of South-east Asia was exercised in a broad sense by the Combined Chiefs. At Quebec, in August, 1943, the direction of the advance was decided. Mac-Arthur, Supreme Commander in the South-west Pacific, was directed to continue his progress along the north coast of New Guinea with the object of reaching the Philippines by the autumn of 1944. The advance across the Central Pacific was entrusted to Admiral Nimitz, who was to move by way of the Gilberts, the Marshalls, and the Marianas and to reach the Ryukus by the spring of 1945. The South Pacific Area—roughly that of the Solomon Islands—was the zone of Admiral William F. Halsey, but at the end of 1943 the Army forces in it came under the strategic direction of MacArthur. The Commander-in-Chief of the United States Navy, Admiral King, was convinced that at some point in these operations the Japanese Navy would have to pick up the glove thrown down and challenge the Americans in a great naval battle.

In the Solomons Halsey's command captured the island of New Georgia with the Japanese airfield at Munda on August 5th, 1943. In October New Zealand troops occupied two islands of the Treasury Group in the northern Solomons, and on November 1st American marines landed in Empress Augusta Bay on the west side of the large island of Bougainville. Here, as at many other points in the Solomons, the Bismarck Archipelago, and New Guinea, Japanese forces were to remain in being until the final surrender in 1945, but the object of the landing was achieved. This was the seizure of a naval anchorage and three airfields within striking distance of the important Japanese base at Rabaul, in New Britain, 235 miles away.

In New Guinea MacArthur's mainly Australian forces, whose capture of Gona, Sanananda, and Buna has already been described, after defeating a Japanese attack on Wau, 120 miles to the northwest, in January, began a long campaign to drive the enemy from his bases at Salamaua and Lae. The threat from the hinterland at Wau attracted the Japanese like a magnet, and month after month they weakened their forces at Salamaua and Lae in order to check it. On September 4th a brilliant offensive was launched. The Australian 9th Division, one of the finest formations in the world, landed in the Huon Gulf, convoyed by the American Navy and protected by American air forces. The 7th Division was landed from the air in the Markham Valley on ground previously secured by American parachutists. Salamaua fell on the 11th and Lae on the 16th. Then a landing from the sea was carried out north of Finschhafen, which fell after fierce fighting on October 2nd and was held after a counter-attack lasting five days. British Matilda tanks were used in these operations, this being the first occasion that heavy or even medium tanks had been employed in New Guinea. Finally the Australians, moving on west, established contact with American troops who had already reached Saidor.

In order to obtain control of the Vitiaz and Dampier Straits between New Guinea and New Britain and to obtain a new link in the chain of bases at Cape Gloucester in the latter island, landings were made on it in December and by March a great part of the western section of the island had been secured. Between February and April, 1944, the Admiralty Islands were captured, providing another harbour and more airfields. The planning sequence would appear to have been: the footing on Bougainville to neutralize Rabaul and other Japanese bases in New Britain; the footing in the Cape Gloucester region of New Britain to assist in covering the Admiralties; and the footing in the Admiralties to provide airfields to support the further advance in a series of bounds along the northern coast of New Guinea and to assist Admiral Nimitz in the Central Pacific.

The first of these leaps, on April 22nd, was to Aitape and Hollandia, direct air support being provided by naval carriers. Only 5,000 Japanese were stationed in the area of Hollandia, which implied that a genuine strategic surprise was attained here. Fifty thousand were cut off to the eastward and it would appear in a sense more complete than could be said of those in other areas which had been "by-passed"—Bougainville, for example, where occasional supplies were received from Rabaul or New Ireland. The Japanese thus isolated were in some cases reduced to a low ebb, but they organized such local resources as they could, fished, and established gardens and farms on a large scale. It may be added that the Allies, the Australians in particular, though their supplies were assured, also made a good deal of local supplies, setting up pig farms and gardens and exploiting the fisheries along the coast, which were fairly well stocked. By July the Americans had made a further bound to the extreme western end of New Guinea. In mid-September they reached Morotai in the Moluccas. The point of the advance was now close to the Philippines.

We now have to turn back to the Central Pacific to note what Admiral Nimitz had been about meanwhile. His first step was the capture of the British Gilbert Islands. After heavy air attacks from carriers to restrain the activities of the enemy in the Marshalls, he occupied islands to the south-east of the Gilberts in September, 1943. Then his Seventh Air Force launched a powerful offensive against the islands of Tarawa and Makin, the vital islands of the Gilberts. Fighting was fierce in both cases, but particularly so on Tarawa, which represented a new type of warfare for the Americans. The enemy was strong in numbers in proportion to the extent of the island, had built numerous concrete "pill-boxes" which covered the beaches with enfilade fire, and had mined the beaches themselves. Only a combination of searching and shattering bombardment followed by assault could overcome the fanatical garrison. Tarawa is a name which will always be remembered in American military annals, coupled with that of the 2nd Marine Division which secured it after heavy sacrifice.

Admiral Nimitz next directed operations against the Marshalls. On January 31st, 1944, troops of his V Marine Amphibious Corps landed on the southern islands of Kwajalein Atoll and on other islands at the northern end. The enemy's desperate resistance was not overcome until February 8th. After another heavy air bombardment from carriers, the Americans secured another atoll, that of Eniwetok, midway between the Marshalls and the Marianas, by the 22nd. They had, it will be observed, so far not entered the Caroline Islands, in which lay Truk, the chief Japanese naval anchorage in the Central Pacific, but this place became virtually useless to the enemy now that they were in control of the Marshalls. It could also be bombarded by long-range aircraft based on the Admiralties, in General MacArthur's zone.

The significance of these coral atolls and their lagoons had been thoroughly grasped by the Japanese long before the war, and they had made exhaustive surveys of them, while barring those in their mandate (Marshalls, Carolines, Palau Islands, Marianas, etc.), from foreign observation. The Pacific is so vast and its waters are so deep that anchorages such as those provided by the lagoons become of immense importance in warfare. The whole Micronesian region in which these groups of islands lie is very deep. To the east of it lies the Miller Deep where the soundings exceed 3,000 fathoms. Between the Philippines and Japan is a zone of similar depth. The Ladrone Basin, in the region of the Carolines and the Marianas, has given a sounding in the Nero Deep, fringing Guam, of 5,269 fathoms, or 31,614 feet, as against the 29,002 feet height of Everest. East of Japan there is a depth of 4,643 fathoms in the Tuscarora Deep. It may indeed be said that only the anchorages afforded by the lagoons make naval operations in the Central Pacific possible.

A pause in the advance in the Central Pacific followed, though in the air the struggle continued, more and more to the disadvantage of the enemy. Admiral Nimitz's next goal was the Marianas; the Japanese must have been aware of it and prepared to meet the attack. On June 15th the V Marine Amphibious Corps landed in great force on the strongly garrisoned island of Saipan, a big island by the standard of this part of the Pacific. Two Marine divisions, followed by an army division, carried out the attack. It took 25 days of hard fighting to subdue the fierce resistance, and even then odd corners of the island concealed small parties of Japanese, some of whom held out for months. On July 21st an infantry division, a Marine division and a Marine brigade of the III Marine Amphibious Corps landed on the island of Guam, where the process was repeated, resistance on this occasion lasting until August 10th. When the Saipan operation was ended the corps artillery which had been landed on that island to take part in it began an artillery preparation against the defences of the neighbouring island of Tinian, and on July 24th elements of two Marine divisions landed here, to secure the island after a struggle of nine days. The support by land artillery firing from one island against another which was to be attacked was a remarkable feature of these operations, though one not unknown in General MacArthur's south-west area. But, needless to say, the most astonishing characteristic of all was the size of the forces engaged in the struggle for these small and remote atolls, which witnessed life and death conflicts between armies larger than those which in old times decided some of the world's most vital battles, whereas on some of these islands there had probably never been twenty white men assembled together at any one time.

And yet it would be hard to conceive any objective in any war which had a greater significance than the Marianas. Their invasion may come to be considered as the most important single step taken in either of the Pacific theatres. Bombers of the Seventh Air Force quickly began to operate from Saipan against Iwo Jima in the Bonins, and the importance of the former island will presently become abundantly clear. But even that did not exhaust the value of Saipan. Before the capture of the Marianas was complete work had been begun both on Saipan and on Guam on airfields which would take the new American giant bomber, the Super-Fortress. From them its great range allowed it to reach the main Japanese island of Honshu. The first great attack on this, the heart of Japan, was delivered on November 24th, 1944.

On September 13th Nimitz reached forward to the island of Peleliu in the Palau group and two days later landed forces also on Angaur, to the south. This move exactly coincided with

MacArthur's advance to Morotai in the Moluccas. Both forces had pushed close to the Philippines. It had already been decided to effect a landing in them with the least possible delay.

In the latter part of August Admiral Halsey had pushed out towards the Philippines and bombarded targets on the island of Mindanao from his carriers. On his return he sent a message to Admiral Nimitz on September 13th recommending that projected operations against Yap, between the Marianas and the Palau Islands, and an attack on Mindanao be cut out of the programme and that a landing be carried out on Leyte, in the central Philippines, as soon as might be. On the same day Nimitz offered to put at MacArthur's disposal for the purpose his 3rd Amphibious Force, which included the XXIV Corps at Hawaii. Two days later MacArthur reported that he could put forward his landing by two months, reaching Leyte on October 20th instead of December 20th, as he had preciously intended. This was, as General Marshall points out in his official report, evidence that the administrative arrangements were remarkably flexible and well balanced by this stage.

The messages reached the Joint Chiefs of Staff at the Quebec Conference (the second conference there, known by the code name of "Octagon", the earlier one, to which reference has previously been made, being "Quadrant", held in August, 1943). Having full confidence in their executants, they agreed. A difficulty now appeared which was brought about by the unfavourable situation in China, where a Japanese offensive was threatening the American airfields and about to cause the abandonment of the eastern of them. This offensive had begun in May with a southerly drive from Tung Ting Lake in Hunan and had recently been supplemented by a westerly drive from Canton. The two offensives eventually met near Liuchow, over-running seven airfields. This naturally caused considerable anxiety, but its effects were confined to China. It had been feared that it might affect MacArthur's progress, since the bombers of Major-General Claire L. Chennault's Fourteenth Air Force in China had been destined to support operations in the northern Philippines. MacArthur, however, remained unperturbed. He considered that Halsey's carrier-borne aircraft had, in the course of the sweep already mentioned, wrought such destruction upon the Japanese air force that he need not rely upon the support of Chennault.

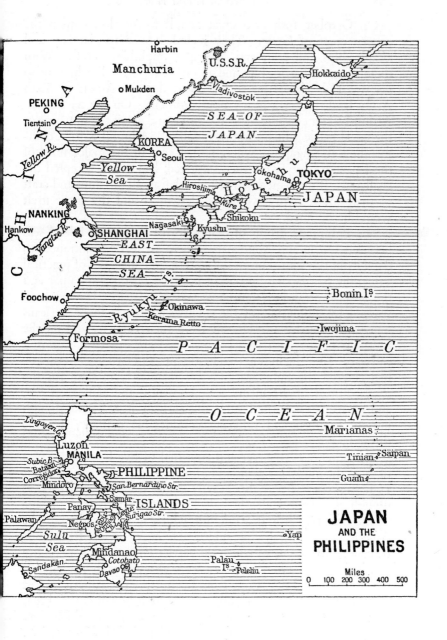

JAPAN
AND THE
PHILIPPINES

Miles
0   100   200   300   400   500

On October 19th two great assault forces closed upon the
eastern coast of Leyte. They included over 300 landing and
assault ships and craft and over 400 amphibious craft. With
them were six battle-ships and 18 escort carriers. Further out to
sea was Halsey's carrier force. Next day the American Sixth
Army landed after a heavy bombardment. On the 23rd Mac-
Arthur bade it consolidate its footholds and await the outcome of
the naval battle which must now follow. Admiral Kurita, commanding at Singapore, where 60 per cent of the major units of
the Japanese Navy were then stationed, had at last accepted the
challenge. If the Americans suffered defeat, all the ships and craft
of their Sixth Army would be destroyed and the force itself
would be doomed.

The Philippine group of islands forms a series of inland seas
between Luzon and Mindanao. There are various entrances to
these from the west, but on the eastern side only two of practical
value, the San Bernardino Strait between Luzon and Samar and
the Surigao Strait between Leyte and Mindanao. Having been
warned by submarines of the enemy's approach, the Americans
sent out reconnaissance aircraft from their carriers, and on the
morning of the 24th two large fleets were observed steaming
eastward. One, including two battleships and two heavy cruisers,
had entered the Sulu Sea and was manifestly making for the
southernmost of the inland seas, known as the Mindanao Sea,
and for its exit into the Pacific, the Surigao Strait. And, though
heavily bombed and suffering considerable damage, it came
through.

The other was stronger and consisted of five battleships, two
of them the modern *Yamato* and *Musashi*, eight cruisers, and about
15 destroyers. It was also heavily engaged and turned back as
though the commander had decided not to force the passage
of the San Barnardino Strait, for which it was heading. The
Americans were meanwhile subjected to heavy attacks from land-
based aircraft, in one of which the carrier *Princeton* was set on fire
and had to be sunk. But there were also carrier-borne aircraft
in the attack, and they came from the north. The Americans lost
no time in tracking them, and at 3.40 p.m. it was discovered that
they were flown from two other Japanese squadrons which were
moving down the coast of Luzon and included four carriers.
These clearly came from Japanese harbours, whereas the other

two were from Singapore. The United States Third Fleet under
Admiral W. F. Halsey turned north to meet the advancing
enemy. In all the Japanese had now disclosed 9 battleships, 4
carriers, 20 cruisers, and about 30 destroyers.

To return to the fleet which had passed the Surigao Strait, it
met with a terrible reception on emerging and a fate which was
merited by its extreme rashness. It came into a terrific volume
of fire from battleships and cruisers stationed to await its arrival—
five which had been involved in the Pearl Harbour disaster and
were now modernized—and was simultaneously attacked by
destroyers. As blow after blow rained upon it it turned back, but
only a small proportion escaped. Either then or early next morning, when American aircraft engaged the fleeing remnant, it was
completely destroyed, with the possible exception of one cruiser
and about half its complement of destroyers. Vice-Admiral T. C.
Kinkaid's Seventh Fleet had gained an overwhelming victory.

The squadrons steaming south from Japan were surprised by
Admiral Halsey while their aircraft, after attacking the Americans,
were refuelling on Luzon. The American air assault sank three
out of the four carriers and damaged the fourth, which was sunk
during the pursuit. But Admiral Halsey could not devote all his
fleet to pursuit in view of the alarming news which reached him
on the 25th. The central Japanese fleet had after all traversed the
San Bernardino Strait during the night and was now threatening
the shipping massed for the landings on Leyte and the escort
carriers and destroyers directly protecting it. The carriers, converted merchantmen, made off eastwards, launching aircraft to
attack the Japanese, but the enemy with his superior speed quickly
closed the range, and had his gunnery and seamanship been as
good as was believed, would have destroyed the whole covering
force. Just when it seemed that it was at last about to do so the
Japanese admiral turned and made off. He had heard of the
destruction of the southern fleet which had entered the Surigao
Strait and of the flight of the northern off the coast of Luzon, and
he was also apparently anxious about his fuel supply.

Next day American aircraft, ranging the waters round the
Philippines, accounted for a few more lame ducks. In all it was
established that two battleships, four carriers, eight cruisers, and
a number of destroyers had been sunk. Many other warships
had been hit, some of them being seriously damaged. The

Americans lost one carrier, two escort carriers, two destroyers and a few lesser craft.

The Japanese strategy had been at fault. It was a grave mistake to split up the Singapore fleet. It was an offence against sound doctrine to attack the force covering the landings while the American main fleets remained in being. Tactically too it was a weakness to have put in the aircraft of the fleet from Japan at such an early stage, so that they had to land on the Luzon airfields to refuel and hardly any were on the decks of the carriers when Halsey engaged them. But apart from these errors the Japanese showed less fighting ability than accorded with their naval reputation. Except for a brief moment off Guadalcanal and in the Indian Ocean when they had but slight opposition, Japanese battleships had not previously been in action, and it cannot be said that they distinguished themselves. It is perhaps unfair to criticize their gunnery, since they had no radar, whereas Kincaid's salved and modernized battleships possessed the latest type, but it was also to have been expected that the Japanese aircraft, whether based on the Philippines or flown from carriers, would have been more effective. The Japanese Navy had held off for a long time, but this strategy of delay and the maintenance of a fleet in being had not been justified by the result when it was at last committed to battle.

CHAPTER XXIX

Closing on Japan

THE greatest naval victory of the war and one of the decisive naval victories in history had been gained by the United States. MacArthur could now go ahead. But while the battle was in progress the Japanese, with remarkable energy and boldness, had been sending reinforcements to the Philippines virtually without interference, and they continued for some weeks to bring them in, though with rapidly growing losses. One of their best divisions was embarked at Shanghai, transported to Manila, and thence transferred to Leyte. On one day alone, November 7th, 1944, seven transports unloaded, the Japanese maintaining sufficient strength in the air to protect them. Two days later four large transports came into Ormoc Bay on the west coast, but on this occasion two were sunk by the Americans. By the middle of December the sinkings had become very heavy and the flow of reinforcements had ceased; even supplies were frequently transported in sailing ships.

The Philippines were not only the seat of a Japanese army headquarters but also that of Field-Marshal Count Terauchi, who exercised supreme command in the whole area of these islands, of the Netherlands East Indies, Malaya, Siam, French Indo-China, and New Guinea. The army commander, General Yamashita, the victor of the Malayan campaign in 1942 and the commander who had wound up the first campaign in the Philippines, was one of the best in the Japanese service. He had at his disposal over a quarter of a million troops in the Philippines. But they were necessarily scattered; many of them could in no circumstances have been moved from Luzon, the main island; and as American air ascendancy became established he was unable to move even such formations and units as could be spared from their stations. The American invasion of the Philippines depended for success essentially upon the same factors as the allied invasion of France: the ability to prevent the enemy, with his over-all superior strength, from concentrating against the original landing force, and the piece-meal defeat of the defence without its ever being able to establish local superiority at any point.

By December 1st the Americans under General Walter Krueger had seven divisions ashore and five airfields in operation. Six days later a new American landing was carried out in Ormoc Bay and shortly afterwards the town was captured with large quantities of Japanese supplies. By the end of the year all organized resistance on the island had ceased. Then other forces took over the task of mopping up and Krueger's Sixth Army went on to one more vital.

In the first week of January, 1945, a vast American convoy which had assembled east of Leyte sailed through the Suriago Strait between that island and Mindanao, and entered the Sulu Sea. On the 9th the Sixth Army effected a landing on the island of Luzon in Lingayen Gulf, the historic landing-place of invaders. Despite the distance which the convoy had had to cover, a remarkable measure of surprise was gained and heavy resistance did not begin until the advanced guard, moving southward in the direction of Manila, had covered half the distance to the capital and reached the old American aerodrome of Clark Field. On the other flank the Japanese were entrenched in the hills and had for the time being to be contained, since resources to drive them out were not available.

On January 29th another landing was carried out, this time by troops of the Eighth Army, on the west coast near Subic Bay. This force at once began to thrust eastwards to cut off the peninsula of Bataan, where it might be anticipated that the Japanese would make a determined stand, just as General MacArthur had three years earlier. On the 31st another division landed, without opposition, south-west of Manila, while at the same time troops from the north were also approaching the capital. The Japanese resisted stoutly in the city, which suffered a great deal of damage in the course of the struggle lasting until February 23rd. Meanwhile yet another landing took place on the 15th at the southern end of Bataan. Corregidor, the fortress which the Americans had held so heroically, had been under heavy air bombardment since January 23rd. On February 16th a parachute regiment was dropped over it, while at the same time assault boats grounded on the shore of the island. Once again the Japanese fought to the last, finally blowing up the tunnel system and the majority of their own survivors with it. Early in March Manila Bay had been opened to American shipping, but resistance in Luzon was by no means over. As in other islands, it was never to be entirely subdued until the final surrender.

On March 10th MacArthur secured a footing on the westernmost point of Mindanao, the largest and most strongly held of the Philippine Islands after Luzon. During the same month he landed forces on intervening islands, Panay, Negros and Cebu. On April 17th the Eighth Army put a large force ashore midway along the west coast of Mindanao near Cotabato. Driving across the island, it captured the city of Davao on May 4th. In mid-May another force landed on the north coast, under cover of Filipino partisans, who were here operating in strength, and seized the town of Del Monte.

Some of the Australian troops had shown much impatience that they should have been left behind when the Americans took up the offensive from them in New Guinea and swept on to the Philippines. On May 1st an Australian force with some Dutch troops attached landed on Tarakan island, off the north-east coast of Borneo. This was a rich oil-field of the highest quality, which it was important to deny to the enemy and would be useful to the Allies if they could exploit it. By the end of the month all the installations of the island had been secured by the Australians. On June 10th their 9th Division got ashore unopposed in Brunei Bay, on the north-west coast, securing further oil-fields. They also seized air-fields, and in General Marshall's words, "completed a chain of mutually supporting strategic bases from which allied air and naval forces could cover the Asiatic coast from Singapore to Shanghai". On July 1st the Australians made a third landing on the great island, this time at Balikpapan, on the southeast flank. They quickly secured the harbour, which was open to shipping within a few days of its capture.

While the conquest—at least the effective conquest—of the Philippines had been in progress, the direct advance upon Japan in the Central Pacific had not ceased. On February 19th Admiral R. A. Spruance, commanding the Fifth Fleet, escorted the V. Marine Corps to Iwo Jima, 775 miles from the Japanese main island of Honshu. The Japanese fully recognized the importance of Iwo Jima and put up a defence even more fanatical than usual. The island was finally cleared in mid-March. The great value of Iwo Jima was that fast fighters could be stationed on its airfields to escort the Super-Fortress bombers now attacking Japan, while many of the latter, too badly damaged to reach their own airfields in the Marianas on their return from their missions, could also land there.

The Americans were, however, planning to come to much closer quarters still. Aircraft based on the Philippines now dominated the Japanese airfields on Formosa and to a great extent on the coast of China. It was possible to obtain a footing in the Ryukyu Islands lying between Japan itself and Formosa. This was the vital move in the great American scheme, which had been built up step by step. If it succeeded the doom of Japan was certain. But the Japanese knew the fact, and they had made what preparation they could.

The first landing was effected on March 26th on Keramo Retto, west of Okinawa. Within the next few days the neighbouring small islands were secured. On April 1st the great blow was struck. Covered by an intense naval bombardment, the III Marine Corps and the XXIV Corps of the Tenth Army landed on the west coast of Okinawa. Little resistance was met with; nor was there for the first few days any hint of what was to come. But the American command was not deceived. It knew that there would be a bloody fight for possession of the island.

The Marine Corps went northward, still meeting with only moderate opposition, but after clearing the northern end had to send a force to the south to aid the XXIV Corps, which had become engaged in a terrific struggle. Here the main Japanese garrison lay in a previously selected position which had been elaborately entrenched and otherwise fortified. It was between sixty and seventy thousand strong with 500 guns, numbers of mortar, and batteries of rockets. The ground was rough and contained many caves, impervious to fire, which the enemy had included in the organization of his defences.

Almost for the first time since the earlier stages of the war the Japanese also launched heavy and effective air attacks on American shipping in the neighbourhood of the island. During the fighting in the Philippines the Americans had had some experience of Japanese "suicide" bombers, which the pilots directed straight on to the target, to perish themselves in the explosion on impact. Now, however, the Japanese exploited in considerable numbers a more deadly weapon. This was the Baka aircraft, a small, rocket-accelerated machine which was brought into action fixed underneath a normal bomber. The Baka carried over a ton of high-explosive in its warhead. At a suitable moment it was released from the parent aircraft and driven by its "suicide" pilot into a dive on the target. By the time the fighting came to an end the Americans had lost 33 ships sunk and 45 damaged, mainly by aerial attacks. The Japanese concentrated on this deadly weapon, till in August, 1945, they possessed more "suicide" than normal aircraft, but fortunately for the Americans just too late.

The hostile land forces put up the most stubborn resistance yet encountered. Week after week went by marked by very slight American progress won at terrible cost. From Japan a message was sent to the troops to inform them that the whole fate of their country depended upon their repelling the attack on Okinawa. They could not have responded with more determination and courage. The battle raged on through April, May and into June. At the end of April a Japanese naval intervention from the west was defeated and the battleship *Yamato*, one of the greatest warships in the world, was sunk by aircraft. On June 18th the commander of the Tenth Army, Lieut.-General S. B. Buckner, was killed directing the final offensive. He was succeeded by the veteran General Stilwell, who had been relieved of his post in Burma on account of differences with the Chinese Generalissimo. But Buckner's work was accomplished. Three days later organized resistance came to an end. The conquest of Okinawa had cost the Americans 39,000 casualties, including over 10,000 personnel of the fleet. They claimed to have killed over 100,000 Japanese, and they had captured nearly 8,000, whereas in many previous battles Japanese prisoners of war had been numbered only by tens or scores. In the air the Americans had lost over a thousand aircraft. They claimed 3,400 Japanese shot down over the Ryukyus and the southern Japanese island of Kyushu, besides hundreds destroyed on the ground.

Before dealing with the final terrible scenes in the Japanese homeland it may be well to take a glance back at the situation in the Pacific in rear of the forces which had closed in with the object of dealing Japan her death-blow. Vast Japanese forces were cut off in the ocean. In some cases they were completely isolated; in others they maintained a feeble and intermittent system of intercommunication. In New Britain, for example there was still fuel in the much-bombed Rabaul and occasional aircraft flew across to Bougainville. They had stacks of ammunition originally dumped for operations against Australia. In the South-west Pacific American forces had been withdrawn and the area had been handed over to the Australians. Why it was considered necessary to put on the pressure against the Japanese garrisons has not been adequately explained, but certain it is that the Australians, taking over fronts which had of late been quiet, stirred them into high activity.

The most important of these offensives was on the northern flank of New Guinea, where, after immense exertions in bad weather the Australians crossed the Torricelli range to hunt down bodies of Japanese who had penetrated some distance inland. They also closed upon the base at Wewak from the west, taking two valuable airfields in Mardi. In New Britain the Fifth Division advanced in two columns along the coast and finally penned the Japanese into the Gazelle Peninsula at the northern end of the island. In Bougainville two Australian divisions on a reduced establishment made some progress after sharp fighting both in the north and in the south-west, but did not possess sufficient resources owing to the calls upon shipping elsewhere to press their advantage home. New Ireland, where there was a strong Japanese garrison, was not invaded.

In all these areas the Japanese were present in strength superior to that of the Australians, their total numbers in the Solomons and New Guinea being over 100,000. There were also large numbers of the enemy in the Central Pacific. In the Gilberts they still held Nauru and Ocean Island on the fringe of the group. In the Marshalls there were 14,000 troops on the three atolls remaining in their hands, without communication for over a year with Japan except by the visits of occasional submarines. In the Marianas, now one of the great Super-Fortress bases and the headquarters of Nimitz, Spaatz and Twining (on Guam), there remained 5,000 Japanese on other islands. In the Palau Islands there were 30,000. But by far the greatest number were in the Carolines, which had not been included in the American stepping-stones. At the great base of Truk, once a name of awe, now nearly useless, there were estimated to be 50,000 Japanese, and over 20,000 more in the islands. These figures are in themselves further proof of the suc-

cess of the allied strategy in rendering almost innocuous a quarter
of a million men. The Americans simply had to assure themselves
by air reconnaissance to look out for long-range aircraft or even
ships which might endanger their supply routes. They also visited
the Kuriles, and here made occasional bombing raids on shipping,
still present in these northern harbours.

Against Germany the experiment had been made of attempting
to put out of action by air bombing a great industrial country.
Even now there is dispute as to what extent it succeeded. It was,
in short, inconclusive. It is clear, of course, that bombing immensely reduced Germany's industrial capacity and, in the
broadest sense, the mobility of her armed forces; but it required
great land campaigns, Russian and British-American, from both
flanks, with long-drawn-out and costly battles, to reduce Germany to submission, and behind the latter sea power, transporting
men and material and maintaining their communications.

The American campaign against Japan in the Pacific followed a
different pattern. In this case, sea, land, and air forces, working
in the closest co-operation, fought their way forward from island
to island till they reached the outskirts of Japan. The Navy held
off the Japanese fleet, defeating it—with the aid of air power—in
several battles and finally crushing it in the Philippines; it protected the convoys—again with the aid of air power—and covered
the landings by bombardments. From its carriers it launched air
attacks directly against the Japanese islands. Its submarines played
a part even greater than that of aircraft in reducing the Japanese
merchant fleet to 20 per cent of its strength at the outbreak of
hostilities. The Army and the Marine divisions won the new
bases required for the Navy and the American Air Force. These
land forces fought the heaviest battles and suffered the highest
losses. The A.A.F. made use of the successive vantage points
gained for it by the other services with its own aid, till finally it
was able to launch continual attacks against the heart of Japan of
ever-increasing strength.

So far it was an equal partnership. Yet in the last assaults upon
Japan it was the A.A.F. which dealt the overwhelming blows.
"Fully recognizing the indispensable contributions of other arms,"
wrote General H. H. Arnold, Commanding General of the
U.S.A.A.F., "I feel that air power's part may fairly be called
decisive." So, though the air attack could never have been

launched without the co-operation of the other services, when the approach to Japan had been completed the other services stood by while the A.A.F. took over the final work. It is true that all preparations had to be made, and were made, to invade Japan, but there was always at the back of the planners' minds the hope that this might not be necessary and that air power would first batter Japan into surrender. It did so. And since Japan surrendered before a hostile foot had been set upon the shores of any of her home islands and her surrender was due not merely to her inability to meet invasion owing to the terrible bombardments to which she was subjected but even more to her inability to go on enduring these bombardments, it is correct to say that the combination of destruction and terror put Japan out of action. In other words, the experiment succeeded here.

It was indeed a terrible experiment, since it aimed at pure and indiscriminate destruction. As a killer pure and simple the aircraft did not prove voracious. It was one of the surprises of the war how relatively few were killed in proportion to the destruction wrought by air attacks. Yet in all the air attacks directed against Japan she lost in casualties more than all those suffered by her land forces. And over nine million people were rendered homeless—the majority of these being subjected to incredible misery. Some 15 square miles of Tokyo were practically burnt out in a single night's attack by Super-Fortresses, on March 9th, when the Americans first resorted to low night flying and substituted incendiaries for high explosive. It is estimated that 57 per cent of the great city of Yokohama was destroyed by fire, and that Hiroshima suffered to the extent of 41 per cent destruction before the dropping of the atomic bomb. It was the "all-out" attack in perfection. That it saved thousands, perhaps hundreds of thousands, of American lives, and probably Japanese lives too, is certain. But even so the last word upon its effect upon civilization and the future of the world has not yet been spoken.

CHAPTER XXX

The End in the Far East

THE Americans reorganized their command for the last phases. On April 6th MacArthur assumed command of all United States Army forces in the Pacific. He divided them into two, Western Pacific under Lieut.-General W. D. Styer, and Middle Pacific under Lieut.-General R. C. Richardson. In early July, with the arrival of air reinforcements from Europe as a result of the defeat of Germany, the air forces were combined under the headquarters U.S. Army Strategic Air Forces commanded by General Carl Spaatz from Guam. They consisted of the Eighth Air Force (Lieut.-General J. H. Doolittle) at Okinawa and the Twentieth (Lieut.-General N. F. Twining) in the Marianas. The development of the Okinawa airfields was fantastic; even the American engineer and his wonderful equipment had never before accomplished anything like this. The construction of 23 strips was taken in hand, and by the end of hostilities the A.A.F. alone was operating 18 groups of heavy and medium bombers and fighters from Okinawa and its little neighbour, Ie Shima. If invasion had been necessary at the beginning of November, 47 groups of Army, Navy and Marine aircraft would have been operating from these islands. The efficiency of the Super-Fortresses was so high and their bomb-load so much superior to that of any earlier aircraft that far fewer bases were required than in Europe.

The improved situation in the Atlantic and in European waters and particularly the destruction of the *Tirpitz* on November 12th, 1944, had rendered it possible for the British to transfer greater naval resources to the Pacific, and they were anxious to do so not merely for strategic reasons but also for the sake of their prestige. When it was announced that this was the case some sections of American opinion received the information coldly, arguing that the United States was fully capable of conducting the Pacific war alone and that the British would have to acquire the special technique. This attitude was not reflected in the statement of the American naval authorities. Before the end of 1944 the appoint-

ment of Admiral Sir Bruce Fraser to the British Command in the
Far East was announced and it was stated that the fleet would
initially be based upon Australia. From that country his words:
"We must get nearer to Japan", were welcomed at home because
they recalled the famous signal of Nelson: "Engage the enemy
more closely". Australian ships were already serving with the
Americans and had taken part in the fighting in the Philippines,
and now it was arranged that the British should also serve under
the direction of American admirals. The first ships to go into
action were incorporated in Admiral Spruance's Fifth Pacific
Fleet and took part in operations at the end of March, 1945, when
they bombed the southern islands of the Ryukus and helped to
cover the Okinawa landing.

The end of the war in Europe made it possible to reinforce the
British fleet in the Pacific, and in July it was announced that no
major warships remained in European waters. The battleships
Howe, King George V, Duke of York, and the carriers *Formidable,
Illustrious, Indomitable* and *Victorious* were in the Pacific, while the
Queen Elizabeth, Valiant, the French *Richelieu* and the *Renown*
were with the East Indies Fleet. The British Pacific fleet took part
in constant attacks on the Japanese home islands, chiefly from its
carriers, though on occasion it also brought the guns of its battleships into action against Japanese ports.

In the bombing attacks on Japan the carrier-borne bombers
shared the task with the Super-Fortresses, though of course the
bomb-load of the latter was by far the heavier. The strength of
the attacks grew steadily. The maximum number of Super-
Fortresses engaged in any one attack on Japan in 1944 was one
hundred. On May 28th, 1945, 450 of these aircraft attacked Yokohama; on June 2nd 600 were engaged against the naval base of
Kure and other towns; in early August 801 went into action. In
the five largest cities attacked over one hundred square miles were
burnt out. It was estimated by the Americans that the destruction
of propeller plants alone, without any further attack on aircraft
industry, would have reduced the Japanese output of aircraft
by November, 1945, to 41 per cent of that of January of the same
year. It was unendurable, and there can be no shadow of doubt
that Japan was utterly and hopelessly defeated before the dropping
of the first atomic bomb. She was already making peace feelers,
but was apparently prepared to use her one bargaining counter,

the fanaticism of her troops and their power to inflict enormous casualties upon the Americans, before yielding.

It was for this reason that the Americans decided to use the atomic bomb, in the hope that it would bring about the end quickly and save the lives of thousands of their soldiers, sailors, and airmen. They had prepared for a great invasion, the first phase of which was to take place in the late autumn. It was to be carried out by the Sixth Army with three corps, two from the Army and one from the Marines, containing ten divisions, against the southern island of Kyushu. A fourth corps, with three divisions, was to feint against the island of Shikoku and then to become the floating reserve. The second phase was to follow in the spring of 1946, four months later. The Eighth and Tenth Armies, with nine infantry, three marine, and two armoured divisions, were to initiate the invasion of the main island of Honshu by landing in the Kanto Plain east of Tokyo. These two armies were to be followed ashore by the First Army with ten infantry divisions and one airborne. General Hodges of the First Army, who had taken so prominent a part in the subjugation of the enemy in Europe, was thus to provide the final reserve for the last battle in the Pacific. Division after division had been hurried across the Atlantic to the United States, there to be stripped of personnel in the groups entitled to early release, made up to strength, re-equipped so far as that was necessary, and then shipped across the Pacific. The air support was by the last stage of the campaign to have reached a strength of about fifty groups.

This would have been a stupendous operation. To have brought 38 divisions with equivalent air strength to the attack on Japan would have been a far greater administrative feat and would have involved a heavier strain than the task of transferring 67 divisions to Europe and maintaining them there, together with a considerably greater air force than it was ever intended to employ in the Pacific. In the European theatres there was much that was of immense value for the conduct of the war. It was, it is true, not often that a prize such as the port of Antwerp, one of the largest and best equipped in the world, fell intact into the hands of the Allies, but the African ports, Naples—damaged as it was—Toulon, Marseilles, even the methodically demolished Cherbourg were ready-made bases. Above all the United States had at its disposal the great base constituted by the United Kingdom, and it must not be forgotten that though the aid which America afforded to Britain was vast, there was also a considerable return under "Reverse Lend-Lease". In the Pacific there was nothing outside Australia, which was off the direct route to Japan, and a few scanty facilities acquired in the Philippines. Natural harbours were not wanting, but every piece of equipment, even of the simplest kind, had to be transported across the water, and the Pacific distances were far greater than those of the Atlantic.

And invasion of Japan would have been bloody. The outstanding characteristic of the Japanese soldier was that he did not surrender in any appreciable numbers and nearly always fought to the last. Suppose that he were to repeat the performance of Okinawa, make little or no attempt to prevent a landing on Kyushu, but simply dig himself in upon a favourable position on that long and narrow island, heavy casualties to the invading forces were unavoidable. Japan still possessed thousands of aircraft, which had been husbanded during the terrific American attacks. So the Americans decided to drop an atomic bomb. The decision was taken at the conference then being held at Potsdam, where the Allies were thrashing out the problems of their victory in Europe and of the future of Germany and her former satellites. The chief representative of the United States was, as often before, the President, but the President was no longer the great man who had hitherto guided the destinies of the nation. Franklin Delano Roosevelt had lived long enough to know that victory was assured but not long enough to see it finally accomplished, even in Europe. He had died on April 18th. In a record of this sort it is unnecessary to speculate whether, had he now been present instead of his successor, Mr. Harry Truman, the decision to make immediate use of the new weapon would have been taken. It is more pertinent to consider the justice of the decision from the point of view of military expedience, political prudence, and morality. Even here it is not easy to form a judgment.

The Americans knew by experiment that the effects of the bomb would be far more terrible than those of any single weapon hitherto employed in warfare since the beginning of time. They must have realized that it would create a new and disturbing feature of international relations in the future. On the other hand, there was that powerful argument of life-saving. It has been suggested that if the bomb had been dropped upon some isolated and thinly populated portion of Japan the demonstration would have served its purpose and the enemy would have been brought to heel just as quickly. There is some doubt whether this would have been so, and in any case the disclosure of the bomb and its potentialities would have been equally alarming to the world, though perhaps the possibility of its being used by any nation which contrived to produce it would have been rather less. At all events the desire to make certain of avoiding the casualties to be expected in an invasion prevailed. It was not inevitable that invasion would be called for. The Japanese might well give in first, and in fact evidence coming from Japanese sources since the end of hostilities make it clear that the Emperor and the Government were determined to make peace at almost any price. The Americans were, however, not absolutely sure of this. So the bomb was to be dropped. There would be no great difficulty in selecting a site or in sending the necessary aircraft over it because the Japanese policy of holding back their air force, which has already been mentioned, played into American hands in this respect.

For several years American science and engineering, with British and Canadian aid in the former field, had been working upon the principle of atomic fission, and vast plants had been created for research and production. It was known that the Germans had also made their experiments in this field, and a daring British airborne raid had been carried out to interrupt their production of "heavy water" at a plant in Norway. But the Germans had fallen behind in the race and the Americans were at the winning post. The first bomb was detonated in a desert in New Mexico, with results even more formidable than had been expected. General Spaatz was ordered to drop a bomb over one of four cities and chose Hiroshima. The bomb was dropped on August 6th, creating almost unimaginable devastation. Still no offer of surrender in clear terms came from Japan.

The bomb had another remarkable effect. On August 8th Russia declared war on Japan and crossed the Manchurian frontier. In the previous April the Soviet had denounced the pact which bound the two countries and now disregarded the clause by which it had pledged itself not to undertake hostilities so soon after the termination of this treaty. Russia's main object was not, it need hardly be said, to assist her allies, who had already completely defeated Japan, but to secure territory which she coveted on the Asiatic mainland and to stake out a claim to participation in the dictation of terms to the conquered foe. A strong army had been built up and some of the ablest commanders, with experience of the European front, had been sent out to the Far East. Considering the reputation of the Japanese Kwantung Army in Manchuria, resistance was surprisingly weak. The opposition dissolved and the Soviet forces swept down into Manchuria at top speed, to reach the city of Harbin. Further south mobile forces crossed the Gobi desert, heading for southern Manchuria.

On August 9th the second atomic bomb was dropped by the United States Strategic Air Forces. This time the target was Nagasaki. The bomb displayed greater blast than that dropped over Hiroshima, the smoke rising 50,000 feet, but owing to the conformation of the ground the loss of life appears to have been considerably less. This was the end. The Japanese could endure no more. They abandoned the round-about attempts at negotiation in which they had been engaged. On the following day, August 10th, the Japanese Government sued for peace on the terms laid down by the Allies at the Potsdam Conference. Peace of a kind had arrived after very nearly six years of warfare.

A General Survey

THIS book has been for the most part, as was intended, a sketch of events. To survey the war and note its tendencies and characteristics briefly is no easy task; in fact, another volume of the length of this might well be devoted to the background. It may, however, be worth while to attempt a short commentary.

First of all, it must be noted that there were two wars, which had little or no connexion. The Japanese and Germans exchanged friendly sentiments, but they exchanged no secrets. They did not in any sense plan together or co-ordinate their operations. That might have happened had the Germans over-run the Middle East while the Japanese over-ran India, so that the two powers joined hands in the Persian Gulf. The fact that it did not make matters easier for the Allies. In this respect the Second World War did not resemble the First, in which, though the theatres were so widespread, the struggle was a single whole.

If, however, Germany be considered alone, there is a strong resemblance in her situation in the two wars. On each occasion she went to war better prepared than her opponents, but certain of the shrewdest and longest-sighted of her citizens believed that a great mistake was being made and were consumed with anxiety for the future. On each occasion these fears appeared to be belied and it did not look as though she could be defeated. On each occasion she overtaxed her strength and went down before the blows of more powerful forces. The main differences were that in the First World War Germany received a sharp check at an early stage on the Marne which coloured all subsequent operations, and that her final collapse was far more sudden, though it was less complete and disastrous. It may also be said that, though she committed rash acts and embarked upon scarcely justifiable gambles, her leaders displayed no such insensate daring and folly as on the second occasion. But the exploitation of the warlike tendencies of the German people, the sound preparation, the highly competent military leadership, the failure to clinch success before the foes became too numerous, are common to the First and Second World Wars.

The terminations of the struggles against Germany and Japan are strikingly different. Germany was completely crushed. Her great armies, victorious all over the world, were reduced to frightened mobs, seeking only to surrender. In the cities of Japan the ruin was almost as great as in those of Germany, but the army was never seriously weakened and the greater part of it never came into action. The biggest Japanese land forces which suffered defeat were those in Burma and the Philippines, but they were small by comparison with the total strength of the army, over one hundred divisions. Japan was battered into surrender by the merciless bombing of the American air fleets, which had in their turn been brought within effective range of the Japanese homeland by a long series of combined operations carried out by the forces of sea, land and air. The Japanese surrendered because their armed forces could not protect the civil population.

It is almost a commonplace now to say that the first characteristic of the war is that it was "total", and this in the double sense that no resources were left untapped by the belligerents and no holds were barred. This is not only the most prominent but also the most sinister aspect of the Second World War because it is the most unpromising for the future of civilization. The devotion—one may call it the prostitution—of thought and effort to the purposes of war is in itself a calamity for mankind. There had been wars in the past century and a half, the Napoleonic Wars, the American Civil War, the Franco-German War, and above all the First World War, in which this tendency had appeared, but not nearly to the same extent as in the Second World War. This may, in fact, be considered not so much a new development as a reversion to the ancient savage or primeval wars of annihilation.

The future is made to appear even darker by the increasing absence of scruple and disregard of convention and of that loose and uncertain but none the less valuable code which is called "the laws of war". This is to be observed above all in the infringement of neutrality, which was practised in particular by the Germans but from which the foes of Germany did not altogether abstain. It is also seen particularly in the war at sea. Unrestricted submarine warfare is in itself an offence, but so is a bombing attack on a merchantman without the remotest prospect of providing for the rescue of the crew, and that became a commonplace. The deliberate bombing of civilians is a natural development of total war because when the greater proportion of industry is devoted to the purposes of war it necessarily follows that the destruction of housing and the terrorizing of workers causes disintegration of the enemy's war effort; but it is none the less one of the most terrible and ominous characteristics of warfare up to date.

The increasingly effective harnessing of science to the offensive is manifestly the most dreadful feature of all. The creation of explosions, of a force hitherto not conceived, by means of atomic fission is the outstanding portent of the last war, but it was responsible for only a fraction of the ruin. It was never used against Germany and it was used against only two of the cities of Japan; but the most frightful devastation was caused in those two countries and to a lesser extent in others by weapons of more normal type, and even these were only reaching their greatest potential force when the war came to an end, and have already been in some cases rendered obsolete by improved types. Moreover, advanced science has clearly not said its last word in the production of the atomic bomb. Bacterial warfare was not exploited, but it is not to be doubted that fruitful experiments in this form of attack were carried out. When these facts are linked with the absence of scruple already mentioned they become even more sinister.

Rhetoric and the powers of persuasion were abused and profaned like so much else. To sift the truth from the lies and distortions became an almost impossible task. The extent to which all official statements were coloured by propaganda became so obvious that they came to be received with scepticism and cynicism, but they nevertheless exercised a profound effect upon thought and opinion, especially national thought and opinion, the effects of which have by no means died out. This is true even of nations like our own and the United States, which are now open to all opinion, but even more so in the totalitarian countries, most of which are virtually closed even in time of peace to any form of opinion conflicting with that of the party in power.

Revolutionary changes in political thought are no new features of great wars, and if this war marked the end of a political age the same may be said of its predecessor. Partly as the result of a general tendency but even more because the aggressor nations lived under a totalitarian rule vaguely associated with the "right wing", the movement of opinion was generally "leftward". It is, however, the case that opinion did not move very far leftward except when it was compelled or encouraged to do so and probable that no country in Europe, with the possible exception of Yugoslavia, would now be under a government of the extreme left were it not for the influence of Soviet Russia. It is also the case that the substitution of totalitarianism of the left for totalitarianism of the right marks but a slight change in organization or in method. All the features which appear most odious to genuine democracy are to be found in both, and certain of them have infiltrated into democracies under the guise of controls and those forms of "planning" which cover a multitude of fooleries and some knaveries. The democracies cannot be absolved from responsibility for the difficulties which they have had to encounter since the war. Because revolutionary left-wing opinion favoured the cause of the Allies for ulterior motives after Russia had been brought into the war, they encouraged its growth, tolerated its abuses, and misled their peoples as to its significance. Now they have to pay for this complacency.

Glib expositors of opinion found so many "turning points" in the war that, if one agrees with their appreciations, it must have been turning like a teetotum nearly all the while. The turning points were in fact fewer than was pretended. One of the most vital features of the war was the Battle of the Atlantic, the submarine war. Fortunes varied, those of the Allies improving in the latter stages, but there was no single turning point. There were, nevertheless, certain episodes or decisions which from time to time exercised a deep influence upon the course of the war, in some cases temporary only but in others persisting throughout. The first of these was the Russo-German pact, concluded before the outbreak of war. This had the effect of giving Hitler a free hand in the early stages and providing him with a steady supply of oil. It enabled him to finish with Poland more rapidly than would otherwise have been possible, a matter of considerable moment to him because in 1939 he did not possess the military resources to maintain a war on two fronts and was bound to transport the bulk of his forces to the west at the earliest possible moment. On the other hand it afforded Soviet Russia a period of preparation for her struggle with Germany, both by the improvement of her fighting forces and the advance of her frontiers at the expense of her weak neighbours. Hitler, an extremely loquacious individual, had long before announced that he might be led to enter into a pact with Russia, with no intention of observing it longer than suited his convenience, but though the Russians were suspicious they were to a certain extent hoodwinked and were among the last to realize that Germany was about to turn her arms against them. The Russo-German pact was a principal factor in the early victories of Germany.

The second episode of importance was the success of the German invasion of Norway. The British and French had not failed to recognize the strategic value of that country. During the Finnish War they had in fact made up their minds to combine philanthropy or knight errantry with profit by opening up lines of communication through Scandinavia for the purpose of sending aid to Finland and then maintaining their hold upon the Norwegian coast in order to prevent Germany from exploiting it. Even after Finland had been defeated they did not abandon their designs on the Norwegian coast, but they were forestalled by Germany and their effort to eject the Germans came too late. In view of what happened in France and the Low Countries just afterwards it must be open to doubt whether they could have maintained themselves in Norway even if they had established a footing there, but there can be no doubt about the advantage which Germany derived from possession of Norway. That country, and especially its ports of Trondheim and Bergen, provided invaluable submarine bases throughout the war, while the fjords provided relatively safe anchorages for German surface warships engaged on the task of raiding either the Atlantic convoys or those passing to northern Russia round the North Cape. Had it not been for German possession of Norway the despatch of convoys to northern Russia would have been comparatively safe and easy. Norway was never again invaded—except when the Russians penetrated its Arctic fringe in the Finmark—and the powerful German army stationed in the country remained undefeated to the end, the only German force of which this could be said.

The next "turning point" is, needless to say, the brilliant German offensive in the west and particularly the break-through on the Meuse and exploitation to the Channel. This was one of the masterpieces of war. At a single stroke it deprived Britain of her one powerfully ally and placed her in imminent danger of extinction. It was to take another four years to obtain a new footing in Western Europe, while apart from that the effects of the fall of France were experienced all over the world. They were at their most dire in the Far East, where the infiltration of Japan into French Indo-China paved the way for the conquest of Malaya, the Netherlands East Indies, and Burma.

The next land-mark is commonly given as the Battle of Britain, but it is sometimes forgotten that that great victory was conditioned and made possible by a vital decision taken before the French Armistice. Earnest appeals were made to the British Government to throw its last reserves of fighter aircraft into the campaign in France on the ground that it was German air superiority which constituted the gravest handicap to the Allies. The Government did increase the number of fighter squadrons in France, as has been shown, but it resolutely refused to strip Britain of fighter defence to the bone. From what had been seen of the French Army in action there appeared little reason to suppose that all the increased air support in the power of Britain to give would turn the scale, while if the last squadrons were dissipated, as they would almost certainly be, Britain herself would be left destitute of her most powerful defensive weapon. There is no need to insist that the Battle of Britain was decisive. The dispute between those who aver that Hitler never intended to invade this country but simply to batter it into impotence and then to occupy it and those who talk of the defeat of the planned German invasion is largely a matter of words. However far the Germans went in weakening the country by the destruction of its defences, the obliteration of its ports, and the cutting of its Atlantic supply routes, there would always have been some resistance to a landing. But all the evidence points to the belief that before they risked their forces on the water the Germans intended to carry the process of "softening" very far.

Next comes the German decision to invade Russia. This was taken by Hitler against the advice of his ablest military advisers, but there is no justification for the belief that it was in itself fatal to his cause. Had the operations been conducted more prudently at certain critical phases, the campaign need not have brought a catastrophe upon Germany. The last offensive against Moscow he winter of 1941 was one of the gravest and most far-reaching of German errors. It led not only to material and moral defeat but also to a serious straining of the army's capacity for resistance in the following months. Had the Germans withdrawn to the line Kharkov, Briansk, Smolensk, Lake Ilmen, the Russians would have been virtually impotent to injure them that winter.

The divergent operations in the Caucasus and on the Volga in 1942 were equally rash. If the Germans did not realize that the Soviet reserves had not been committed at Stalingrad their intelligence must have been exceedingly faulty. It would appear that Paulus was forbidden to retreat while there was still time partly because German prestige seemed to depend upon the capture of Stalingrad, which Hitler had announced as a certainty, and partly because retreat would uncover the flank of Kleist in the Caucasus. As it proved, the armies of Paulus were virtually destroyed, whereas Kleist extricated himself brilliantly. The Russian conduct of the counter-offensive was not wholly successful, since it failed to block the door to the Caucasus armies at Rostov; yet it accomplished more than is commonly achieved by the greatest victories in routing one group of armies and compelling the other to retreat post-haste and to abandon the vital objectives which it had all but attained. It is a commonplace that Stalingrad was one of the genuine turning points of the war. After that defeat the Germans gained no more major victories.

It is equally obvious that the Japanese attack on the United States was another landmark of the first importance. If it was to prove in the end fatal to Japan herself, it was equally so for Germany. It was the intention of President Roosevelt to go to war with Japan if she attacked Great Britain alone, but it is mere speculation to what extent he would have carried the country with him, whether American efforts would have approximated to what they actually amounted to after the slap in the face of Pearl Harbour, and whether, or how soon, the United States would have been drawn into the war against Germany, supposing that Germany had not declared war upon the United States.

The decision of the British Government and the Chiefs of Staff Committee to cling to the Mediterranean and to the Middle East when it seemed to many observers that the only means of preventing worse disaster would have been to withdraw from them was another big factor in allied success. There may be a question whether the Italian offensive should have been broken off after the capture of Rome or even earlier; there can be none of the correctness of the strategy of launching the first offensives against Germany in the Mediterranean and incidentally driving her chief European partner out of the war. Even on the point of training and experience alone, the Mediterranean campaigns were an indispensable preliminary to the invasion of Europe from the north-west. And here Alamein takes its place as a turning point as important as that of Stalingrad, which shortly followed it. Montgomery was concerned in another turning point, the decision to broaden the frontage of assault in France, even though the assault was thus delayed. The margin of success was smaller than appeared, and the narrow front would have led to failure.

The exceptionally close co-operation between the United States and the British Commonwealth in all theatres was one of the most valuable elements in victory. It was due in great measure to President Roosevelt and Mr. Churchill, but though they could lead their horses to water they would not have been able to force them to drink unless they had been so inclined. In this respect credit must be given to the senior staff officers, especially to Sir Alan Brooke (to-day Lord Alanbrooke) and to General Marshall, but most of all must go to General Eisenhower. It was he who first put the system into force and laid down the lines which it was to follow, and he who brought to it the spirit of loyalty and comradeship without which no formal rules would have availed.

In the war against Japan there was really only one major turning point, and that was reached when Japan had achieved her greatest expansion and found herself unable to increase it or to seize the further objectives which might have made her position more secure. In all theatres there followed a series of step-by-step advances by the Allies, methodically planned and executed. There was no single event, hardly even the naval battles of the Coral Sea and the Philippines, possessing in itself a significance equal to that of Stalingrad. The war would undoubtedly have dragged on far longer, with effects upon opinion in the United States and perhaps also in Britain which are difficult to estimate, but for the strategic genius of MacArthur and Nimitz. Yet the fact remains that the Japanese, for all the brilliance of their early successes, were not of the calibre of the opponents whom they so lightly engaged and that they would have been defeated considerably earlier had it not been for the priority justifiably accorded to operations against Germany.

The industrial capacity of Japan has been estimated to have been only about one-tenth of that of the United States. If one cause rather than another can account for the success of the allied strategy in closing upon Japan, it is the damage inflicted upon her carriers. Of the ten with which she started the war six were sunk in 1942. She constructed or converted from other types a total of twelve more, not counting five escort carriers, but in 1944 she lost seven more. Another seven were finally lost in her home waters as the result of attacks by submarines or aircraft. A far-reaching source of weakness was inability to train her air reinforcements. She trebled their numbers, which rose from 12,000 to 35,000, but whereas at the outset the pilots were among the best in the world, having had from 500 to 800 hours' flying experience and in many cases operational experience in China, the quality fell off. Towards the end she began concentrating on the production of Kamikaze or "suicide" aircraft, but just too late. With these weapons she damaged 15 battleships and 12 carriers, besides a number of other vessels, the sinkings achieved being mostly of destroyers. The Americans estimate that had this form of attack been rather more powerful and concentrated it might well have caused a revision of their strategy and tactics. Yet another grave Japanese handicap was the loss of her merchant shipping. She began by allotting two-thirds of it to transport work in the service of the Navy and Army, always hoping that after the perimeter was consolidated she could return many ships to the task of transporting raw material from the conquered countries. This hour never came, and presently the merchant shipping failed to suffice for her operational needs.

Though the great British victory in Burma contributed only indirectly to bringing Japan to ruin, it was so thorough and complete in itself that it is worth while remembering that, like the victory in the Pacific, it also was conditioned by air superiority. But in Burma it was the platoons of men, the equipment, ammunition, stores, and rations carried in the aircraft which provided the air's decisive contribution to victory. The bomber did its work; the fighter made the air safe for both bomber and transport aircraft; but in this theatre, alone of those of the war, the *beau rôle* was reserved for the unarmed "air lorry".

One characteristic of the war which no Briton can afford to neglect but which is sometimes slurred by propaganda is the shift of the balance of power. In the First World War the major victors were the British Empire and France, after Russia had been driven out of the field in defeat and anarchy. The French Army remained to the end stronger numerically than the British, but the British Navy was by far the most important factor at sea, while the Royal Flying Corps was superior to the French aviation. Moreover, the British divisions on the Western front, though numerically inferior to the French, had not like them been involved in disaffection amounting in many cases to open mutiny in 1917, and they were on the whole sounder and more aggressive in the concluding months of victory in 1918. In that year the British Empire played the predominating part in achieving victory in the west, while conducting two other major victorious campaigns (Palestine and Mesopotamia) entirely with its own resources and taking an appreciable part in a third (Macedonia).

The United States, entering that war relatively late, rendered vital service and may have made the difference between victory and defeat on the Western Front in 1918. Yet the country never developed its full strength. Its land and air forces were for the most part equipped with British and French material. Quantitatively they were only approaching their full strength when the war came to an end. Two American armies were in action in Western Europe. Except in potential strength the United States cannot be regarded as a first-class power in the First World War.

It was a very different matter in the late war. Then the United States had been given no more time to prepare than a generation earlier and had been dealt a severe blow at the very outset. But she entered the war full fledged as a first-class power and as time went on further developed her strength in a manner truly astonishing. She dominated the war against Japan, and in the air and on land took a far greater part in the war against Germany than the British Empire. One factor in this change in the balance of power is doubtless to be discovered in the fact that Britain had suffered considerable exhaustion in maintaining the war against Germany single-handed from the fall of France to the German attack on Russia; but a far more important cause was the vast expansion of American industry in the period between the two wars and the great superiority in imagination, boldness, and initiative of the administration of President Roosevelt over that of President Wilson.

The military power of Russia gave evidence of an even more remarkable expansion. In the First World War Russia engaged a very much smaller proportion of the German Army than was the case in the second, yet suffered continuous defeat at the hands of Germany and her allies, finally being driven out of the war long before it had been concluded. Throughout the period of her belligerency in the Second World War she always engaged at least two-thirds of the German Army, as well as a considerable proportion of the *Luftwaffe*; from the winter of 1942 onwards she inflicted upon the Germans and their allies defeat after defeat, and in the end routed them entirely and captured the capital of Germany and the capitals of all Germany's allies except Italy—and Finland, whose capital she could have entered at will. The causes of this transformation are to be found in the growth of industry, the superior strength and determination of the régime, a certain improvement in education which made the fighting forces more formidable, the fact that the national spirit did not crack as it had under the obsolete administration of the Tsar, and the greater foresight and generosity of Russia's allies in supporting her with supplies of all natures, from tinned food to tanks.

The result of this shift of power was that, whereas Britain had been the foremost of the victors of the First World War—even though the French believed sincerely that France had occupied this place of honour—she came third in the late war. Her effort in maintaining the war alone or virtually so between the summer of 1940 and that of 1941 was a vital element in victory, though it may be noted that she did not suffer heavy loss of life in that period. Her sea power once again proved to be her greatest contribution. Nevertheless, her decline by comparison with Russia and the United States is a portent, and its effects have been observed in the period of the aftermath. One consolation to British minds is the fact that the men who most highly appreciate the efforts of Britain and the Commonwealth in the late war are the most highly instructed American naval and military officers, and they, alone of their countrymen and perhaps in the world, are in a position to know.

In sheer fighting the British were superlative in all fields. The palm must be given to the pilots of the Battle of Britain, but the sailors of the Battle of the Atlantic and the soldiers of Egypt, Tunisia, Italy, Burma and Western Europe, run them close. The self-sacrifice of the bomber crews engaged in the night attacks on Germany was unsurpassed. In a certain concentration camp in Germany there was found one of the architects of the early German victories, General Halder, the former Chief of the Staff of the Army, fallen out of favour with Hitler and lucky to be still alive. Halder was a talkative man and opened his heart on many matters to a companion in detention, a distinguished soldier of a small country. Leaving out the numerical element, he assessed the quality of the armies which the Germans had faced thus: first British, second American, third Russian, fourth French. Britain has produced great formations in the past, but it is doubtful whether she has ever excelled some of the divisions and independent brigades which fought in the late war.

Yet it would be folly to neglect an element which gives cause for a certain disquietude even in this pleasing picture. British divisions could be raised to a far higher standard of skill than was possible in the earlier war, in which they were trench-bound and in which they continually suffered casualties so high as to wipe out the experienced core of officers, non-commissioned officers, and trained soldiers time after time. The science of creating physical fitness and endurance had also made progress, so that troops were able to stand the strain of constant fighting and movement in a manner which their fathers would not have found possible. Yet it is more than doubtful whether British—or for that matter American—troops were as stiff as they were in the First World War. They did not appear to be able to take casualties and preserve their offensive "bite" in the same way. If desertion—not going over to the enemy, but disappearance on the eve of an offensive—became prevalent in a division, as occurred in one or two cases, this was attributed to the heavy losses which that division had suffered; but in point of fact these were rarely more than one-third of the casualties suffered in the First World War by divisions which maintained a high standard and in which desertion was virtually unknown to the end.

Again, the theory upon which the composition of infantry brigades of the Indian Army was based was that the single British battalion normally included would set a standard and provide an example to the Indian battalions. Good as were many of the latter in the First World War, this was how things commonly worked out in practice. That also was the case in the Second World War to start with, but here the British battalions did not as a rule remain at their best as long as the Indian and Gurkha battalions. By 1944 it could not be said that these were in any need of an example set by Europeans. Again, the relative status of Indian divisions such as the 4th, 5th, 8th and 17th, to name but four, was certainly far higher in the Second World War, though it is possible that this was in part due to a direct improvement in the Indian Army for which British instructors, administrators, and leaders deserve much of the credit, while some must go to a raising of the educational standard in India between the wars.

The point which it is desired to make is that the conditions in this country during the last generation had resulted in a certain softening of the young manhood. With patience and skill they could be raised to a degree of efficiency in war higher than that of their fathers, but they required much more careful handling and there was much more dross to be sweated out of them. And this dross was mental or spiritual as well as physical. The fighting forces went far to master this problem, but the revelations of war-time should not be forgotten or obscured by propaganda in time of peace. The recruit of 1914 may have been worse educated and may even have had less initiative and intelligence than the recruit of 1939, but he possessed a better poise, was mentally healthier, and less brittle as a soldier. The younger generation became in many cases the better soldiers, but it required a great deal more trouble to make them so. The best results were obtained above all in the Guards and in certain armoured divisions and it was undoubtedly because a stiffening element with rock-like discipline was needed that so many brigades of Guards were formed.

After every great war the prospects of the next have tended to become more sombre owing to the development of more formidable weapons. It was a commonplace after the First World War that, bad as affairs then appeared, civilization had narrowly escaped a much more serious disaster than it had suffered and that, if there should be another war, material destruction, suffering, and the subsequent dislocation would be very much greater.

That proved to be the case. Evil as was the aftermath of the earlier war, it took less than ten years to restore Europe to prosperity and in several countries to a standard of life higher than that of before the war. There can be no hope of a comparable recovery this time.

Moreover, on this occasion the harnessing of science to war, as already achieved or manifestly impending, has reached a stage at which any further advance is practically superfluous and can but duplicate the destructive effects already at the disposal of great nations when they go to war. The bare maintenance of civilization is by no means as inevitable as has commonly been assumed. In contact with the new forces it is in fact relatively fragile. The late war has given us sufficient indication that it would not be difficult to disrupt the basis of civilization altogether and to plunge this planet and its inhabitants into chaos. We have been warned.

Index

The general principle on which officers are indexed is that they are entered under the final rank under which they appear in the text.

PRINTED IN GREAT BRITAIN BY
EBENEZER BAYLIS AND SON, LTD.,
THE TRINITY PRESS, WORCESTER, AND LONDON